KING SAUL

THE TRUE HISTORY
OF THE FIRST MESSIAH

ADAM GREEN

The Lutterworth Press

The Lutterworth Press
P.O. Box 60
Cambridge
CB1 2NT

www.lutterworth.com
publishing@lutterworth.com

ISBN 978 0 7188 3074 8

British Library Cataloguing in Publication Data
A catalogue record is available from the British Library

Dedication

To the memory of my late grandfather, Harry Pizan,
whose constant presence during my childhood was
a more than adequate compensation for an absent
and wayward father. It was he, my gentle and sage
zaida, who instilled in me an abiding intolerance of
injustice, great and small, which directly resulted in
this book. It is an ironic certainty that as a devout,
traditional Jew my grandfather would have been
appalled by my unflinching dissection of his beloved
David. Nevertheless, this work is dedicated to my
zaida, who was truly a follower of Saul, though he
never knew it.

Levites Carrying the Ark

Contents

Illustrations and Maps
by the Author

Preface

In an attempt to retain the interest of the general reader while avoiding academic opprobrium, I have relegated much scholarly detail to the chapter endnotes and the appendices at the end of the book.

Out of deference to non-Christian readers, throughout the text I have used the abbreviation BCE (Before the Common Era) and CE. Similarly, I have avoided wherever possible the use of the Tetregramatton, when discussing the Israelite deity/ies (*E* and *J*), and restricted myself to the 'God' appellation.

All translations of biblical quotations are based on the version contained within the Jewish Publication Society's "Tanakh – The Holy Scriptures" 1985 Edition.

Throughout the main text I refer to the writer(s) of the first book of Samuel as 'the author,' the 'pro-David (or Pro Saul) author,' the 'Davidic (or Saulide) author' or redactor, the 'monarchist' author and the 'anti-monarchist' author or redactor – depending upon the section of narrative under discussion. Those interested in the theories (including my own) about the actual evolution of the Samuel text should see Appendix A.

Following lengthy consideration I decided to avoid, as far as possible, the issue of the comparative chronologies of ancient Israel and her neighbours. In spite of the fact that David Rohl's revisionist position in particular would in some ways support my hypothesis, I concluded that the subject was beyond the scope of this work and would do as much to cloud the core issues as underpin my arguments. However, I have no qualms in stating here that I regard the 'New Chronology' as a valid and useful aid to all those interested in studying biblical history.

In the text, I refrain from what many scholars would regard as a misuse of the term *Hebrew* and restrict myself to the appellation Israelite when referring to Saul and his compatriots.

My illustrations are based on three sources. The drawing style is derived from an ivory panel discovered at Megiddo (now in the Rockefeller Museum, New York), dated to the Late Bronze Age, depicting the court of a Canaanite king, and a relief of a battle between the armies of Rameses III and the 'Sea Peoples', including the Philistines, from the walls of the temple of Rameses III at Medinet Habu. 'The crown of Saul' is copied from a bust discovered in Jordan and *purported* to be that of an Ammonite king from the time of the united monarchy. The bust, from the collection of Moshe Dayan, is now in the Israel Museum, Jerusalem.

Adam Green
Malaga, Spain, 2006

Acknowledgements

When I began this project some eleven years ago, I sensed even then that the task ahead of me would be as epic as the subject matter itself. Over the course of that time there were several people who sustained me, technically, financially and emotionally.

At the top of this small list I must name two scholars who I have never had the privilege to meet. First of these is the late, truly great and genuinely heroic Immanuel Velikovsky, whose brilliance and courage inspired me as an unpublished writer "to dare" to start out upon this long and arduous path. Secondly, I owe a debt of gratitude to Professor Baruch Halpern, whose articulate and highly academic re-evaluation of King David proved so emboldening to my own enterprise.

For his literary expertise and guidance I must extend my love and my thanks to Stanley Marcus for his tireless efforts in helping me turn my initial scrawls into a readable and cogent manuscript, and in the process, convincing me that I really could write a book. And, for his invaluable technical input, his vast knowledge, his patience and enthusiasm, and for convincing me of the soundness of my own scholarship, I pay special thanks to David Rohl.

Adrian Brink and Lutterworth Press deserve much praise for their brave and highly complimentary decision to publish this work, opening the door of authorship to an unknown academic 'outsider'. I would also like to express my gratitude to Ann Parry for her excellent index

More special thanks and love go to my mother Hannah Green, for her constant encouragement, her extreme patience, for being my 'soundboard' and for her numerous readings of the drafts.

Finally, I thank my wife Dido, for being my rock and my support, and for the unswerving faith she has shown, throughout the last decade. Without her incredible love, her strength, her resolve and her sacrifice, "Saul" would have remained an unattainable dream.

Glossary

Humash *(Heb.)*, *Five books of Moses plus related chapters from other sections of the Hebrew Bible*

emrods *(Heb.)*, *An unidentified plague that afflicted the Philistines, according to 1 Sam*

keshet *(Heb.)*, *Bow (as in 'bow and arrow')*

Massoretic text, *Standardised Hebrew text of the Bible (Finalised in the 12th century)*

melech *(Heb.)*, *King*

meshiach *(Heb.)*, *Anointed (Gk.* Christ-*; Lat.* Messiah*)*

nagid *(Heb.) Captain/Prince*

navi / nabi *(Heb.)*, *Prophet*

Septuagint *(Gk.)(LXX)*, *Ancient Greek translation of the Hebrew Bible*

Seranim *(Heb.)*, *Philistine rulers, normally translated as 'Lords'*

shofet *(Heb.)*, *Judge*

shul *(pronounced SHOOL) (Yid.)*, *Common term for synagogue among Ashkenazi Jews*

Talmud *(Heb.)*, *Primary collection of ancient rabbinical commentaries on all aspects of Judaism*

Targum *(Aram.)*, *Ancient Aramaic version/translation of the Hebrew Bible*

Tanakh *(Heb.)*, *The Hebrew Bible*

Tehillim (Heb.), The Psalms

Torah (Heb.), The Five Books of Moses

Zaida (Yid.), Grandfather

Key to Abbreviations

AB	*Anchor Bible*, 1980
ABD	*Anchor Bible Dictionary*, 1992
AEHL	*Archeological Encyclopedia of the Holy Land*, 2001
AHOTHP	*A History of the Hebrew People*, Kent, C.F., 1910
AHOTJP	*A History of he Jewish People*, 1976
Ant	Antiquities (Jos)
ATOT	*A Test of Time*, Rohl, D.M., 1995
BAR	British Archaeological Review
BOTB	*Battles of the Bible*, Gichon, M., 1997
Chron.	Chronicles
CAH	Cambridge Ancient History
CBQ	Catholic Bible Quarterly
cf.	Compare
Deut.	Deuteronomy
DSD	*David's Secret Demons*, Halpern, B., 2001
EA	Amarna Letter
EJ	Encyclopedia Judaica
Est.	Esther
Ex.	Exodus
Ezk.	Ezekiel
ff.	Following pages
Gen.	Genesis
Heb.	Hebrew
Hos.	Hosia
Is.	Isaiah
Jem.	Jeremiah
Jg.	Judges
Jos.	Josephus
Josh.	Joshua
JSOT	Journal for the Study of the Old Testament
K.	Kings
Lev.	Leviticus

Mac.	Maccabees
Matt.	Matthew
n.	note/reference
Num.	Numbers
OTH	*Old Testament History*, Wade, G.W., 1928
Ph.	Philippians
POT	*Personalities of the Old Testament*, James, F., 1939
Pss.	Psalms
Qs.	Qumran Scroll
Sam.	Samuel
SATM	*Saul and the Monarchy*, Brookes, S., 2005
TAOTB	*Times Atlas of the Bible*, 1989
TBU	*The Bible Unearthed*, Finkelstein, I., & Silberman, N.A., 2001
THOI	The History of Israel, Noth, M. 1958
TI	*The Israelites*, Isserlin, B.S.J., 1998
TOCB	The Oxford Companion to the Bible, 1993.
TOHBW	*The Oxford History of the Biblical World*, 1999
TOTC	*Tyndale Old Testament Commentaries*, (Wiseman, Donald J., General Editor), *1 and 2 Samuel,* Joyce Baldwin, 1988
VTS	Vetus Testamentum Supplements
ZFDAW	*Zeitschrift für die alttestamentliche Wissenschaft*. Berlin

*Regional map showing the nominal territories of the Israelites
and their neighbours, circa 1020 BCE*

Dramatis Personae

FROM 1 SAMUEL

Abiathar: son of Ahia (House of Eli) – High Priest

Abijah: (first) son of Samuel – Judge

Abigail: wife of Nabal – 'third' wife of David

Abinadab [a]: (Levite from Kirjath-Jearim) – Guardian of the Ark

Abinadab [b]: (third or fourth?) son of Saul – Royal Prince

Abishai: son of Zeruiah/brother of Joab – Companion of David

Abner: son of Ner, cousin of Saul – Commander of the Army of Israel

Achish: (Philistine) – Lord of Gath

Adriel: Husband of Merab

Agag : King of Amalek

Ahia/Ahimelech: son of Ahitub – High Priest

Ahinoam [a]: daughter of Ahimaaz – Saul's Queen

Ahinoam [b]'of Jezreel' – 'second' wife of David

Ahitub: (first) son of Phinehas – Father of Ahia/Brother of Ichabod

David: (eighth) son of Jesse – Judahite prince and pretender to the throne

Doeg: (Edomite) Saul's chief herdsman

Eli: High priest and judge of Israel

Eliab: (first) son of Jesse – eldest brother of David

Elkanah: son of Jeroham/father of Samuel

Gad: (Judahite) Prophet

Goliath: (Philistine) giant warrior

Hannah: (first) wife of Elkanah and mother of Samuel

Hophni: (first) son of Eli – Priest

Ichabod: (second) son of Phinehas – brother of Ahitub

Ishboshet/Ishbaal/Ishui: (second) son of Saul/second King of Israel

Jesse: son of Obed/father of David – Judahite prince

Joel: (second) son of Samuel – Judge

Jonathan: (first) son of Saul – Crown Prince of Israel

Kish: son of Abiel/father of Saul – Benjaminite Prince

Merab: (first) daughter of Saul

Melchishua: (third or fourth) son of Saul

Michal: (second) daughter of Saul – 'first' wife of David and wife of Phalti

Nabal: Calebite Prince of Judah and husband of Abigail

Nahash: King of Ammon

Peninah: (second) wife of Elkanah

Phinehas: (second) son of Eli – Priest

Phalti: son of Laish – Husband of Michal

Samuel: son of Elkanah – Judge and Prophet of Israel

Saul: son of Kish – King of Israel

'Woman' of En-dor: 'Pagan' priestess

FROM 2 SAMUEL

Absalom: (third) son of David – rebel leader against David

Armoni: (first) illegitimate son of Saul (by Rizpah)

Bathsheba: daughter of Eliam/wife of Uriah – (eighth?) wife of David/ Mother of Solomon

Elhanan: son of Jarre-Oregim – Israelite champion and slayer of Goliath

Joab: son of Zeruiah – Brother of Abishai/Commander of the army

Mephiboseth/Meribaal [a]: son of Jonathan

Mephiboseth/Meribaal [b]: (second) illegitimate son of Saul (by Rizpah)

Nathan: Prophet

Rizpah: daughter of Ahia – Concubine of Saul

Solomon: (seventh?) son of David (with Bathsheba) – fourth King of Israel

Sheba: son of Bichri – (Benjaminite) rebel leader against David

Shimei: son of Gera – abuser of David

Uriah: (Hittite) high ranking officer in David's army

Zadok: Jerusalemite high priest appointed by David

Introduction

"The task of the ancient historian, of any historian, is in the end to recognise and reconstruct the cacophonous constructions of historical realities, the competing and merely alternative narratives, the possible alternative narratives that were or in some cases might have been pertinent to the historical agents, the human beings, involved in historical transactions. It is the historian's burden to elect his or her narrative that includes, privileges, excludes, or repudiates elements of all those agents' voices." (Baruch Halpern. 2001)

Around the time I was beginning this book, an article by an Israeli academic was published. It claimed that Goliath, the infamous nine-foot Philistine, suffered from a condition known as *giantism*.[1] If true, he would have exhibited an assortment of physical handicaps, such as 'shambling gait,' back pain, and most particularly, myopia. The significance of this hypothesis is that the man from Gath may have been far less ferocious than previously believed, and young David's slingshot victory over him was considerably less significant than legend would have it. To put it bluntly, the son of Jesse may have been not so much a hero as a persecutor of the disabled.

The publication, the subsequent broadcasts and the tenet of that report is symptomatic of the reasons why I felt compelled to write *Saul: The Forgotten Messiah*. What on the surface seems to be an amusing observation, casting doubt upon the relative heroism of David, fails to take account of a far more serious and damning probability.

This book is a discussion of that probability and its many inferences with regard to the characters in the First Book of Samuel and the alleged roles they played in laying the foundation of messianic tradition.

As will become clear, David's reputation is inversely related to that of Saul. Therefore, as my revised account of David and his early career brings him down to earth, it raises his predecessor from relative inconsequentiality to a pinnacle of significance. A true picture of the anointing and reign of King Saul, which I have tried to present in these pages, reveals the uniqueness of his messianic credentials.Moreover, it will be shown that the betrayal of the one true Messiah was perpetrated not at Golgotha but over a thousand years earlier, on the slopes of Mount Gilboa.

A Gift from 'Gob'

When I was a boy, most Saturday mornings I was to be found sitting, standing, and dutifully bowing by the side of my grandfather, my *zaida*, in our local *shul* (synagogue). I was a moderately observant child from a North London suburb who had a reasonable grasp of the orthodox liturgy. Nevertheless, the only part of going to shul that I ever enjoyed was returning home after three hours of boredom.

Over the years, I developed a survival strategy for dealing with the tedium; namely, reading the *Tanakh*.

Tanakh is the Hebrew word for what non-Jews refer to as the Old Testament, while for Jews, of course, it represents the one and only testament. It was within the pages of my *zaida*'s *Tanakh* that I discovered redemption from boredom. Each week, I would read an episode from one of the more action-filled books such as Joshua or Judges. I particularly enjoyed Judges, with its rambling account of Israel's violent and protracted settlement within the land of Canaan. It was epic stuff, strewn with battles and scenes of covenant, and packed with heroes such as Deborah and Gideon. Chaotic perhaps, probably inaccurate, and as for the 'signs and wonders,' they were just good fun. Historicity was not an issue to a young boy, who felt that these sagas were reaching out to him across three millennia. It seemed to me that these pages were an attempt to describe the genesis of my people. We had been born in blood and glory, out of the union of faith and passion. Here was the whole weighty record, with a tenuous thread to me and my imagined offspring.

But while Judges thrilled my young spirit, it was from the pages of the books of Samuel that I received the gift of wonder. Whereas the former seemed obscure and remote in style, the latter was crisp and sharply defined. It was in Samuel that I sensed the beginnings of a concrete history. Moreover, with its often-sublime blend of fable, myth and history, I found it eminently readable. Thus it was that, while engrossed in the pages of the second book of Samuel, I came upon verse 21:19:

And there was another battle in Gob[2] against the Philistines, where Elhanan the son of Jaare-Oregim, a Bethlehemite, slew *the brother of* Goliath the Gittite, the shaft of whose spear was like a weavers beam.

Funnily enough, if it had not been for the fact that the phrase '*brother of*' was printed in italics, I might have merely skimmed over the verse without a backward glance. But those italics caught my eye. I knew that in traditional translations of the Bible such as the King James Version, and that which I had before me that morning in Shul, italics were used for one of two reasons. The more common was to show conjunctions and suchlike that had been inserted to improve the flow of the language. The other was to indicate that words had been added to *make sense* of a passage that would otherwise be obscure.

Although my Hebrew was rudimentary, it was proficient enough to allow for direct comparison between the English translation and the original Hebrew, which appeared side-by-side in the Tanakh. Thus, it was a simple matter to check on any curiosities.

The 'brother of Goliath' verse struck me as especially odd for two reasons. First, I had never heard that the terrible Philistine had a brother, and second, I was left puzzled by the fact that the brother was unnamed. Failure to mention people's names is very rare in the Bible, and especially so within passages such as the one in question – a list of heroic Israelite champions and the enemies they had vanquished in the service of King David.

My eyes quickly darted across to the right-hand side of the page, to the classical Hebrew printed in neat columns. To my amazement, I could find no mention of a brother. The reason the English translation had omitted to name Goliath's brother was that the Hebrew text mentioned no such person. The Hebrew was clear; except for the name of Elhanan's father Jarre-oregim,[3] it consisted of particularly familiar words and phrases – 'brother of' not being amongst them.

Reading about Elhanan and Goliath was like suddenly discovering that the Garden of Eden had been inhabited by Adam and Esther. Shocked, I naturally turned to my learned zaida for an explanation, and was aghast when he told me he didn't have one.

From that instant, I was a deeply perplexed little boy.

Dozens of questions spun around in my head – the foremost of which were: Who on earth was Elhanan? Why had no one ever pointed him out to me? How had he killed Goliath – with a slingshot or a spear? If Elhanan killed Goliath, why had the deed been claimed for David?

However, by far the most disturbing implication for me to digest was the possibility that David had not killed Goliath.

What was I to make of it? For the whole of my short life, I had been taught to regard David as the ultimate Jewish hero, the standard against which all other heroes were to be measured. Every revered national leader from Judas Maccabaeus to Moshe Dayan had been compared to David. In times of adversity, Jews have constantly sought and found solace and encouragement in the tales of his epic deeds, none of which is evoked more often than his vanquishing of the giant Goliath, wielder of the weaver's beam.

Over the following days, I became obsessed. I spent every spare minute reading and rereading any book I could find on the subject. With my return to boarding school – Carmel College – a week or two later, I enjoyed access to one of the finest and most comprehensive libraries of Judaica and bible studies in the world. There I discovered dozens of theories, concerning 'early versions' and 'late versions,' this tradition versus that tradition, this possible error and that probable mistranslation. I emerged more confused than ever.

I sensed early on however, that part of the problem lay in the common perception of David himself. Only the most pious regard the biblical personalities prior to the Samuel narrative as more than semi-mythological. Similarly, all but the most 'minimalist' biblical historians fail to regard David as an historical character. This being the case, why had he, or those who came after him, invented the story of his slaying Goliath? And even more perplexing, having gone to all that trouble, why then allow the competing Elhanan episode to slip through the net?

If somebody has been telling lies to make David look good, might they also have been trying to make his famous *bête noire*, King Saul, look bad?

There is nothing new in the suggestion that David did not kill Goliath and that he was, in all probability, a usurper[4] – many of whose psalms are exquisite manifestations of his obsessive need for self-justification. Neither is there anything original in the recognition that David was a far from perfect personality; indeed, his litany of misdeeds is well documented in the second book of Samuel (e.g. 2 Sam. 11; 24 / 8:17). What may be less appreciated, however, is that a probing examination of the young (and supposedly heroic and saintly) David is capable of casting a new and revealing light on the life and personality of King Saul.

The first objective of this work is to bring these facts to the attention of a wider audience, who may never have heard of Elhanan. The second aim is to reveal the extent to which David's campaign of messianic self-promotion was driven by guilt and his consequent need for self-vindication. The third and central thesis of this work arises out of the first two and is meant to reveal a truer picture of Saul.

The story of Elhanan provided me with stark evidence of why the biblical text should never be taken at face value, and if a single anomaly could tell me this, surely it would be worthwhile examining as many other problems in the text as possible. As long as one remained objective and level-headed, a new plateau of understanding might be reached. My main problem from the outset, however, was my distinct subjectivity. Certainly, in common with many others, I had always sympathized with Saul because of the harsh treatment meted out to him by Samuel. Yet David remained my ultimate biblical hero.

Part of the reason it took so long for this project to come to fruition was an innate reluctance to accept what my research had suggested to me. Nevertheless, the radically simple act of looking at what was in front of my face eventually convinced me that I had stumbled on a history of Saul and David truer than the one I had inherited. I hope many of my readers will arrive at the same conclusion.

This book will demonstrate:
· how the only person with a genuine claim to the title 'king-messiah' was traduced by the biblical chroniclers and consigned to an almost forgettable role in the national and spiritual history of the Jews;
· how he was betrayed by David, a prince of Judah;
· how he was pierced with arrows and then dispatched by a sword on the slopes of Gilboa;
· how pagan warriors mutilated his body before nailing it to the walls of the city of Bet-shean;[5] how it was rescued by his adoring subjects and lovingly interred;
· how his remains were later raised and moved to lie with those of his family;
· and finally, how his own usurper resurrected and immortalized his spirit by writing an exquisite lament.

Furthermore, this book will show that, by the time of his death, David had succeeded in weaving a mythology for his entire rise to power. He created not only a fantastical tale, but also a fabulous alter ego in the form of the wonder-boy warrior and 'beloved of God' who, moreover, enjoyed a son/father relationship with the deity. David established – if not to his own inner satisfaction, at least to the satisfaction of every subsequent generation of Jews and Christians his messianic credentials.

For Jews and Christians of the past two millennia, the term *messiah* has denoted a unique agent, or expression of God, whose role is to redeem the universe and usher in an era of peace. Jews have longed for his coming, and Christians have yearned for his return. However, the ancient Israelite notion of royal Messiahship was of a very different, and humbler, order – exemplified by Saul, the virtuous and courageous first King of Israel. The elevation of the term to its current status can be traced to Saul's usurper, David, whose vaulting ambition led him to falsely claim royal-messianic importance. Both Judaism and Christianity have been grievously led astray by this fabulist's brilliant propaganda.

The Meaning of 'Meshiach'

The word *messiah* is widely taken to refer exclusively to Jesus Christ. Yet *messiah* is simply the anglicised form of the Hebrew word *meshiach*, meaning *anointed one* or *the anointed* – nothing more and nothing less.

In the time of King Saul of Israel, anointing was a common practice associated with many religious and secular appointments. It was a form of certification of office. The more senior the appointment, the more venerated the certificate. This is not to diminish the importance of the rite, but merely to point out its pluralistic nature.[6]

The exact constituents of the anointing liquid have always been a mystery to scholars.[7] Everything from olive oil and bitumen to semen and the juices of a menstruating woman have been suggested, not to mention exotic recipes which include all of the above and many other rare ingredients. In his highly controversial, not to mention courageous, masterwork *The Sacred Mushroom and the Cross*, John Allegro discussed the origins and symbolism of the anointing rite and produced convincing evidence of its deeply sexual connotations.[8] (Whatever the fluid was, it seems to have been intended not to wash away easily, but rather to leave a stain and an aroma that would serve as a lasting mark of office.) However, this is a subject beyond the scope of the present work. The ceremony itself is only of passing interest. What matters here is that regardless of the actual nature of the anointing, the ritual became the symbolic key to the gates of power.

Theories also abound over the number of anointings a person would undergo for a given task. For instance, it may be that in the case of a military commander, he (or she, in the case of Deborah) was anointed before every battle, just as the Spartans would ritually comb olive oil through their hair on the eve of combat.[9] (We shall learn how this multiplicity of anointings led to confusion over the length and nature of the reign of King Saul.)

Thus, we find ourselves presented with a rite that, from a purely historical perspective and for all its sanctity, was far from unique. Anointing was simply a form of sacred confirmation in a world where everything – from high cultic ritual to the act of defecation, was regarded as a manifestation of the divine.

In this regard, as we shall soon see, the importance of the second and third anointings of Saul lay not in the acts themselves but in the particular levels of certification they conferred.

In his first elevation, to the rank of ruler, (*nagid*) he had merely joined a long list of past and current officials, including judges and princes. It was only when he was crowned king of Israel that Saul received an anointing which was novel, by virtue of his becoming the first Israelite monarch. His subsequent success in uniting, and for a while securing, the kingdom added to the status implicit in his special anointing by investing him with the qualities of supreme *redeemer* and, more important from a retrospective point of view, *saviour king*. Nevertheless, in this context, it must be stressed, that the messianic element itself was not of special significance in the person of Saul (in later generations, Israelite scribes attributed the title to gentile rulers such as Cyrus the Great – Is. 45:1) but rather the level he attained by being anointed.

For the Israelite nation, the other main novelty, which sprang from the anointing of Saul was the royal-dynastic constituent.

We know from the story of Gideon and Abimelech in the Book of Judges (Jg. 8:22; 9:2) that for several generations prior to the events recorded in the first book of Samuel, there had been some degree of acceptance or expectation of hereditary succession. In 1 Samuel, the stories of Eli and his heirs and of Samuel and his two sons indicate that this trend had become firmly established. Thus, it must be the case that when the people asked Samuel to anoint a king, they were also opting for royal-dynastic rule. Moreover, if the 'House of Saul' represented the first Israelite royal dynasty, its overthrow by David resulted, paradoxically, in the consolidation of the royal-hereditary concept.

The Seed of Jesse
At this point, it is important to say a little about the long, complex, not to say mysterious, development of the Judeo-Christian *meshiach* tradition.

During the previous two thousand years, from a time before the destruction of the second Temple in Jerusalem until the gates of Auschwitz, wherever and whenever things became desperate for the Israelite people, they would pray and hope for messianic deliverance.

The Kingdom of Judah's distinct historical survival, the Kingdom of Israel's disappearance, and a Davidic literary legacy combined to ensure that the people looked in anticipation towards redemption – primarily from the seed of Jesse. With the passage of time, a suffering people increasingly regarded David the giant-slayer – saviour and Lord's anointed – as a larger-than-life hero and a potent symbol of hope.

Faith in the 'House of David' became so entrenched that whenever an alleged messiah sought to establish his credentials, he announced his lineage as going back to Jesse. This has been an imperative from the time of Jesus and his disciples (Matt. 1:1-17; 15:21-28; 20:29-34 etc; Luke. 3:23-38) to the present day. If the theory presented in this book is correct, David was a false king-messiah, a traitor, and usurper of the 'true king-messiah'. The implications are sweeping, for all his supposed 'royal-messianic' descendants, however sincere, have to be false by association. Neither Jewish nor Christian beliefs can easily withstand such a blow.

Competing Messiahs

For millennia, Jewish mystics have brooded over the subject of the *meshiach*. From the earliest times, there has existed a puzzling competitor to the exclusively Davidic tradition: a belief that the saviour would emanate from the 'House of Joseph' or be *'Messiah, son of Joseph'*.[10] With typical pious tenacity, Jews and early Christians found ways of resolving this contradiction in accordance with the peculiar requirements of their own faiths. Jews decided that the 'Josephic Messiah' would come shortly before the 'Davidic Messiah,' as a sort of prologue to the crucial event.[11] Meanwhile, the Christian mythmakers, for whom that event had already occurred, installed a Josephic father/stepfather for the Davidic Christ. Even Jesus' Aramaic name, *Yeshua,* echoes that of the ancient Ephraimite/Josephite spiritual and national leader Joshua, or *Yehoshua* (in Hebrew) – 'God the saviour' or 'God is the saviour'.

These already murky waters are muddied further by the discovery in 1948 of an ancient but apparently distinct *dual messiah* tradition propagated by the Essene sect of Qumran.

According to this inter-Temple-period belief, it seems there were to be two concurrent messiahs of equal importance, one a priest and the other a king (1 QS. 9:1). There are many theories to explain the source for the Essene-tradition, from the exotic pairing of Pharaoh Akhenaten and his high priest Meryre to the relationship of David and his personally appointed high-priest, Zadok.[12] Additionally, scholars of the Jesus-as-Essene persuasion see in the John the Baptist/Christ duality a direct manifestation of the Qumran belief.[13] In this construction, they allude to John's priestly credentials as the son of Zacharias and his role as baptiser/anointer of Jesus, as the legitimate descendent of the house of David (Luke. 1; 5: 3).

Nevertheless, this book will show that the source for the Essene tradition (and all other Jewish and Christian messianic partnerships) is to be found in the original Israelite priest/king relationship of Samuel and Saul.

The roots of the tradition of a Messiah from the House of Joseph is probably a legacy from the time when the tribes of Israel – led by the 'sons of Joseph,' Manasseh and Ephraim – threw off the yoke of Judah and anointed their own king in the person of Jeroboam from the tribe of Manasseh. The rival messianic traditions of David and Joseph persisted and evolved throughout the following centuries. The original Saulide king-messiah went the way of his tribe, Benjamin, which was gradually absorbed, into both the larger tribes of Judah and (the Josephic) Ephraim. Thus, paradoxically, the one genuine royal messianic line was totally forgotten. The confusion over messianic constructs has resulted in a multitude of conflicting traditions – from messiah partnerships to double messiahs, priest-kings to priests *and* kings, one single event to a succession of events, and various permutations of the above.

Nevertheless, the concept of a kingly saviour derives explicitly from Saul. The priestly anointer – with his own special, if subordinate, messianic credentials, is neither Elijah (the favoured candidate of Jews), nor John the Baptist (the 'herald of Christ'), but Samuel. The confusion arose as a direct result of a deceit perpetrated by an ambitious and vainglorious tyrant by the name of David.

It is the tenacity of the Saulide spirit, that survives within the pages of the charming and picturesque first book of Samuel, which prompted the hypothesis presented in these pages. Its editorially chaotic style reflects successive attempts – some more deliberate than others – to erase the imprint of Saul. But the original intent is discernible to the alert eye. The experience is like perceiving what appears to be a pure white garment, then noticing that it contains a barely visible thread of blue. Once the eye becomes aware of the thread, it is impossible to ignore. Finally, one may realize that the faint blue thread holds the entire garment together.

Samuel in the Hill Country

1
Samuel
The Final Days of the Israelite Theocracy

'And I will raise up for Myself a faithful priest, who will act in
accordance with My wishes and My purposes. I will build for him an
enduring house; and he shall walk before my anointed for evermore'
(1 Sam. 2:35).

A Tribal Confederacy

Most commentators place the events of the First Book of Samuel toward
the end of the second millennium BCE, or just over three thousand years
ago. The tribes of Israel were settled within their allotted areas within the
land of Canaan, and the Exodus from Egypt was already a distant memory
– having occurred anywhere from 150 to 500 years earlier.[1] Following
a long, difficult, and often violent conquest of the country, the people
had established themselves as permanent inhabitants of the new 'Israel'.
A temporary torpor that infected the great powers of the time, such as
Hatti, Assyria, Babylon and especially Egypt, had opened a window of
opportunity for the smaller peoples of the region to flex their muscles
and, to a greater or lesser degree, map out their own destinies.[2]

In Israel's case, this national self-expression was initially epitomised
by charismatic, religious, military leaders, usually men (but sometimes
women), who appeared at times of crisis. During intermediate periods
of peace, they would remain in public office as 'judges' (Heb. Shoftim),
hence the naming of the era after them.[3] For the most part, the roles of
the judges were local and tribal (e.g. J. 11), but as time went on and Israel
became stronger and her enemies increasingly formidable, their operations
became pan-national in nature (e.g. J. 5: 14-18).

Under this theocratic regime, despite open rivalries and occasional
disputes, the tribes, mostly, co-operated with each other in the manner of
an amphictyony.[4] Tribal integrity was more or less honoured. By the time of
Deborah and Gideon, the Israelites, having grown more confident, ventured

down from their hilltop strongholds to take on their rivals in ever larger, formal battles for control of the fertile valleys (see Jg. 4; 5).

As the tribal nation became defined, its expanding borders were increasingly contested and its conflicts more international in character. The concept of establishing a king to rule all or most of the nation took root among those who believed that pan-tribal cohesion would lead to greater security and prosperity. The first experiment in kingship began, and ended badly, when Gideon's son Abimelech presumed to anoint himself unilaterally. Although he ruled a large part of the central hill country for three years – thanks to a combination of ruthlessness and the non-readiness of the populace for a monarchy – his half-brother Jotham was able to topple him and restore the regime of the judges (Jg. 9).

Nevertheless, the old theocratic system, so well suited for dealing with local and tribal emergencies, began to fail with the arrival on the scene of a potentially catastrophic threat, in the form of the mighty Philistines.

The Philistines

Exactly who the Philistines were, like everything else in this period of history, is a subject of incessant debate, raising issues related to demography and Near Eastern chronology. Suffice it to say here, that they were an eastern Mediterranean people – possibly of Cretan or Cypriot origin.[5]

The two characteristics of the Philistines which were of particular concern to the Israelites were, firstly, in contrast to their other mostly nomadic neighbours, they, like Israel, were a settler people. Thus, whereas an invasion by the nomadic, tent-dwelling Edomites normally meant a temporary inconvenience, the Philistines intended to stay put. Secondly, the Philistines were fine soldiers, rich in iron weaponry and chariots, and therefore well capable of securing their settlements within the fertile lowlands of the coastal plain. In the event, it was not long before the newcomers settled along the entire southwest coast of Canaan, where they established five city-states (a pentopolis), ruled by lords (Heb. seranim), which acted as a confederacy in times of war.[6]

It was apparently the arrival of the Philistines which resulted in the displacement of the hitherto maritime tribe of Dan to its second home in the north.[7] Hence, from very early on, large areas of Judah and Israel were under the yoke of this formidable 'Sea People'.

The transition from tribal theocratic amphictyony to monarchy was ultimately forced upon Israel by the ever-growing threat posed by the Philistines. Around 1020 BCE, the inevitable happened: after numerous skirmishes, the protagonists clashed in a large formal battle for control of the strategically important and agriculturally rich central lowlands.[8]

Geopolitical Cauldron

At the time of the great battle, Canaan comprised three main power bases (see map, p. 14):

1. The Philistine confederacy, as already stated, had dominion over the southwest;

2. Bordering the Philistines to the east (with the River Jordan forming the eastern extremity) was the mountainous territory of Judah (and nominally Simeon[9]);

3. To the north and east of these two regions lay the lands of the northern tribes, dominated by the powerful 'Joseph block' of Ephraim and Manasseh. These lands comprised the central and northern-Galilean uplands separated by the fertile Jezreel plain; the former of which, contained the religious cult centre, Shiloh.[10] This was by far the largest of the three areas, extending deep into Trans-Jordan – the territories of Manasseh, Gad, Reuben and (the possibly Canaanite) Gilead.[11]

A sizeable Canaanite community, including Jebusites and Gibeonites, occupied a significant enclave in the heart of these three areas. It is even speculated that several of the northernmost Israelite tribes – Asher[12] in particular – were native peoples who had either converted or been absorbed into the body of Israel during the course of settlement. There seems little doubt that this is what also later happened to most of the indigenous Canaanite population and, some hundreds of years later, to the Philistines themselves.[13]

Surrounding the entire area were;

1. to the north, the early (proto-) Phoenicians of Lebanon (possibly a 'northern settler' constituent of the Sea Peoples, who also included the 'southern settler' Philistines);[14]

2. to the east, the Ammonites and Moabites;

3. to the southeast, the Edomites;

4. to the strategically vital southwest, the Amalekites and Kenites.[15]

Such was the highly volatile national and political geography of the region in the eleventh century BCE.

The attention of the Philistines was focussed upon the agricultural valleys of central Israel. So, in the cause of survival, all the northern tribes flocked around mighty Ephraim and Manasseh to defend the lands so recently wrested from the original Canaanite owners (see Josh. 13). Conspicuous by their absence from the host of Israel were Judah, the strongest of the tribes, and Simeon. One reason may have been the memory of a possible reversal suffered during earlier encounters with the Philistines. Another cause for absence of the main tribe descended from Leah (Jacob's first wife) may have been a feeling of rivalry with the main northern tribes (principally descended from Jacob's second wife, Rachel, reflected in Gen.36: 23-26).[16] Another cause of possible resentment towards the Rachel tribes, was probably connected with the legacy of the long dead Joshua.[17]

Shiloh, Capital of All Israel

When Joshua placed the Ark of the Covenant at Shiloh in Ephraim, he was serving notice of the special place his own tribe occupied in the heart of the Creator (Josh. 18:1). The larger and more powerful tribe of Judah would have harboured an ever-increasing resentment over this slight, as evidenced in the early years of David's reign over all Israel by his removal of the Ark to Jerusalem (2 Sam. 6). This envy of the Joseph tribes, along with a sense of relative military security, may explain Judah's apparent isolationist policy in the early days of Israel's struggles with the Philistines and David's later readiness to ally himself with those enemies of Israel. Also, Shiloh's location had implications for the other tribes, especially the priestly tribe of Levi.[18]

While Israel remained a theocracy ruled by judges, the constant power in the land was the priesthood. Judges could come and go, but Levi remained the spiritual authority in Israel and Judah. Among the Levites, none were more influential than those who guarded the Ark of the Covenant and oversaw the sacred rites at the shrine in Shiloh. But once the theocratic regime was superseded by a monarchy, the supremacy of the Levites, and particularly the 'sons of Aaron' (Jos. *Antiquities* 5: 11. 5) would be fatally compromised.

Priests, Levites and Benjamin

Although they constituted a tribe, individual Levite clans (or 'houses') aligned patriotically with their host tribe (Josh. 21), just as in recent European history, priests of a trans-national church found themselves on opposing sides in war. The House of Eli, blessed with the sacred duty of officiating over the Ark and the sanctuary, was identified with Ephraim.[19] The same was true of Samuel and his family. The tribe of Benjamin, descendants of Jacob's youngest son (by Rachel), was in a position of strategic importance out of all proportion to its minimal geographical size and military strength. Wedged between Ephraim to the north and Judah to the south, the tribe was, on the one hand, vulnerable to the domination of its mightier neighbours. On the other hand, posing minimal threat, and by virtue of its central position, Benjamin uniquely qualified to provide Israel with leaders acceptable to the whole nation.[20]

Nazirite, Levite and Judge

Our story begins with the Ark of the Covenant housed in modest lodgings in Shiloh, the spiritual capital of All Israel, in Ephraim. Shiloh was the seat of Eli the high priest and his sons, ministers and judges to the people of Israel.

1 Sam. 1-3: During the long judgeship of Eli, there was a man by the name of Elkanah, (an Ephrathite) of Ephraim,[21] who had two wives, Hannah and Peninah. The latter had children, but Hannah was barren. In desperation, Hannah prayed that she might conceive, and even made Nazarite vows on behalf of the prospective child, dedicating him to the service of God for the duration of his life.[22] Her prayers were answered and she bore a son, calling him Samuel ('In God's Name').

Hannah was as good as her word, and from a young age Samuel spent his time in service at the shrine in Shiloh.[23] Because Eli's two sons, Hophni and Phinehas, had proved to be corrupt and wicked, Samuel – an honourable young man, became the high priest's main protégé.

One night in the shrine, while Samuel slept close to Ark of the Covenant, God called to him. The young lad, mistaking the voice for that of his master, went to Eli, who sent him back to bed. After this sequence of events was twice repeated, the high priest realised that it was the Lord's voice the boy was hearing, and he instructed Samuel that, if he were to hear the voice again, he should respond, 'Speak, Lord, for your servant is listening.' When he did so, the solemn words he heard spelled doom for Eli and his descendants, who were to pay the price for the wickedness of Hophni and Phinehas. The following morning, Samuel was afraid to convey the divine message to his mentor. However, unable to defy his master's interrogation, he eventually told Eli all that the Lord had said. The old priest accepted the terrible prophecy with phlegmatic piety.

By the time Samuel reached manhood, his reputation gradually spread beyond Shiloh through the entire land of Israel and he gained respect as a man of God.

The dramatic verse which heads this chapter, from early in the first of the two books that bear Samuel's name, probably emanates from the pen of an enthusiastic monarchist. In the Tanakh, 'my anointed' is a divine utterance used uniquely for describing Israelite kings, while the phrase 'walk before' is indicative of the relative importance of Samuel's role as herald and proclaimer of the king-to-be, in the same way as the patriarch Abraham "walk[ed] before [God]" (Gen. 17:1). Thus, in the quoted statements – supposedly uttered by God when speaking to Eli – the Lord Himself was actively preparing for a monarchy even before Samuel was born.

This linkage of future judge with future king illustrates the ancient perception that Samuel's role was intimately interwoven with that of Saul. It is also the first scriptural mention of the symbiotic relationship between 'priest' (i.e. prophet) and monarch that was to have such profound ramifications down the ages for the Judeo-Christian messianic tradition.

The text states that Samuel spent his childhood serving Eli at the shrine of Shiloh (1 Sam. 3:1). This must have been a typical education for a young Levite in that era. There is no reason to question that Samuel was an especially gifted and charismatic pupil of the old judge, well suited to the task the Lord was about to lay upon him.[24]

1 Sam. 4:1-11: The Philistines mustered their army at Aphek,[25] where they confronted the warriors of Israel. The early skirmishes went badly for the Israelites, so they sent word to Shiloh that their sacred talisman – the Ark – be brought to the field of battle. It duly arrived, escorted by Hophni and Phinehas. The triumphant roar that met the arrival of the Ark into camp momentarily unsettled the Philistines, who nevertheless proved too strong for Israel in the ensuing battle. The defeat was total. Thousands, among them the sons of Eli, were slain, and worse still in the eyes of the Israel, the Ark was lost to the victorious heathens.

The Transfer of Power

The narrative mentions the tribe of the future King of Israel for the first time:

1 Sam. 4:12-17: *A Benjaminite runner who survived the battle brought the dreadful tidings to Shiloh.*

'A Benjaminite man ran from the battlefield and reached Shiloh the same day; his clothes were rent, and there was earth upon his head.'

On receiving the news, Eli fell from his seat, broke his neck, and died. Phinehas' wife died after giving birth to their son, Ichabod.

On the face of it, this is merely telling us about a messenger arriving at Shiloh to inform Eli of the bad news from Aphek, and but for the partial identification of the runner, that would be all it is. However, the common biblical formula would have been to describe the messenger simply as a 'man of Israel'. We may therefore conclude that the runner's tribal identity is more than a gratuitous dash of colour added by the writer. The information – bearing in mind the forthcoming drama – is at the very least redolent with symbolism and perhaps, highly significant.

Saul son of Kish, as a prince of Benjamin – well into his forties at the time – was in all probability a leading combatant at Aphek. If Saul was there, his fellow clansmen, possibly including his eldest son, Jonathan, and his cousin Abner most likely accompanied him. It is not implausible, then, that the runner was one of these three men or another of their relatives. The probable presence of the Kish clan at the defeat of Israel also means that Saul and his family may have witnessed the loss of the

Ark and the deaths of Hophni and Phinehas. Apart from the profound impression such an event must have had on the minds of devout men, there is an added symbolic resonance to consider. For, here we observe the effective termination of the House of Eli as a power in the land. This was witnessed in all probability by a member of the House of Kish, to which the same power would – in the style of the biblical narrative – shortly be transferred.

In the same way that some commentators regard the scenes of Saul tearing the cloak of Samuel (1 Sam. 15: 27) and then later, David cutting off the corner of the cloak of Saul (1 Sam. 24:5), as power transference allegories,[26] the graphic image of an exhausted, battle-scarred warrior of Benjamin (possibly a clansman of the future king) delivering the fateful news to Eli is rich with symbolic drama. This would be one of the few pristine pro-Saul fragments to have survived the later editorial purges of the first book of Samuel.

For the moment, however, Samuel continues to command the stage.

According to the narrative, by the time of the Aphek battle, Samuel was established as a notable holy man and judge in his own right. Thus, in the wake of Israel's darkest hour since the crossing of the Jordan under Joshua, there was a man well placed to respond to the emergency and to begin rallying the people.

Judges, Generals and Sacred Chests

The spiritual and national ideal for all the judges of Israel was enshrined in the character of Moses – the ostensible founder of the Israelite religion, whose many roles included those of miracle-working shaman, guide, and teacher in all the affairs of life – both spiritual and secular.

Moses' deputy was Joshua, who, after the great leader's death, combined judgeship with military command. Subsequent to Joshua, and as Israel established itself in the land of Canaan, most of the succeeding judges seem to have copied his example, in that they were originally charismatic warrior chieftains who 'retired' (or, as in the case of Deborah, 'returned') to the role of judicial and spiritual leaders in times of peace.

The progression seems to have worked something like this:
- An enemy (often nomadic) would invade, conquer and oppress a part of the country.
- Typically, the tribes so afflicted would eventually rise up in revolt to throw the invader out.
- The hero who led the revolt would continue bearing judicial and social authority until the day he or she died. Thus, the leader became, or returned to being a judge.

The common and essential ingredient in all judges, from Moses to Samuel, was charisma – referred to in the Bible as 'the spirit of God'. This charisma, blended with a burning faith in the God of Israel, was a powerful spiritual and political force.

Another source of power for the soldiers of ancient Israel was the gold-plated, cedarwood box known variously as the Ark, the Ark of God, the Ark of the Covenant, and the Ark of the Testimony.[27] With its capture by the Philistines, the narrative informs us, 'the glory . . .departed from Israel'.

What did the Israelites of this period believe the Ark contained? The tradition that it held both sets (broken and whole) of the tablets bearing the Ten Commandments and other artefacts, may date from a period later than the events described in Samuel. However, far more important to the Israelites than the Ark's contents was that the Shechinah – the very presence of God on Earth – hovered above its lid (known as the Mercy Seat), between and under the outstretched wings of two gilded cherubim (Lev. 16:2-3; 13-15). This 'knowledge', that God resided within the midst of the army, infused the warriors of Israel with the belief that they were invincible.

1 Sam. 5-6: The Ark spent seven months on display as a trophy throughout the lands and cities of the Philistines. But then it began to wreak havoc among the victors, causing destruction and an outbreak of disease. In an attempt to halt the devastation, the Philistines decided to return the Ark to Israel, together with gift offerings to the Israelite God. It was placed on an ox-drawn cart, but en route its destructive influence persisted, resulting in the deaths of the Israelite inhabitants of Bet-Shemesh.[28] The Ark was eventually housed in the home of Abinadab, a priest of Kiryath-jearim[29] in Benjamin, with whom it remained for twenty years.

The books of Joshua and Judges imply that the Ark had been moved to Shiloh during the earliest days of the settlement, remaining there until the Battle of Aphek (Josh. 18:1). There is no definite record of its use in battle by any of the judges after Joshua. The army's demand for it at Aphek after unsuccessful encounters with the Philistines reveals the scale of the conflict and the level of military desperation. Yet this was as nothing compared with the entire nation's despondency when the army was subsequently routed by the Philistines and the Ark was lost. Its return seven months later must have done much to restore the people's flagging morale.

1 Sam. 7: Samuel now became leader in Israel. After gathering the army at Mizpah, he defeated the Philistines and went on to liberate most of the recently conquered land. Meanwhile, his judgeship continued and a peace treaty was signed with the Amorites.[30]

Chapter four shows that both 'Samuel's victory' and the peace treaty are events that are both misplaced and misappropriated in the narrative.

Two Pairs of Bad Sons

At this point in the Samuel narrative we are introduced to the concept of hereditary succession amongst the ruling, non-priestly, elite of Israel.

1 Sam. 8: As Samuel grew old; he appointed his two sons, Joel and Abijah as his deputies and sent them out to judge in Israel and Judah (from their base at Beer-sheba).[31] However, they were corrupt and accepted bribes. The disillusioned people asked Samuel to install a king over them – a request that mortified him. Despite his warnings and entreaties, the people persisted in their demands. The Lord, though angered at this rejection of His own divine rule by Israel, instructed Samuel to yield to the popular clamour. The prophet reluctantly did so.

Unlike Joel and Abijah, destined to take over only one of Samuel's roles (that of judge), Hophni and Phinehas had been set to inherit Eli's priestly mantle as well as his judgeship. But neither pair of sons actually succeeded their father, and the Tanakh casts all four men as sinners: ". . . Now Eli's sons were scoundrels; they paid no heed to the Lord" (1 Sam. 2:12).While, the sons of Samuel, ". . . did not follow in his ways; they were bent on gain, they accepted bribes, and they subverted justice." (1 Sam. 8:3).

Samuel's sons sinned primarily against their fellow men, while Eli's sinned directly against God – a far more serious crime in the eyes of the pious compilers of the final narrative. Moreover, Eli, in apparent contrast to Samuel, is implicated in the wickedness of Hophni and Phinehas because of his awareness of, and failure to adequately respond to their sins. Hence, all three men died prematurely, and the House of Eli was subsequently terminated in the time of Solomon. Samuel and his sons, on the other hand, suffered only the second part of the penalty, in so much as they seem to have survived, even though nothing more is heard of the 'House of Samuel' beyond these passages.

There is much to learn from this double episode. By this time, the position of judge was hereditary, like the high priesthood.[32] But, this heritability presented the author with the challenge of explaining why the sons of two saintly men – Eli and Samuel – never succeeded their fathers. The premature deaths of Eli's sons are passed off as direct punishment for their sins. Within a generation the 'House of Zadok' had superseded Eli's priestly dynasty. This was explained as a consequence of the sin in which Eli himself was implicated.[33] This is a prime example of 'pious' redaction that embellishes the narrative while at the same time obscuring the underlying history.

Although both pairs of sons probably existed, their alleged wickedness offers a first example of expedient repetition. In reality, all four men may have been of good character. Yet for the sake of the author's overall agenda, their reputations became tools with which to shape the narrative. Apart from any association with the House of Saul, the houses of Eli and Samuel may have been considered credible rivals to David in their own right.[34] It requires little imagination to see a Davidic agenda as the source of what were probably gross libels – a pattern repeated through the narrative.

> ## Conclusion 1
> The stories of the 'wicked sons' in the book of Samuel confirm that hereditary rule was established in Israel before the end of the era of the judges. These stories represent an attempt by pro-David partisans to consign potentially competing dynasties to oblivion.

How many Samuels?

Whatever the truth regarding the character of the sons of Eli and Samuel, as just concluded, it seems clear that the people were firm in their desire for a monarchy. The success of their petitions leads us to the second and main character of this work – Saul.

1 Sam. 9:1-9: At the time when Samuel agreed to the people's request for a king, Saul was searching the countryside for his father's lost asses. He was about to give up and return home when his servant pointed out that there was a local holy man in the nearby town who might be able to assist them.[35]

"There is a man of God in that town, and the man is highly esteemed; everything he says comes true. Let us go there; perhaps he will tell us about the errand on which we set out."

This is how we are introduced to Saul, soon-to-be first King of Israel. It is intriguing that Saul is ignorant of the prophet Samuel, when one considers that, according to the narrative, 'All Israel from Dan to Beersheba knew that Samuel was trustworthy as a prophet of the Lord' (1 Sam. 3:20). The apparent discrepancies can be explained in several ways:

1. Samuel's fame may have been exaggerated – implausible given that he had already won an important victory over the Philistines at Mizpah.

2. The young farmer Saul may have been unworldly or sheltered – hardly consistent with leading an army of All Israel a week later.

3. We might conclude that the story of Saul's first meeting with Samuel is apocryphal, either in whole or in part.

The textual anomalies over Saul's first anointing are, however, almost entirely due to confused chronology. Untangling this confusion reveals answers to many more problems within the First Book of Samuel.

The importance of Saul's 'first' anointing is anyway reduced by the mass witnessing of his later sacred immersions at the hands of the great prophet and judge. Nevertheless, this story has taken on a different significance which has done much to convince the scholarly community of a dual authorship for this section of 1 Samuel.[36] This view holds that the grafting together of contrasting traditions has resulted in two distinct Samuels in the person of one character. The first is the great prophet of Israel – commanding huge assemblies, leading vast armies, working portents and wonders. The second, more historical, character is merely a local holy man, revered in his native territory of Ephraim and Benjamin. The latter is the Samuel who began a small-scale resistance movement, later taken over by Saul. In this construct, Great Samuel was an anti-monarchist, while Minor Samuel was an enthusiastic kingmaker. The polarised attitudes of the two Samuels are said to reflect the eras in which the two authors wrote. Because of its more elaborate linguistic style, and hostility towards kingly rule echoing the words of Hosea (mid-eighth century BCE), Great Samuel is dated to a time of pious disillusionment with the monarchy of his own day. This is later than the period from which Minor Samuel's earthier and simpler style would have emanated. The monarchist author of Minor Samuel could have been Davidic, Israelite, or both.[37] The well-established 'double Samuel' hypothesis is cogent and almost credible, but is only required because of a perverse faith in the sequencing of events in the superficial narrative. Preoccupation with textual form forces commentators to postulate the existence of what are, in effect, two caricatured personalities. Stronger focus on the textual substance however, reveals a single, plausible, Samuel, rooted in history.

Regardless of the number of different authors, there is no requirement for two Samuels if we order the narrative text into correct historical sequence. For instance, if we accept that, at their first meeting, Samuel was relatively unknown and Saul was young, this explains the son of Kish's ignorance of the prophet. This illuminates the historical picture more than any convoluted critical theory. The re-establishment of a single, evolving Samuel is the first step in untangling the chronological confusion that afflicts so much of our received understanding of the first book that bears the judge's name.

Conclusion 2
A confused chronology permitted the personality of the single Samuel to be fragmented and pressed into service by a variety of agenda-driven authors, thus obscuring the historical Samuel.[38]

Prince Saul

2
Saul
The Prince of Israel

There was a man of Benjamin, whose name was Kish . . . a man of
substance. And he had a young son, named Saul, an excellent young
man; no one among the Israelites was handsomer than he; he was a
head taller than any of the people (1 Sam. 9:1-2).

A Judge without a General

After the battle of Aphek, the Philistines occupied much of northern
and central Israel. The death of Eli and his sons, the loss of the Ark, and
the probable destruction of Shiloh led to popular disaffection with the
priestly leadership (Jem. 7: 12&14 and 26: 6&9 imply that Shiloh was
destroyed). Any sense the Israelites may have had that they deserved their
fate – that it was divine retribution for the collective sin of doing 'right
in their own eyes' (Jg. 21:25) – was overshadowed by the consciousness
of the Ark's apparent fallibility. Moreover, their religious leaders had
been found wanting.

Samuel was no doubt charismatic and revered, but he was fundamentally
a man of God. This association may have compromised his leadership in
the eyes of his god-forsaken compatriots. While his earlier good works
and years of sound judging in his hometown of Ramah[1] confirmed his
Ephraimite credentials, his previous affinity with the house of Eli provoked
a general mistrust. Even if Samuel possessed military skills, after the dismal
performance of Hophni and Phinehas at Aphek, the men of Israel were loath
to follow another holy-man into battle. Therefore, Samuel's first task as
leader of his people was to find a man to be his general.

Samuel would have learnt three very important lessons from the
Israelite defeat at Aphek. First, that the northern tribes alone, without
Judah in the ranks, had little chance of victory against the mighty Philistine
army in formal battle. Second that unity was essential to win back and
then maintain the independence of All Israel against such a formidable

foe. Finally that no army of Israel should ever again go into battle without
strong and decisive leadership. Nevertheless, Samuel knew how difficult
it would be to persuade Judah or Ephraim to follow a general from the
others tribe, or from any of the main rival tribes. Neither would they
deign to follow a prince from any of the peripheral tribes. This left only
one acceptable tribal candidate from which Samuel could choose his
charismatic military leader.[2]

As we have seen, Benjamin's uncomfortable geographical location
ensured the trust of its larger neighbours. Despite its diminutive size,
Benjamin enjoyed a sound military reputation. In fact, during the times
of the judges, this small tribe had not been afraid to take on the larger
tribes in battle and had gained a reputation as an adversary to be reckoned
with (Jg. 19-21).

Nonetheless, it might not have been easy for Samuel to convince the
tribal elders. Bruised sensibilities and a substantial degree of resistance
were unavoidable. What was needed was a military victory, however
modest, which would ensure the rallying of all Israel to the banner of his
chosen general.

'Among the Prophets'

The following presents the narrative's version of just how Samuel – with
God's guidance – chose his Benjaminite:

1. Sam. 9:11-10.1: *After Saul had decided to seek out the 'holy man', a
group of girls directed him to the 'high place' where the seer was making
sacrifice and eating with a number of men.[3] Samuel had been forewarned
concerning the approach of the young Benjaminite by God Himself, who
had told him that Saul was His 'chosen one' to be prince over Israel.*

*'. . . I will send a man to you from the territory of Benjamin, and you
shall anoint him ruler of my people Israel. He will deliver My people
from the hands of the Philistines . . .'*

*Samuel reassured Saul about the lost asses and invited him to join the
feast. To his surprise, Saul found himself seated at the place of honour,
and served the choicest portion. The next morning, Samuel escorted Saul
from the town.*

*'Samuel took a flask of oil, and poured some on Saul's head and
kissed him and said: "the Lord herewith anoints you ruler over His own
people".*

For a Benjaminite to command the loyalty and obedience of his Josephic
brethren, he would need to possess exceptional qualities. Samuel found
these abundant in Saul – fine looks, imposing stature, charisma, and

proven courage in battle. Additionally, as we shall come to learn, Saul would prove to be a man of humility, dignity, and mercy (1 Sam. 9: 21; 10: 16, 21-22, 27; 11: 12-13).

This combination of attributes fitted him perfectly for the role of a leader required to inspire both awe and affection. Samuel was aware that men would lay down their lives for such a captain. Meanwhile, in an apparent contradiction, the narrative also portrays Saul as an innocent young man, more concerned with his father's mules than with the prospect of leading the liberation of Israel. However, there is an often overlooked clue in the narrative that seems to suggest that the choice of Saul was not merely based upon his personality, but also on his familial provenance – when Samuel says to his somewhat dubious guest, "And for whom is all Israel yearning, if not for you and all your ancestral house?" (1 Sam. 9: 20) Be he the proven soldier of this hypothesis or merely the innocent stripling of messianic presupposition, Saul's pedigree was such as to have made him the natural and apparently active choice of the people even before he had ever led them into battle.

1 Sam. 10:2-16: Before they parted, Samuel told his new sceptical captain of a series of auspicious events and signs which would occur on his way home. These would convince him of his destiny. Samuel then commanded Saul to meet him in seven days at Gilgal, where he would give him further instructions. Everything happened exactly the way Samuel foretold, culminating in Saul's being overcome with prophetic fervour. A great change was noted in Saul by everyone.

' . . . the people said one to another, "What's happened to the son of Kish? Is Saul too among the prophets?"'

Upon Saul's return home, his uncle[5] enquired about what had occurred between him and Samuel. However, Saul related nothing of his recent experiences.

Whether there is any truth in the story of the lost mules is academic. The two traditions that (a) Saul was a young farmer and that (b) Samuel was not yet a national figure (but merely a local holy man) when they first met is, as stated previously, of fundamental importance.

The genuine reason for their meeting could have been any number of things. Most likely, it had something to do with 'anointing' – though not to the captaincy of Israel. We know that the families of both Saul and David were wealthy (1 Sam. 9; Ruth 2:1). Their respective fathers, Kish and Jesse, were – according to other parts of Samuel and the Book of Ruth (in the case of Jesse) – rich landowners well before their sons' rise to power. Almost certainly, Kish and Jesse were tribal princes[6] who on occasion would have encountered, and perhaps employed, Samuel.

Anointing with sacred fluids by holy men was the common method by which anyone was promoted to any rank of importance in the biblical world.[7] In the light of this, and bearing in mind the relative proximity of Ramah and Zelah (2 Sam. 21: 14), the hometowns of Samuel and Saul respectively, it seems safe to assume that Samuel did indeed anoint Saul at their first meeting. Anointing was merely an everyday duty in the life of an eleventh-century BCE holy man and a common rite of passage for a youth of free and high birth in ancient Israel (somewhat akin to a modern-day bar mitzvah). This was interwoven, however, by the scriptural mythmaker, with the much later captaincy anointing, and embellished with apocryphal signs and wonders.

One sign, which we ought to take seriously, given what we understand about the charismatic nature of Saul's military predecessors, is the statement that he was 'among the prophets'. Whatever may have been involved in Samuel's first anointing of the youthful Saul, there is no doubt that the second ceremony (raising him to the office of Prince of Israel) effected his initiation into the sacred rites of the 'prophets' of Israel. These rites (which, according to some biblical scholars, may have involved the use of powerful narcotics and possibly culminated in veritable hallucinogenic orgies) were the expected preparation for a man destined, and most importantly, authorised by God to liberate his people.[8] It was not enough for Saul to be endowed with extraordinary human charisma. In the eyes of the people, it was imperative that their new leader should be infused – literally – with the spirit of God. In other words, Samuel gave added authority to his captain by making him a fellow initiate. Whether this did anything for Saul's soldiering abilities at the outset of his career was less important than his being invested with a prophetic charisma that might make him – this obscure Benjaminite – acceptable as a general to the army of Israel.

All this would occur long after his first meeting with Samuel.

> ## Conclusion 3
> The first meeting between Saul and Samuel occurred long before the disaster of Aphek, when Samuel had not yet achieved national standing, and Saul was still a youth. This meeting became confused with an occasion following the battle of Aphek when Saul received a low-key, military-related anointing as 'captain' of Israel.[9]

Too many Mizpahs?

Meanwhile, 'Samuel summoned the people to a gathering at Mizpah;' (1 Sam. 10:17) In the days of the judges, when an assembly of some or all of the people was necessary, they were summoned to a 'high place'. In

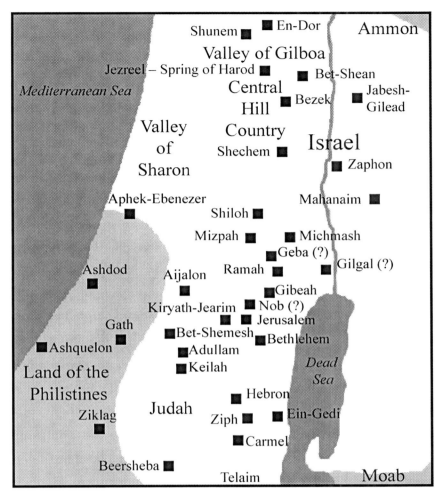

Saul's Kingdom and his main sphere of influence and activity

the first book of Samuel, the most common reason for such gatherings was a mustering of the levy. The high place would serve as a convenient, strategic, and defensible gathering area for the troops and a perfect setting for the customary pre-combat rites.[10] Places such as Mizpah and Gilgal were typical sites; thus, at first glance, there is nothing of particular significance in the fact that Samuel is said to have gathered the army at Mizpah on two separate occasions. Yet, further scrutiny reveals certain anomalies.

· The first gathering preceded the military victory at Mizpah in which 'General Samuel' reversed the gains the Philistines had made at Aphek: 'Samuel said, "Assemble all Israel to Mizpah, and I will pray to the Lord for you . . ."' (1 Sam. 7:5)

· The second was for the election and coronation of the new king.

This is all very plausible. However, if Samuel's victory following the first Mizpah gathering was as conclusive as the story would have us believe – 'the Philistines were humbled and did not invade the territory of Israel again; and the hand of the Lord was against the Philistines as long as Samuel lived' (1 Sam. 7:13) – we are bound to ask ourselves: Why was it that, at the start of Saul's reign, the oppression of the Philistines was still effective? This burdensome rule over the greater part of Israel included the territories of Saul and Samuel. If 'Samuel's victory' at Mizpah had been so total, why, at the outset of Saul's campaign, does the Bible state that the Philistines had control over all metal (and in particular arms) manufacture within their newly conquered lands? 'No smith was to be found in all the land of Israel, for the Philistines were afraid that the Hebrews[11] would make swords and spears' (1 Sam. 13:19). If Israel had been freed by Samuel at Mizpah, there would have been no need for Saul's subsequent war of liberation. Furthermore, if Samuel was indeed a successful general and leader (even allowing for the alleged shortcomings of his sons and his priestly connections), why is it that in the next episode, immediately following the prophet's victory, the people called for a king?

The author of the Samuel narrative attempts to explain these obvious incongruities, interpolating a long interval between the two Mizpah gatherings – sufficient time for Samuel's supposed gains to be reversed. Yet, this does not hold water because, as we recall, 'the Philistines were humbled . . . as long as Samuel lived'.

All of which leaves us with a confused picture. On the one hand, there is the superlative judge who subdued the Philistines 'all his days', while on the other hand, a perversely unappreciative people demand a king whose primary task is to reverse the enemy's gains – a task allegedly already accomplished by Samuel.

Once more, the application of common sense will deliver us from confusion.

The major points are these:
· First, there is the common denominator of Samuel mustering the people at Mizpah;
· Second, there is the location of Mizpah itself, in the land of Benjamin.

It is almost unknown, prior to the establishment of Jerusalem by David, for the same location to be chosen twice for a gathering place of the people as Mizpah was by Samuel. On both occasions, Israel was about to fight an important battle against the Philistines.

This apparent duplication may in reality be merely an attempt by an anti-monarchist author to mask the true role of Saul in the Israelite overthrow of Philistine oppression. 'The hand of the Lord' which was against the Philistines 'as long as Samuel lived' was an allegorised reference to the very human victor of the battle of Mizpah – the Israelite hero, Saul.

Conclusion 4
'Hand of the Lord' was a metaphor for Saul – the genuine victor of a single battle of Mizpah. The description of General Samuel was an invention of a later anti-monarchist author.[12]

Ultimately, we shall see that the single gathering and subsequent battle at Mizpah occurred much later in Saul's career than the biblical narrative suggests and that it was the grand culmination of his war of liberation against the Philistines. It will be shown not only that Mizpah was Saul's victory (rather than Samuel's) but also how his success forced Samuel to anoint the victorious Benjaminite warrior as King of Israel.

We have now reached a critical point in our analysis.

Orthodox Sequence	Major Variants
1 Sam. 8: Samuel has two wicked sons.	
The people demand that he make them a king; Samuel fails to dissuade them.	
1 Sam. 9: Saul, the son of Kish, is wandering in country of Ephraim searching for the lost asses of his father; he approaches Ramah.	
Samuel is forewarned by God of Saul's arrival; Samuel entertains Saul at his house.	
1 Sam. 10: Samuel anoints Saul 'captain' of Israel; he instructs Saul to meet him in seven days at Gilgal to receive instructions.	Saul was anointed 'captain' of Israel by Samuel at the outset of the war of liberation against the Philistines, by which time he was a respected and seasoned warrior, well into middle age.
Samuel gathers the people at Mizpah.	

Saul Turns Ahia away

3
Saul
'The Hand of the Lord'

Do you see the one whom the Lord has chosen? There is none like
him among all the people. (1 Sam. 10:24)

The 'Choosing' of Saul

Because of its oral origins, for the sake of an unbroken story, biblical
narrative nearly always places individuals or eras in convenient
juxtaposition. Messy historical transitions are minimised or ignored in the
interests of telling a straightforward story. This sacrifice of reality for the
sake of narrative conciseness has produced many chronological puzzles,
including the confusion that surrounds the supposed second meeting of
Saul and Samuel.

Whatever the exact truth, it is likely that Saul, between his initial
youthful anointing and the Battle of Aphek, demonstrated sufficient
prowess as a warrior to convince Samuel that he should be promoted
to the position of general – or more properly, in Israelite terms, nagid
(ruler or captain). Thus, the gap between their first meeting and Saul's
anointing as nagid was considerably longer than the stated 'seven
days'.

We shall see, however, that the myth/tradition of the 'seven days' does
nevertheless contain interesting clues that will enable us to trace the genuine
chronology of Saul's rise through the ranks from nagid to king.

According to 1 Samuel, the people were unaware of the identity of their
king-to-be until the very moment of his 'election' by divine lots:[1]

*1 Sam. 10:17-21: The people of Israel gathered at Mizpah once more,
where Samuel grudgingly informed them that the time had come to elect
a king. Following the drawing of lots, Saul was chosen.*

On the face of it, the story of Saul's 'election' to the kingship by the
drawing of lots seems to contradict the assertion that Saul had already been

chosen by God. This apparent conflict has been one of the bases of the multi-authorship theory. The earlier story of lost asses and divine selection is generally seen as apocryphal, while the later account is normally regarded as more historical. Additionally, the first story is perceived as being sympathetic to Saul – and therefore, older. The academic consensus appears to be claiming, counterintuitively, that the more ancient tradition (and thus closer to the events described) is less accurate than the more recent one.

It seems equally plausible, however, that the ceremony of the lots was merely a symbolic and graphic ritual to confirm what was in effect a fait accompli.[2] In other words, it was imperative for Samuel to show the people that their choice was endorsed by the Lord himself. That the lots would necessarily have been rigged would not have posed a problem to an experienced holy man such as Samuel, and neither would the morality of such an election. The historical Samuel we are sketching wanted what was best for Israel, and thus, what was best for God.

Saul, by any other name

The subject of Saul's name is one that commands a rare degree of scholarly consensus. Pious and secular scholars are as one in affirming that the name of Israel's first king is apocryphal (i.e. traditional). In support of this hypothesis, they point to the Israelite meaning of Saul's name, 'asked for' or 'was asked for', and the fact that it reflects the people's demand of Samuel and God that they be given a king.[3]

> Then all the elders of Israel assembled and came to Samuel at Ramah, and they said to him, "You have grown old and your sons have not followed your ways. Therefore appoint a king for us like all other nations." (1 Sam. 8:4-5)

In his thought-provoking book, *A Test of Time*, David Rohl suggests an additional name for Saul.[4] Adapting a technique developed by Immanuel Velikovsky, he readjusts the chronologies of Israel and Egypt to align the Amarna period in Egypt with the lives of Saul and David. In doing so he asserts that many of the central characters of 1 Sam. are mentioned in the famous royal correspondence discovered at Tel-el-Amarna in Middle Egypt at the turn of the last century – in the form of clay tablets engraved with cuneiform syllabic script. Indeed, Saul is revealed as one of the correspondents. Names similar to those of David (Dadua or Tadua), Jesse (Yishuya), and Joab (Ayab) are adduced to support the theory. In stark contrast, however, the name of the central personality of Rohl's Amarna drama – bears no resemblance to the biblical name of Saul, whom he equates with the Amarna correspondent Labayu (or Labaya) – meaning 'Great Lion of God'.

The 'revisionist' Rohl concurs with the conventional theory that Saul was merely a later insertion by the compiler of the Samuel narrative, while neither he nor the conventional position hesitate to accept the genuineness of the stated 'given' names of David et al. The simple possibility that Saul was, in fact, Saul – just as David was, probably simply David – is never considered.[5]

The problem of Saul's name only arises because, unlike for example, the treatment of Samuel or Moses, the stories of Saul and David omit details of their births, as well as the usual anecdotes explaining why they were given their names. It may be that Saul's mother gave him that name because she had asked for a child from God, in much the same way as Hannah had prayed for Samuel.[6]

Conclusion 5
Saul was simply Saul.

Right War, Wrong Time

The time has come for us to return to Mizpah, which is about to become the scene in a defining moment in the history of Israel – the coronation of its first king.

1 Sam. 22-26: Saul, terror-stricken at his selection, fled the scene and hid among piles of baggage. He was soon found and presented to the people, most of whom were eager to acclaim him as their king. Samuel then wound things up by recording the 'laws of kingship' in writing and laying them 'before the Lord'.[7]

Saul also went home to Gibeah[8] accompanied by upstanding men, whose hearts God had touched.[9]

Saul would not liberate his future capital for some time. Hence, his return to Gibeah at this point seems unlikely. If Saul went anywhere with his band of men, it may have been to Zelah[10] – his ancient family home – at the very outset of the liberation campaign, following his historical anointing as nagid. (This presumes that Zelah was not itself occupied by the Philistines.)

His return to Gibeah, with a substantially larger body of men, did not happen for another year, following his great victory at Mizpah and his subsequent anointing as King of Israel.

The Bible informs us that Saul's first great military crisis sprang from the opposite side of the map to that inhabited by the Philistines.

1 Sam. 11:1-11: *A short while later, Nahash, the King of Ammon, besieged the town of Jabesh-Gilead[11] in the Trans-Jordan section of Israel. He said he would accept the town's surrender only on condition that the right eye of each inhabitant be put out. The elders of Jabesh-Gilead requested a seven-day respite from attack, during which they could seek aid from other sources, and this was granted. When their pleas reached Saul, he became enraged and told his subjects, in the strongest terms, what he expected of them.*

'And he took a yoke of oxen and cut them into pieces, which he sent by messengers throughout the territory of Israel, with the warning "Thus shall be done to the cattle of anyone who does not follow Saul and Samuel into battle!" Terror from the Lord fell upon the people and they came out as one man.'[12]

Saul mustered an army of 330,000 men from Israel and Judah at Bezek,[13] under his and Samuel's joint 'banner'. He sent a message back to Jabesh-Gilead that the town could expect deliverance the next day. The Gileadites then misinformed Nahash that they would surrender the next morning. In fact, the only thing the Ammonites experienced the following day was a terrible defeat at the hands of Saul's army, which took them by surprise and destroyed them.

Gibeonites and Benjaminites
Saul now reveals the forgiving side of his character.

1 Sam. 11:12-13: *After Saul's election, one group of men, 'the children of Belial',[14] had refused to send tribute to their new king, saying he was a poor choice. Saul had not reacted to this act of defiance. Now, in response to a public demand that members of the group be executed, he again showed leniency.*

Saul replied; 'No man shall be put to death this day! For this day the Lord has brought victory to Israel'.

Saul's evolution from captain of hundreds to king over thousands – with the capacity to launch massive campaigns such as the one against Ammon described later in the narrative – was a gradual process. Certainly, at the outset of his reign, he was in no position to take action against neutral or dissident Canaanites. For the same reason, the story of his war with Nahash is obviously misplaced.[15]

Saul's two displays of leniency towards the children of Belial (literally 'sons of darkness' and/or 'scoundrels') raise several interrelated issues concerning his character and his style of leadership.

Similarly, the extent to which Saul ruled over or merely cooperated with various peoples would have reflected, to a greater or lesser degree, how those tribes perceived the Philistine encroachment. In the case of the Gibeonites, and possibly the Amorites (i.e. all other Canaanites), there was a shared interest with the Israelites in resisting the Philistines. These were all fundamentally pastoral peoples whose lack of walled cities and heavy weaponry made them especially vulnerable to massed chariots and ironclad phalanxes in open battle. Their main hope of resistance lay in a unified effort. Thus – so far as their fear of the Philistines was concerned – they were natural allies.

Perhaps the greatest of all Saul's apparently non-Israelite allies came from among the Gileadites, whom he liberated during his first royal campaign. Although most scholars, especially those of a pious Jewish persuasion, see the term Gileadites as simply a generic appellation for the Trans-Jordanian half of the tribe of Manasseh, some academics believe that a significant minority of this population was of non-Israelite stock. While the former point to the name Gad hidden within the G-ile-ad-ite title, the latter regard the fact of a distinct identification as evidence that the Gileadites were indeed a separate, non-Israelite people.[16] As we will learn, a close reading of the various texts tends to support the latter position, and thus it does seem that the close association with Israel was of the pragmatic variety rather than through blood ties (Josh. 10). This appears to be further evidence of both the considerable range and the racial diversity of Saul's nascent realm.

Many other tribes and peoples preferred to maintain neutrality vis-à-vis the Israelite kingdom. These were mainly urban Canaanites, such as the Jebusites and the inhabitants of Bet-shean, who dwelt in the relative safety of walled cities.[17] They were conscious that so long as the Israelites and the Philistines were preoccupied with each other, they had little to fear. They could postpone committing themselves to one side or another until an obvious victor became apparent. Saul's display of leniency towards the children of Belial and any other possible waverers within this fragile environment was thus as pragmatic as it may have been humane.

Nevertheless, pragmatism as well as mercy are useful qualities in a leader, and Saul was to demonstrate both on several occasions during his reign.

God and Baal
Another intriguing issue raised by Saul's leniency is the ambiguity of his own religious leanings. Although Saul was a passionate devotee of the God of Israel, it does seem that, in common with many of his Israelite contemporaries, he had more than a passing flirtation with indigenous Canaanite religion.

Later in the story when his daughter Michal helps her husband David escape from an irate Saul, we are informed that: '. . . Michal then took the household idol, and laid it on the bed . . .' (1 Sam. 19:13) In addition, several of the names contained within Saul's family tree contain the Baal[18] element – as 1 Chronicles (9:35-40) states: "The father of Gibeon, Jehiel lived in Gibeon. . . . His first-born son, Abdon; then Zur, Kish, Baal. . . . Kish begot Saul, Saul begot Jonathan . . . and Eshbaal . . . and the son of Jonathan was Merib-baal. . . .

In 1 Samuel, some of these names have been given the alternative ending boshet – for example, Ish-(Esh)-Boshet. Boshet is normally translated as 'shame' and would thus seem to represent an anti-Saul or pious corruption of the original names. Allowing for a measure of post-Davidic slurring of the Saulide name in all of these verses, and bearing in mind the cultural melting-pot that was tenth-century BCE Canaan, it is probable that the influence of the Canaanite Baal found its way into the names and superstitions of the family of Kish.

It is also possible that the relationship between the indigenous people of Gibeon (not to be confused with Gibeah – Saul's eventual capital) and Benjaminites resulted in personal and religious interchange as well as cultural.[19] Indeed, the strong and persistent association of Gibeah with Saul casts an ambiguity over all Benjaminite tribal origins, which may help explain why the daughter of Israel's first king kept a life sized idol in her sleeping quarters.

Conclusion 6
The cultic practices of eleventh-century BCE Israelites and their new king were syncretistic.[20]

How many Anointings?
Following their victory over Nahash, the people decided to confirm Saul as king at the high place of Gilgal.[21] 'So all the people went to Gilgal and there at Gilgal they declared Saul king before the Lord' (1 Sam. 11:15). This verse must be considered in conjunction with two earlier passages, the first of has which already been cited: 'Samuel took a flask of oil and poured some on Saul's head and kissed him, and said, "The Lord herewith anoints you ruler over his own people." ' (1 Sam. 10:1). And, 'Samuel said to the people, "Do you see who the Lord has chosen? There is none like him among all the people." And all the people acclaimed him, shouting, "Long live the king!" ' (1 Sam. 10:24).

These three passages have provoked endless scholarly debate, and they are consistently cited as proof of multi-authorship. A perceived enthusiasm (within the academic community) of Samuel for the job in hand, as portrayed in the first version of the anointing of Saul, is naturally said to reveal a pro-Saul and therefore older tradition. Whereas, the Gilgal episode, with Samuel's subsequent tirade against kingship is said to represent a late, anti-monarchist tradition.[22]

This hypothesis presents us with the same problems as the two distinct Samuels narratives and personalities discussed earlier, and again, as many difficulties are created as are resolved. For instance, is the so-called older tradition more reliable, because it was 'closer' to the events described? Indeed, is it truly an older tradition? If so, are the more public ceremonies described later less likely to have occurred? And therefore, was Saul, like David, anointed by Samuel on only one occasion, and in secret? If so, why? The questions are legion.

This is not a situation, however, where the historicity of one event necessarily precludes the actuality of others. There is no reason to dispute that all three accounts were memories of real happenings. If one account is better written, that fact alone does not confirm or negate the veracity of the other. Neither does the fact that the third account provided fertile soil for the seeds of later editorial prejudices.

Once again, the application of common sense and detailed inspection of the text yields interesting results. The primary clue to a resolution of the apparent conflict is the level of office that Saul attains at each event.[23]

1. A low-key affair where, in the aftermath of the Aphek catastrophe, Saul was anointed nagid, or Prince of Israel.

2. His election as melech, or king, over Israel following his spectacular reversal of the Aphek defeat.

3. After Saul's total victory over Nahash, when he is 'renewed' as king of both Israel and Judah.

The failure of multi-authorship hypothesis to acknowledge these distinctions is almost as mysterious as much of the Samuel text itself. In fact, the matter could not be simpler, without the need for any preclusion. What is described – albeit a little clumsily – is the evolution of a leader into a king.

After we have completed the untangling of the narrative's twisted chronology, this gradual development from nagid to king will be seen in an even clearer light.

1 Sam. 11:15-12: Saul's second coronation was celebrated with many sacrificial offerings and great joy, but the mood was tempered by a long oration from the embittered Samuel, who prophesied hardship and strife for the people and their king should the laws of God be forsaken.

Conclusion 7
The triple anointing of Saul reflects his historical evolution from nagid (Prince) of Israel, to melech (King) of Israel, to melech (King) of *All Israel*.[24]

The Length of Saul's Reign

The only statement regarding the length of Saul's reign is nonsensical: 'Saul was a year old when he became king, and he reigned over Israel for two years.' (1 Sam. 13:1)

The Saul of our hypothesis was well into middle age by the time of his coronation over Israel (without Judah). Moreover it is impossible that he was a babe-in-arms at this point in the narrative. Thus, the inescapable conclusion to be drawn is that in this instance we are dealing with a mistake in the text. Luckily for us – in spite of its erroneousness – 1 Sam. 13:1 represents the first example of a 'formula' – for regnal lengths – repeated many times in the following narratives of 2 Samuel, Kings and Chronicles. Thus, by juxtaposing the verse above against a later example we can deduce the nature of the mistake and suggest a possible correction.

The next example in the biblical narrative of the formula, describes the age and regnal length of Saul's son and successor when, in the second book of Samuel in verse 2:10 we are informed that 'Ishboshet was forty years old when he came to the throne of Israel and was king for two years. . . .' From Ishboshet onwards the formula in Hebrew is clear and consistent,

1. Age (at accession);
2. Name;
3. Statement of accession;
4. Description of realm (i.e. Israel, Judah or All Israel);
5. Regnal length.

To sort out the confusion over Saul's age at accession we should compare the Hebrew age descriptions in the two verses above:

· In the case of Saul, it reads – 'Ben-shana . . .' – i.e. 'Son of year[s]. . . .'

· In the case of Ishboshet, it states – 'Ben-arbaim shana' – i.e. 'Son of forty year[s]. . . .'

It does not take much to see instantly and clearly the nature of the textual error. It simply amounts to a missing word – and in this case the missing word is the number pertaining to the age of Saul. What that missing number should have read is a subject with which we will deal shortly.

Bearing in mind the overtly Davidic nature of 1 Samuel, the sloppy editing about Saul's regnal formula is unsurprising.[25] Nevertheless, the lack of detail over Saul's chronology is marked when compared with that of almost any other Israelite leader mentioned in the Bible. For example, the lengths of nearly every individual judgeship are recorded, including that of the obscure Tola son of Puah (Jg. 10: 1). In addition, both ages and regnal lengths are listed for all of Saul's Benjaminite, Judahite, and Israelite successors.[26] It is only with Israel's first king that we are left to guess.

The main factors responsible for this vague historicity are, as stated, the carelessness and selectivity of the pro-David authors, the gradual nature of his ascent, and the confused chronology of the 1 Samuel narrative.

As with most of the Bible's historical conundrums, scholars have resorted to outlandish 'translations' of the Hebrew text to solve the riddle. One commentator renders the verse cited above, 'Saul was fifty years old when he became king, and he reigned over Israel for twenty two years..'[27] Another insists that 'Saul was fifty-two years old when he became king, and he reigned over Israel for two years.'[28] These and many other versions display the skill – not to mention imagination – of the various commentators concerned as they go about their learned numerical-cum-philogical contortions, but the Hebrew gives no warrant for these numbers. The main obstacle to determining the length of Saul's total reign is the 'missing' final formula that should appear immediately following the story of his death at Gilboa. Fortunately, however, the Tanakh offers some further information that clarifies how long Saul reigned, both over Israel – as described in the formula above – and later over All Israel (with Judah):

· Following the Battle of Aphek, the Ark was in the hands of the Philistines for seven months;
· After its return to Israel – except for its appearance before the battle of Michmash (1 Sam. 14:18) – it was placed in the care of Eleazer son of Abinadab of Kiryath-Jearim, for twenty years (1 Sam. 7:2);
· This period included its move to Gibeah[29] (2 Sam. 6:3) down to David's capture of Jerusalem, seven-and-a-half years after the death of Saul.

If these figures are more or less correct, and assuming Samuel made Saul nagid – immediately or very soon after Aphek – we can deduce that the length of Saul's total rule, including all three stages from nagid to his death, was about thirteen years.

On the other hand, if we regard the notorious and perplexing formula verse as alluding to the possibility that Saul was nagid for one year and king of Israel alone for two years, then the subsequent reign over a united Israel and Judah would have lasted through the following decade. This hypothesis is given added credence when the text explicitly places Saul's numerous military campaigns within his time as King of All Israel. Only in that role would he have been strong enough and sufficiently influential to undertake such wide-ranging and ambitious military adventures. That Saul subdued five enemies (1 Sam. 14: 47-48), as well as his continuing struggle with the Philistines and his forthcoming contest with David means he must have been ruler of Israel and Judah for the longest of the three periods.

The 'twenty-two years' of reign chosen by most translators is based on Josephus' assertion that 'Saul reigned for eighteen years with Samuel and twenty-two years on his own', but in the absence of any corroborative evidence, and considering the clues already mentioned in the text, we have no reason to give credence to these words of the famous Jewish historian. It seems that Josephus – probably out of piety – was eager to grant Saul the symbolically important total of forty years (Jos, *Ant*. 6:14: 9).

Another basis for the exaggerated reign length may have been confusion over Saul's probable career as a Benjaminite clan chieftain (a minor nagid, so to speak) in the years prior to the battle of Aphek. Saul's possible early succession to the eldership/princeship within Benjamin may have contributed further to the muddle over his multiple anointing – and especially so if Samuel had some role in more than one of these rites.

Conclusion 8
Saul was Captain of Israel for one year, King of Israel for two years, and king of All Israel for ten years.[30]

The 'Ages' of Saul

All this raises the question of Saul's age when anointed by Samuel to be nagid of Israel in the aftermath of the battle of Aphek.

Saul's second-born son, Ishboshet (also Ishui/Ishbaal) was forty when he succeeded his father (2 Sam.2:10), following the battle of Gilboa.[31]

The contemporaneous custom of entering into fatherhood in the mid-teens and siring children at one-year intervals, taken simply, could mean that Saul was as young as fourteen when his eldest son Jonathan was born and fifteen at the birth of Ishboshet. By this reckoning, the youngest Saul could have been at his death was fifty-five, making him forty-two at the commencement of his captaincy of Israel.

If we then allow for the probability of failed pregnancies and infant mortalities, we may permit ourselves to adjust the numbers upwards.

Thus, we can propose an outline for the career of Saul up to his coronation as King of All Israel:

· Saul was either a child or in his early teens when he first met Samuel;
· He was about twenty, married to Ahinoam, and already the father of two or three children when he succeeded his father Kish as a Benjaminite clan chief;

- Over the next twenty years or so, he earned a reputation as a charismatic warrior and developed a working relationship with Samuel;
- Together with his older sons and his cousin Abner, Saul was present at the battle of Aphek;
- It was a Benjaminite runner who brought the terrible news of defeat to Shiloh;
- Within a matter of days, Samuel decided that the forty-five-year-old veteran was the perfect choice to help him rally the people; therefore, he anointed Saul nagid;
- About a year later – for reasons that will become clear shortly – Samuel found himself compelled to promote his nagid to the position of King of Israel (without Judah);
- Two years later, Saul became King of Israel and Judah.

> ## Conclusion 9
> Saul was middle aged by the time he became king over All Israel.[32]

Now that we have this chronological framework for Saul's route to the throne, the next task is to put historical flesh on these dry bones.

Orthodox Sequence	Major Variants
1 Sam. 10: At the gathering at Mizpah, the reluctant Saul is elected and anointed King of Israel; Saul and a band of men return home to Gibeah. Some people, unconvinced with the new king, refused to pay him tribute.	The Mizpah coronation of Saul as King of Israel was a direct result of his victory at the same site, and thus its placement here is premature by about a year.
1 Sam. 11: Nahash, King of Ammon, invades Gilead; Saul leading a huge army of Israel and Judah, beats Nahash, and liberates Gilead.	The account of Saul's war against Nahash is erroneously placed. He would not be strong or influential enough until he had liberated Israel from the Philistine yoke, completed his restructuring and training of the national levy, and established his alliance with Judah. This would take another two years (see chap. 5).
Saul pardons those who had withheld tribute.	
Samuel anoints Saul King of All Israel at the victory celebration at Gilgal.	This anointing is likewise incorrectly placed by two years.
1 Sam. 12: Samuel makes his great anti-monarchist oration at Gilgal.	

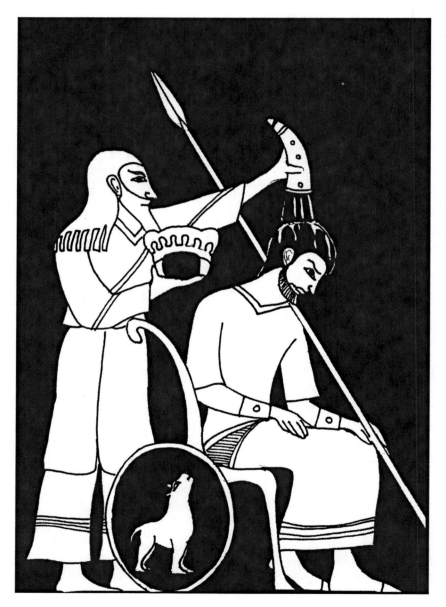

Saul Anointed King of Israel

4

King Saul
A Nation is Born

And the Lord said unto Samuel, "Heed their demands and appoint a king for them". (1 Sam. 8:22)

Holy Haemorrhoids!
As mentioned in chapter 1, the Philistine victory at Aphek was a near-total disaster for the people of Israel. Not only did the Israelites forfeit all the finest agricultural land west of the Jordan, also many were reduced to virtual serfdom, with their weaponry confiscated by their new masters and their continued engagement in metallurgy proscribed. Furthermore, they suffered the indignity of having to go to Philistine smiths to sharpen their agricultural tools (1 Sam. 13:19-20).

The remnants of the army that survived in the hills under the leadership of Samuel and his new nagid, Saul, must have been totally demoralised. There would have seemed to be no immediate prospect of mounting any meaningful resistance. Judah could have made a difference, but, in common with other 'neutrals', they chose to wait and see. The future for the Israelites looked bleak – until something quite unexpected occurred.

Less than a year after the battle of Aphek, the ranks of the Philistines were decimated by a mysterious disaster. The Israelite text calls the destructive agents ophlim, a word that has been translated as everything from a bombardment of meteorites to a unique plague of haemorrhoids (or 'emrods') in the standardised versions![1] Whatever the ophlim were, they were nasty and lethal on a massive scale. The Philistines ascribed the scourge to the presence of the Israelite Ark of God in their midst and, dreading further devastation, they hastily returned it to its original owners.

Unfortunately for those Israelites who lived nearest the Philistine homeland, the ophlim seem to have been virulently contagious – many around Bet Shemesh also died.[2]

Thus, the recent victors of Aphek found themselves suddenly brought low. Only their garrisons within the recently conquered Israelite hill country apparently remained unaffected. But even these outposts were weakened, for the devastation back in the Philistine homeland had virtually eliminated the possibility of their receiving relief or reinforcement in the event of an outbreak of hostilities.[3]

Conclusion 10
The ophlim disaster which struck the Philistine homeland provided a window of opportunity for the start of the Israelite resistance.

Samuel and his military deputy Saul must have been fully aware of this seemingly miraculous chance that had been offered to them. However, a mere seven-and-a-half months after Aphek, Israel was still militarily weak and could take only limited advantage.

By the time of the return of the Ark, Saul had managed to rally a small guerrilla force comprising about six hundred men (1 Sam. 14:2), mostly from the Rachel tribes and friendly Canaanites, organised into two groups under his command and that of Jonathan, his eldest son. Whereas formerly Saul and Samuel could do no more than irritate the Philistines with small, lightning raids on enemy supply trains linking the garrisons with their motherland, it was now possible to set their sights a little higher.

Saul's first targets were strategic. As things stood, Benjamin and southern Ephraim were separated from their brothers in the northern part of the central hill country by the Philistines garrison at the strategic Michmash pass.[4] Before all-out war was feasible, Saul had to secure a safe corridor between the divided 'halves' of his territory. The other main enemy positions were at Gibeah, and the town of Geba.[5]

Once again, due to confused chronology, the narrative presents a muddled picture of these episodes. One moment Saul is based in Michmash, while the next moment he is attacking the very same place – now a Philistine garrison:

1 Sam. 13:2-7: *Saul's long duel with the Philistines began when, as King of Israel and Judah, he formed a standing army of three thousand elite fighters, with two-thirds under his command and the rest in the charge of his eldest son and heir, Jonathan. Saul stationed himself at Michmash, and Jonathan at Gibeah in Benjamin. Jonathan began the war of liberation by overrunning the enemy garrison at Geba. Following this success, the entire army mustered once again at Gilgal for battle. The Philistine response was to reinforce their large, well-armed force at Michmash, from where they launched attacks deeper into Israel. In the face of such an awesome foe, much of the Israelite army became dispirited and fled back into caves in the hills.*

To defeat Nahash, Saul had mustered a vast army of Israel and Judah. Yet, if we are to believe the narrative, just a short while after that spectacular success and his coronation as King of All Israel, he can barely raise a platoon. This is clear evidence of more confused chronology, which is further compounded when we are informed that Saul: 'waited seven days, the time that Samuel had stipulated. But when Samuel failed to come to Gilgal, and the people began to scatter.' (1 Sam. 13:8).

Samuel's original instruction for Saul to meet him at Gilgal in seven days dates back to the time of the first anointing. Yet, according to the biblical chronology, two coronations, an enormous military victory, and the beginning of the war of liberation separate the instruction from the Gilgal event. This makes no sense:

1 Sam. 13:8-23: Samuel's delayed arrival to perform the pre-battle rites depressed morale even further. Saul, fearing the loss of his entire army, decided to conduct the ceremony himself. Samuel turned up just as Saul was finishing the ritual, and was incensed at Saul's presumption. Despite the king's pleading, the judge stormed off in a rage, claiming that by his injudicious act Saul had forfeited the kingdom and that his dynasty, which would otherwise have lasted forever, would end with him, while a man more worthy than he would take his place.

By now, Saul's army had dwindled to six hundred men. Unable to attack, they remained confined to Gibeah and could only watch as the enemy strengthened its hold over the king's own territory. In addition, the strict controls on metal forging imposed by their conquerors meant that the warriors of Israel found themselves lacking in weaponry.

This is yet more evidence of the chronological chaos inherent in the text, since the shortage of Israelite military hardware was mysteriously unapparent only a short while before, in the victorious battle of Jabesh.

1 Sam. 14:1-23: Eventually, Jonathan and his armour bearer launched a surprise attack on Michmash – which they did not disclose to Saul – spreading panic throughout the Philistine camp. After sending the high priest Ahia and the Ark[6] away, Saul learnt of Jonathan's expedition and joined the fray. At the sight of their king, the Hebrews within the enemy camp turned on the Philistines. Encouraged by Jonathan's and Saul's example, the Israelites who had been hiding in the hills poured down upon the fleeing foe.

Hebrews and Israelites

This is one of the relatively few mentions in the 1 Samuel narrative of 'Hebrews' (Heb. Ivrim) in contrast to Israelites.[7]

Many scholars see the Hebrew and Israelite distinction as a substantiation of the hypothesis that the two were separate peoples, but the conventional view is simply that the two words are interchangeable. In this instance, the former represent the Ivrim within the Philistine camp as mercenaries who turned upon their employers to assist Saul. The latter believe that the Ivrim were Israelite prisoners who, encouraged by the attack of their king, rose up against their captors. The issue depends upon what meaning one attributes to the Hebrew word saviv. It can mean – amongst other things – 'turned', as in *turned traitor*, or equally, 'turned', as in *turned upon* one's captor. The other references to Ivrim contained within the Michmash episode are equally equivocal and open to scholarly speculation.

As far as this book is concerned, whether or not Hebrews and Israelites were distinct or identical is only of academic interest. That there may have been ostensible compatriots of Saul who proved less than reliable – of that we can have no doubt. Indeed, that fact lies at the core of our hypothesis.

1 Sam. 14:24-46: Saul forbade the eating of any food by his men until the battle was over, swearing a curse of death on the first warrior to disobey. Jonathan, who had not heard the edict, took some honey from a tree during a break in the fighting. On learning that he was now the object of his father's curse, Jonathan remained unperturbed and voiced criticism of the king's approach to the military encounter.

The victorious Israelites chased the Philistines all the way to Aijalon.[8] The hungry and exhausted Israelites gorged themselves on the spoil, not stopping to drain the blood from the flesh. Saul put an end to this ritually unclean feasting and, by way of atonement, made a sacrifice and in God's name set up an altar on the very spot. [9]

Because of Saul's failure to act on his earlier curse, he was unable to obtain from the high priest's oracles any guidance on continuing the battle. When he discovered that Jonathan was the guilty party, he was adamant in calling for his son's execution. But the people could not contemplate the death of their beloved hero, and they made sure he was protected from harm.

At a stroke, the nagid recaptured a handful of vital strategic positions in Benjamin and Ephraim. Suddenly, the Israelites had new heroes, and most importantly, the myth of Philistine invincibility had been shattered. The spirits of the Israelites were lifted, and within a short time Saul's band of guerrillas had swelled into an army of about three thousand men (1 Sam. 13:2).

The capture of Michmash achieved three goals for Samuel and Saul. First, it was a severe reversal for the enemy. Second, it restored the Israelites' strategic advantage in central Israel by re-establishing a link between north and south. Third, it sent a signal to any waverers within Israel, and also to Judah, that the Israelite tribes were capable of turning the tables on a formidable – albeit weakened adversary.

> ## Conclusion 11
> Saul's first campaign was not against Ammon, but against the Philistines when he was still only a nagid.[10]

A Reluctant King

Samuel had might have assumed that the success of his chosen general would have cemented his own authority in the eyes of his people, but if so, his powers of seership were wanting. For instead, the Israelites, in fear for their continued existence, found in Saul a charismatic focal point for all their hopes and prayers. The desire to make him their king was heightened by the victory at Michmash. Samuel had not only presented his people with a brilliant general but, inadvertently, had given them a perfect candidate for the title of King of Israel.

If the tradition of Samuel's reluctance to take such a step is true, he had four good reasons to be hesitant:

1. Despite the general clamour, there must have been significant resistance among the princes and elders of Ephraim and Manasseh to the idea of a non-Josephite king.

2. Samuel might have been aware of the antimonarchist sentiment within the hearts of his brother priests, and especially those of the hitherto ruling House of Eli.

3. There may have been a similar lack of enthusiasm for the coronation of an Israelite king among the indigenous Canaanite population, which could have been particularly suspicious of any tampering with a confederate status quo.

4. Last but not least was the apparent, and probably genuine reluctance of Saul himself.

Therefore, for the time being at least, the will of the people was ignored and the son of Kish remained merely their faithful nagid. For about a year, Saul, together with his sons, his clan, and an ever-growing band of fearsome guerrilla troops, carried on a war of attrition against the invader. Little by little, he secured his own hill country and the towns of Benjamin and of Ephraim. Following the battle of Michmash, he established Gibeah as the base of the resistance – the Ark of the Covenant having been brought there by its new guardians from Kiryath-jearim (2 Sam. 6:3).[11]

The Philistines must have become ever-more perturbed, while Judah might have observed events with increasing interest and, presumably, growing admiration.

Samuel and Saul

It is most likely that by now the relationship between the judge and his general had become seriously strained. As Saul's star continued to rise, and the delineation of their respective roles began to blur, Samuel's position would have become increasingly awkward. The alleged confrontation between the two, prior to Michmash, may reflect the growing tension (1 Sam. 13:11-14). However pious Saul may have been, and whether or not he ever was 'among the prophets', his primary motivation was nationalistic and not spiritual.

Saul had witnessed the supposed invincibility of the Ark of God shattered at Aphek and as if to highlight the fact, we are informed that he refused to allow it to be carried into battle (1 Sam. 14:19). The men of Israel had to understand that they would win or lose by their own courage and their own fortune, while honouring God before battle and expressing thanks for victory was merely the custom of the day.

By contrast, Samuel was the consummate man of God, for whom everything was shaped and coloured by the fact of God's sovereignty. Thus, if the two men shared a deep sense of patriotism, they may have had widely differing views on how to satisfy its demands through service and duty.

Thus, the spiritual disposition of his general was propably of increasing concern to the prophet. The more Saul grew in stature, the more unsettled Samuel may have become. Nevertheless, so long as Saul was only his nagid, their tensions remained largely confined to points of pre-battle protocol and the like. But, as Saul's kingship approached, a deeper crisis loomed.

Conclusion 12
The joint rule of Samuel and Saul engendered an ambiguity in their respective roles and tense relations between the two leaders.[12]

Saul's victory at Mizpah [13]

Meanwhile, men flocked to Saul's banner at Gibeah, where, under Abner, they were equipped with captured weaponry and trained in its use.[14] About a year after Saul's anointing as nagid, he would have felt confident enough to face a still weakened Philistine army in pitched battle.

Following their alleged falling out prior to Michmash, it seems that the nagid of Israel was assiduous in granting Samuel the leading role in the ritual of battle preparation, and thus confirming the supremacy of the judge. When a spectacular thunderstorm erupted at Mizpah, it must have seemed as though their plan was being given divine approval. 'The Lord thundered mightily against the Philistines that day. He threw them into confusion, and they were routed by Israel.' (1 Sam. 7:10)

However, once the Israelites fell upon the unsettled Philistines, it was Saul whom they saw leading them to glory, and it would have been to him that they looked for inspiration. In the event, Mizpah proved to be a bloody rout, culminating in the Israelite army chasing the Philistines all the way to Bet-car.[15] The taste of victory was made all the sweeter by the location of the battle's climax. Halfway between Mizpah and Shen, near Aphek, on the very spot where the Ark had been captured the previous year, it was Samuel and his sons, and not Saul, who erected a great victory stele and named it Eben-ezer (1 Sam. 7:12).[16]

In little more than a year, Israel had succeeded in reversing its fortunes. If this seemed miraculous, the only question would have been over the nature of the miracle.

The Second Anointing
As things turned out, Saul and Samuel's apparent attempt to give God and his seer the credit for victory failed to persuade, if not the future compilers of the narrative, at least the army of Israel. They were well aware of the brilliance of their beloved nagid. So aware, in fact, and so joyous at their moment of liberation, that it could have come as little surprise to Samuel when once again the demand that Saul be made king rang in his ears. The irony would not have been lost on either man that what the two leaders had intended to be seen as the victory of Samuel came to result in the coronation of Saul, and this time, there could be no denying the people's wishes, so condemning Samuel to be the last judge of Israel. He at least had the gratification, however, of being the man to whom his people looked for the granting of their wish.

Josephus asserts that Saul's show of humility at his election was contrived (Jos, *Ant*: 6. 4: 5) – equivalent, perhaps, to the feigned reluctance of a newly elected Speaker in the British House of Commons to take his or her presiding seat. If so, it was certainly not a tradition continued by Saul's successors. All the same, from everything one can glean from the pages of Samuel, there is no reason to doubt that this bear of a man was terrified at the realisation that he was to be the first King of Israel. For, if in truth there was a dichotomy in the personality of the meshiach of Israel, it was that behind the heart of a lion breathed the spirit of a vulnerable and gentle man.[17]

In any event, Samuel anointed Saul as king before the people of Israel (without Judah)[18] at Mizpah. Thus, over three thousand years ago, and for the first time in recorded history, the cry went up:

". . . Long live the King!" (1 Sam. 10:24).

At that very instant, a nation was born.

Conclusion 13
Saul's anointing as King of Israel (without Judah) was a direct result of his successful war of liberation against the Philistines.[19]

Orthodox Sequence	Major Variants
1 Sam. 13: Saul recruits 3000 men to his and Jonathan's command.	Since the liberation of Geba historically belongs at the very beginning of Saul's liberation war, 3,000 is probably an exaggeration. The 600 mentioned later is no doubt closer to the true size of the original guerrilla army.
Jonathan liberates Geba – Saul calls the people to Gilgal. The Philistines respond by gathering a huge army at Michmash; The dispirited Israelites return to the hills.	
Having waited for Samuel for the specified seven days, Saul, seeing his army dwindle, initiates the pre-battle sacrifice himself; Samuel arrives and admonishes Saul for disobeying God; He tells Saul his kingdom will end with him, and that the Lord had chosen another nagid.	The 'seven days' make their long-awaited reappearance. However, four key events (battle of Mizpah, coronation of Mizpah, war with Ammon, Gilgal coronation) have been artificially wedged into the historical space between Saul becoming nagid, and his launching of his offensive. A gap of seven days between Samuel's appointment of Saul and the outbreak of hostilities is perfectly plausible.
Saul's army dwindles to 600 men.	
The Philistines send three raiding parties into the Israelite countryside.	
The Philistines prohibit the Israelites from metal forging – only Saul, Jonathan, and their men have proper weapons.	
1 Sam. 14: Ahiah, the great-grandson of Eli, is high priest.	

Jonathan launches a surprise raid on Michmash, and creates havoc in Philistine camp; Ahiah and the ark are turned back from battle by Saul; Saul joins the fray with the remainder of the army; All those who had fled to hills return to the battle; the Philistines are routed;

Jonathan is spared the consequences of having violated Saul's temporary prohibition on eating.

Following his victory at Michmash, Saul wins victories over Moab, Ammon, Edom and Zobah; he has more victories over the Philistines and defeats the Amalekites.

The sequence of wars as presented here is probably correct. The war with Ammon followed Michmash *and Mizpah*. Saul fought Moab before becoming King of All Israel.

Saul's sons are Jonathan, Ishui, and Melchi-shua; his daughters are Merab and Michal; His wife is Ahinoam. Abner, Saul's 'cousin', is made commander of levy. The war against the Philistines persists; Saul continues to recruit elite soldiers.

Ishui is yet another name of Ishbaal/ Ishboshet.

Saul Wearing the Double Crown

5

King Saul the Saviour
The United Monarchy

After Saul had secured his kingship over Israel, he waged war on every side against all his enemies. (1 Sam. 14:47)

The War with Ammon

Saul had been King of Israel about two years when the next crisis arose. We can assume that, during this period, the war of attrition with the Philistines continued, or else there was an uneasy lull while they licked their wounds and continued to recover from their 'ophlim' catastrophe. In either case, Saul must have used this time to consolidate and organise his forces. This consolidation was to undergo its first test not from west (the land of the Philistines), but from the east.

Gilead, the large Trans-Jordan portion of Saul's new kingdom, had its own hostile neighbours with which to contend – The Ammonites, led by their king, Nahash (1 Sam. 11:1).[1] Friction had been recorded between Gilead and Ammon since the days of the judge Jephthah (Jg. 11). From the southern uplands of the Golan (biblical Bashan) down south as far as the northern half of the Salt Sea, the Gileadites occupied the best agricultural and grazing land east of the river. The Ammonites must have looked down on these fertile territories from their arid highlands with envious eyes.

The Samuel narrative implies that Saul's war with Ammon was the earliest campaign of his reign, immediately following his first coronation. Oddly, this sequence is rarely challenged. Yet consider the implications.[2]

If this scenario were true, the Gileadites, invaded by a large army, would have asked for help from an obscure Benjaminite farmer, who then raised an enormous army from Judah and Israel simply by issuing a gory threat (1 Sam. 11:7). The novice general then led his army to a glorious victory. The entire sequence of events, and much more besides, would have taken place between Saul's secret anointing and the start of a war against the Philistine confederacy – a period represented as just seven days (1 Sam. 10:8; 13:8)! But, as we have also noted, following Saul's momentous victory, he could barely muster a handful of men to fight the Philistines (at Michmash). These are the same Philistines who had already been roundly defeated by Samuel (all of which, it should be remembered, was achieved without any iron weapons).

Surely, by the time the men of Gilead appealed to Saul for help, he was already an established king and fully capable of a significant armed response.

Perhaps the reason for the tacit academic acceptance of this part of the narrative is the temptation to see the Ammonite attack against the background of a defeated and vulnerable Israel.[3] Such a perspective is plausible if the event is considered in isolation. However, as we have just seen, as soon as one attempts to reconnect the Ammonite action to the surrounding narrative, everything is thrown into confusion.

An historian with a conventional perspective might suggest that Saul's first campaign against Ammon was on a much smaller scale than that described in Samuel, making a victory based upon his extraordinary prophetic charisma alone more plausible. The time discrepancies must then be swept under the carpet as products of so much fanciful storytelling.

However, this reconstruction suggests equally logical reasons for Nahash's invasion that are more plausible than those offered by most commentators, and with the added virtue of not throwing the peripheral events into confusion. On the contrary, everything falls neatly into place.

The text informs us that, following their crushing victory over the Philistines at Mizpah, the Israelites 'made peace with the Amorites' (i.e. indigenous Canaanites, 1 Sam. 7:14). The biblical terminology, 'made peace with' is most probably a euphemism for 'made an alliance with'.[4] It would make sense politically that Saul desired to secure his embryonic realm by the formation of strategic alliances. We can assume that Nahash, King of Ammon, would have seen the new alliance of Israel (including Gilead), Judah, and the Amorites as both threatening and provocative. Warrior chieftains who feel threatened and provoked tend to respond pre-emptively.

Thus in all likelihood, it was primarily through fear that the warlike Nahash invaded Gilead. He must have gambled that the new Israelite king and his allies were preoccupied on their western borders, and in any event, were too disorganised to mount an effective response to his invasion of Gilead.

His assault certainly seems to have taken Israel by surprise, in both its swiftness and its savagery. Within a short time, Ammon had overrun Gilead and laid siege to the city of Jabesh.

The story of Nahash's infamous terms of surrender and his allowing Jabesh to call to 'all farthest reaches of Israel' for relief has a strong smell of the apocryphal about it (1 Sam. 11:3). Nevertheless, it probably reflects the truth in so far as the siege was of sufficient duration for Saul to organise a response and by the depiction of an overconfident Ammonite king. In the event, Nahash appears to have overlooked two critical factors.

First, Saul, some two years into his reign, had by now established an effective military structure: Abner was placed in command of the main army, which was based on the old tribal levy system, while Saul and Jonathan marshalled a standing regiment of some three thousand professional troops (1 Sam. 17:55; 26:5).[5]

Second, by this time Judah – for reasons that will be made apparent presently – not to mention Israel's new Canaanite allies, were all likely to march under the banner of Saul. Up to this point, Nahash could never have envisaged such an army of All Israel. To his mind, the hitherto disparate Israelite groupings would have seemed as distinct as the Moabites and the Edomites and thus, the King of Ammon had made a fatal miscalculation. Within days he found himself confronted by a powerful army of All Israel reinforced by its Canaanite allies. The Ammonite invasion force was destroyed and Nahash retreated back to his arid mountains. Jabesh, together with the whole of Israelite Trans-Jordan Israel, was liberated.

The victory celebrations following the Gilead liberation was the pinnacle in the career of Israel's first king. Saul's hitherto ambivalent subjects – the so called 'sons of Belial' – had either lost their doubts concerning his appointment or been sidelined in the general acclamation and also, more crucially, Judah and Gilead were now firmly united behind him. Overnight, his tiny mountain kingdom was transformed into a sizeable realm incorporating nearly all the tribes and peoples of the land of Israel.

Within days of the victory, in front of the entire army at the high place of Gilgal, Samuel anointed Saul King of All Israel (1 Sam. 11:15). In effect, the Israelite people were voluntarily united as a nation for the first and only time in their history.

Conclusion 14
Saul was crowned King of All Israel following his victory over Ammon and his earlier successes against the Philistines.[6]

The Wars of King Saul

The Tanakh provides us with scant detail for the decade or so of Saul's rule over All Israel. For the most part, we can merely surmise.

1 Sam. 14:47-52: Following the Battle of Michmash, Saul fought victorious campaigns against all the other enemies of Israel: Moab, Ammon, Edom, Zobah and Amalek. Meanwhile, the Philistine war continued, as did Saul's recruiting of crack troops to his bodyguard.

It is open to speculation, whether the wars against Moab, Edom, and Zobah were offensive or reactive. Saul's action against Amalek appears, on the face of it, to have been aggressive. Yet, bearing in mind that on all available evidence Saul was not a conquering king, we may suspect that there was some element of provocation on the part of the various enemies. We can at least glean from this information and much else besides that Saul was in truth an accomplished warrior, who seems to have, for the most part, achieved strong, defensible borders. We can also deduce from the extensive geographic range of his campaigns that his army was more than the mere guerrilla band depicted by many modern commentators.[7] Given that he was able to conduct successful raids as far south as the River of Egypt (El-Arish[8]) and as far north as central Syria (Zobah), his capabilities must have been far beyond those of a simple mountain warlord.

In this context, it is intriguing to note that clay tablets excavated during the first half of the twentieth century (notably the Cuneiform texts of King Zimrilim) at Mari (modern Tell Hariri), close to ancient Zobah[9] on the banks of the River Euphrates, mention a marauding tribe called Banu-Yamina.[10]

Although this reference predates the campaign of Saul by over a millennium, some scholars believe that the tribe of Benjamin may have originated from the Zobah region. If so, it at least suggests the possibility, that ancient tribal ties and/or obligations may have endured to the time of the Benjaminite King of Israel. Such an intriguing possibility would lend credence to the biblical claim that Saul embarked on some form of military adventure far to the north of his realm.

Despite the dearth of detail, it is not unreasonable to conclude that Saul built a formidable military machine, with a structured command. Both his standing regiment and the national levy were well suited to defensive and offensive tasks. We can logically assume, however, that Saul's primary concern was the constant threat posed by the Philistines. This being the case, any long-term dreams of expansion he may have entertained would have been sacrificed in the interest of securing his home borders.

The Rule of King Saul

The single piece of theocratic legislation ascribed to King Saul is his famous ban on necromancy (1 Sam. 28:3). We shall learn presently, that this was most likely an anachronism – the result of later editorship. Allowing for the certainty that he must have issued at least one or two edicts and decrees, and the fact of a partisan authorship, the evidence does nevertheless point towards a fundamentally passive style of domestic rule. This is hardly surprising, considering both the novelty of kingship and the persistent military distractions Saul had to face and, it seems certain that, domestically at least, Saul behaved more like an old style judge than a king.[11] For example, he seems to have done little to centralise the government at Gibeah. In fact, it is doubtful that he had a royal capital in the accepted sense. He must have thought of himself primarily as a warrior king and the military guardian of his people. He was simply the mortal servant of God, who consciously limited the scope of his rule to the protection of his people. He was, above all else, his subjects' servant and protector.[12]

We can infer from the alleged originality in Israelite terms of King David's census-taking many years later (2 Sam. 24) that Saul probably never subjected his people to institutionalised royal taxation. Nevertheless, even a court as apparently modest and rustic as that of Gibeah would have required some funding, not to mention the payment and upkeep of his standing regiment of three thousand men. According to 1 Sam. 22: 7, Saul's professional troops – or his Benjaminite officers, at any rate – were rewarded with gifts of land, and any additional expenses must have been covered by occasional tribute received from his grateful subjects and Canaanite vassals – and perhaps especially by spoil appropriated from his defeated enemies.[13]

Their military successes gave the people a feeling of national pride such as they had never experienced before, and as a result, Saul commanded a fierce loyalty within the hearts of all his subjects, whether Israelite, Judahite, or Canaanite. However, his apparent diplomatic and political naïveté would in time colour his entire reign and ultimately undermine his military gains.

Foreign Affairs

Apart from the wars and a treaty with the Canaanites (biblical 'Amorites' 1 Sam. 7:14), there is no obvious diplomatic foreign policy recorded for Saul's reign.[14]

The one peaceful border he seems to have consistently maintained was that to the immediate north. Scholars sceptical of biblical historicity cite this as evidence that the northernmost tribes of Israel remained unliberated by Saul and were thus excluded from his kingdom. The theory goes that tribes such as Zebulun and Asher were vassals of either the Philistines themselves or, more probably, the early Phoenicians, and that they remained so until David united them with their brethren to the south. The same school of thought suggests that the maritime traditions associated with these tribes are misattributed, belonging in reality to the Sea Peoples (possibly 'northern' Philistines and/or Phoenicians) for whom they were merely serfs.[15] However, the text is consistent and unequivocal in laying out the extent of the permanent Philistine settlement. Moreover, we are given a graphic description of Saul's non-Judahite domain in a verse from the second book of Samuel: 'Abner . . . had taken Ishboshet son of Saul . . .and made him king over Gilead, the Ashurites, Jezreel, Ephraim, and Benjamin. . . .' (2 Sam. 2:8-9)

Nominally at least, the Samuel scribes considered the House of Saul to be masters of virtually all non-Judahite Israel – even in the aftermath of the battle of Gilboa.[16]

There is no mention in either Judges or Samuel of the northern tribes being occupied for a longer period than those south of the Jezreel Valley. Neither is there any suggestion that Zebulun, Asher, and so on were any less established vis-à-vis their Canaanite neighbours than were Ephraim and Judah by Saul's time. On the contrary, most textual evidence, such as the relative lack of campaigning by Saul and David in the north of their kingdom, might indicate that the area was well settled and securely established by the time of Saul's reign.

It is therefore possible that, from an early date, Israel enjoyed good relations with the rulers of Lebanon – relations that later came to such spectacular fruition under Solomon (1 K. 5 etc).

David Rohl's highly seductive revisionist theory suggests that Saul (in the guise of Labaya) corresponded with the pharaohs of his day.[17] But, even if true, it is hard to deny that Israel's first monarch failed to grasp the nettle of diplomacy and did little to formulate international relations.[18] This insular trait would have resulted in an Israel surrounded, for the most part, by suspicious and potentially hostile neighbours.

A Priest King?

Saul must necessarily have trodden on many more toes in addition to Samuel's as he struggled to define his position in relation to his God and his people. The fact that he occasionally took on the role of priest, when the situation demanded it, is compelling testimony to the nebulous character of his new identity (1 Sam. 13:9-10). Though the text hints at sound reasons for these infrequent actions, and the possible acceptability of a religious component to his role, Saul may nevertheless have been regarded as an heretical usurper by much of the clerical community.

According to Martin Noth, due to its "secular" nature "[T]he institution of the monarchy was bound to come up against internal difficulties within the sacral association of the Israelite tribes . . ."[19] Moreover, as Fleming James points out, "nothing is said [in any of the source material] of Saul's being appealed to as a judge",[20] which seems odd when one considers the proximity of his reign to the era of the Judges. Bearing in mind the tradition of Solomon's famous feat of judgeship in 1 K. 3:16-28, and allowing for Saul's busy military schedule, he must surely have been called upon to make the odd judicial decision – especially once Samuel retired from public life.

Whatever the exact truth of the matter, as our thesis unfolds, it will become increasingly apparent that the descendants of Eli in particular – far from sharing in the universal enthusiasm for the new king – resented their loss of influence. It seems that the bitterness they harboured was to have tragic consequences for themselves and the entire house of Aaron.

The Two Rages of Samuel
According to the narrative, Saul's clash with the established clergy was far less calamitous to his reign than the righteous indignation directed at him by Samuel the prophet.

1 Sam. 15:1-9: *Samuel reappeared and commanded Saul to make war on the Amalekites in revenge for the treatment they had meted out to the Children of Israel during the flight from Egypt (Ex.17: 8-16). Every man, woman, child, and beast, and all spoil, was to be utterly destroyed.*

After mustering the army at Telaim[21] and – out of deference to the memory of Jethro – giving the Kenites warning to evacuate the area, Saul launched his attack. The victory was complete, but Saul spared the life of the Amalekite king, Agag, and allowed his soldiers to take sheep and cattle as spoil.

Egyptian friezes bear gruesome testimony to the custom of 'reserving' captive leaders for later ritual smiting, and this may be what Saul had in mind when he spared the life of Agag.[22] As for permitting the army to take spoil, this was merely consistent with intelligent generalship. However, he was faulted on both counts.

1 Sam. 15:10-28: God then told Samuel that because of Saul's impiety He now regretted his choice of king and that He had chosen another. Samuel was heartbroken and prayed to the Lord through the night. When Samuel

*subsequently arrived at the victory celebration at Gilgal, he was furious
with the king. Saul's excuses and remonstrations were of no avail. Samuel
told him that the Lord had now rejected him as king.*

*And Samuel said to him, "The Lord has this day torn the kingship of Israel
away from you and has given it to another, who is worthier than you."*

It should be remembered that the earlier great reprimand and rejection of
Saul by Samuel had taken place following the mythical seven days. Seeing
his army dwindle before his eyes and with morale plummeting, Saul had
initiated the sacrifice himself. In the eyes of God and Samuel, that was an
heretical act. Thus, Samuel had told Saul (1 Sam. 13:14): 'But now your
dynasty will not endure. The Lord will seek out a man after His own heart,
and the Lord will appoint him ruler over His people, because you did not
abide by what the Lord had commanded you.' In addition to the verbal
similarities of the two reprimands, they both took place at Gilgal.

Given the probable Benjaminite location of Gilgal and its strategic and
cultic importance, it is reasonable to think it was the site of the mustering
of the army prior to Michmash and the victory celebration following the
defeat of Amalek. There can be no such assurance, however, about the
historicity of the two reprimands, which seem to be the result of duplication
– a grafting of the same alleged incident onto two different events.[23]

Apart from the almost identical nature of the two rejections and
punishments, there is another reason for believing that the two passages
describe the same admonishment. After the first event, the very next
chapter begins with Samuel confirming Saul's kingship over Israel – a
flat contradiction. Why would the judge confirm the title of a king he had
just deposed in favour of another? By contrast, after the second event,
Samuel although wary of Saul, immediately carries out God's command
and anoints a new king. Indeed, 'Samuel feared for his life' and, according
to the story, the two former allies 'never met again'. If the reprimand
occurred at all, this second account is the only one that rings true.

If Samuel's double rejection of Saul represents a problem in and of itself,
it pales into insignificance when compared with the attendant chronological
turmoil (already touched on in Chapter 4, when we considered the multiple
major events that were allegedly crammed into seven days). The first
reprimand, which includes the statement that 'the Lord had commanded
[David] to be captain over his people . . .' implies that David became
cognisant of his own calling only seven days after the initial meeting
between Samuel and Saul – prior to Saul's first great victory over the
Philistines and well ahead of Samuel's famous visit to the home of Jesse!

In other words, the (evidently pro-David) redactor, intent on suppressing the genuine history of Saul, bungled his editorial crime and left an unholy mess at the scene.

1 Sam. 15:30-33: *Saul begged in vain for forgiveness, and then pleaded with Samuel to at least honour him before the army by worshipping with him. To this Samuel assented, after which he demanded Agag be brought before him. The judge of Israel promptly executed the defeated king. Saul and Samuel went their separate ways, one to Gibeah and the other to Ramah. They were never to meet again.*

Until and including this alleged falling out with Samuel, Saul's recorded failings were his two acts of disobedience to the divine will. Even if we accept these alleged transgressions at face value, the reader's sympathy for, or antipathy towards, the king very much depends on his or her religious viewpoint. It is the assertion of this study, however, that no such catastrophic falling out between king and prophet actually occurred, and that judgement – pious or otherwise – on the merits of King Saul must, therefore, be reserved.

Nevertheless, the description of Samuel's rejection of Saul at the Gilgal victory ceremony represents sublime tragic literature. The scene of the disgraced hero grabbing hold of the old prophet's cloak as he pleads that Samuel honour him before the army is heartrending. Moreover, Samuel's reprimand of Saul (1 Sam. 15:22-23) constitutes the first and most dramatic example of Israelite/Judaic anti-sacrificial ideology recorded in the religious canon – and it comes across most powerfully in the old standardised translation: 'And Samuel said: "Does the Lord take as much delight in burnt offerings and sacrifices, as in those who obey His voice? For, to obey is better than sacrifice, to hearken than the fat of rams. For rebellion is like the sin of witchcraft, and stubbornness is like iniquity and idolatry. Because you have rejected the word of the Lord, he has also rejected you as king." '

However, the historical Samuel of the mid eleventh century BCE could never have uttered words so derisive of burnt offerings.[24] They are from a far later era when the prophets of Israel and Judah were disillusioned with the ruling institutions, both regal and clerical. The sentiment expressed emanates from the pen of a scribe writing hundreds of years after the events he is recounting. It is an example of ideas close to those expressed by the likes of Hosea (c. 740 BCE) as he railed against the institutionalised corruption of the kings and priests of his own day: 'For I desired mercy and not sacrifice and the awareness of God more than burnt offerings' (Hos. 6:6). These are words that can have little to do with the real Saul and Samuel.

As with so much of this story, we must attempt to free ourselves from the emotions that such powerful writing and imagery are designed to evoke. It is essential to see the broad picture and the given event in its correct historical context. When we take a closer look at Saul's war with Amalek, it will become apparent that hostilities did not stem from the command of an irate prophet nursing a centuries-old vendetta, but was impelled by political expediency.

If Saul felt obliged to launch a massive campaign against a people with whom he had hitherto enjoyed peaceful, or at least tolerable, relations, it had to be for a sound reason. We will soon learn that he had such a reason, and so any tension that might have surfaced between the king and his prophet at this time would have been incidental to the war – not causal.

By revealing a very different cause for the possible tension between Saul and Samuel than that suggested in the Bible, we consign Samuel's genocidal command (or herem, in Hebrew) – to annihilate the Amalekites – to the archives of editorial invention, together with Saul's crime and punishment. However, there remains the persistent tradition of a rift between the two great men. While it is possible that this tradition is a pro-David misrepresentation of Saul's probable falling out with Ahia on the eve of the battle of Michmash, it seems equally likely that the two Gilgal episodes do reflect one historical dispute between Saul and Samuel. In both accounts, Samuel alludes to an already established rival nagid (i.e. David). In addition, each version describes Samuel as being angry with Saul over sacrifices carried out before his arrival. We can deduce from these commonalties the probable where, when and why of the actual event.

· Where? at Gilgal.
· When? following the victory over Amalek.
· Why? a dispute over religious protocol.

To complete the scene, we can add one more important ingredient: the Amalekite king, Agag.

As stated above, near-Eastern rulers of Saul's era are often pictured as the actual executioners of important captives. If this was a practice imitated by the kings of Israel, it is notable that it is Saul's holy man, Samuel, who kills the captive King Agag. As supreme leader, had he so desired, Saul could surely have executed the Amalekite himself. He, however, chose not to, instead leaving the task to Samuel.

At this point, it is useful to take a step back from the anti-Saul scene painted in Samuel and imagine how a scribe more favourably inclined toward the King of Israel might have recorded it:

> The conquering hero and his army returned from their magnificent victory over Israel's most ancient enemy.
>
> They gathered at the high place of Gilgal to celebrate and give

thanks to God by sacrificing thousands of the finest animals from among the spoil.

While waiting for the arrival of Samuel, who was to officiate over the festivities, the men became impatient and restless, intoxicated as they were with wine and victory.

To avoid potential trouble among his overexcited troops, Saul initiated the sacrifices himself so that the party could begin.

Samuel arrived. He was furious; he felt insulted and accused Saul of heresy. The two men had a blazing row. Samuel said that if Saul were not careful, God would abandon him, and then alluded to the growing influence of David.

Saul sought to pacify Samuel. He even ceded his royal privilege to the old judge and allowed him the honour of the ritual slaughter of the captive King. Samuel then left, vowing to retire from public life.

If this is anything like the true course of events, we can again see how easy it must have been for a later author to alter the narrative to the advantage of the Judahite king. Later still, this scene would lend itself to further embellishment with powerful anti-monarchy imagery.

Conclusion 15
The chronologically confused records of Saul's two reprimands by Samuel are the result of the anti-monarchist perspective superimposed upon an earlier pro-David narrative.[25]

Orthodox Sequence

1 Sam. 15: Samuel commands Saul to wipe out Amalekites; Saul musters a vast army of Israel and Judah at Telaim; Israel is victorious; Saul allows his men to take plunder and he spares Agag, King of Amalek; Furious with Saul for his failure to obey God's commands, Samuel announces that God has forsaken Saul in favour of another; Samuel slays Agag; Saul and Samuel never meet again.

Major Variants

This is unquestionably a fabrication of the Davidic author. The war against Amalek did not occur until very late in Saul's reign, by which time David was a warlord, established at Ziklag (see pp. 123-125). It was his belligerent presence on the Amalekite frontier, and not Samuel's vendetta, that provoked the war.

This claim of a final meeting is at odds with both our heterodox reading and the biblical narrative itself, where Saul meets Samuel again in Chapter 19 (while in pursuit of the fleeing David). Though the latter meeting does not fit our revised chronology, Saul and a living Samuel did meet prior to the battle of Gilboa.

David Plays for Saul

6
David
The Terrible Price of Unity

And the Lord said to Samuel, "How long will you grieve over Saul, since I have rejected him as king over Israel? Fill your horn with oil[1] and set out; I am sending you to Jesse the Bethlehemite, for I have decided on one of his sons to be king" (1 Sam. 16:1)

The Young Shepherd
If Saul's performance as Israel's first king is worthy of mixed reviews, especially for his lack of political acumen, by contrast, his achievement in gaining the devotion of the tribe of Judah is deserving of great credit.

As we have seen, both he and Samuel must have understood from the earliest days of their leadership that a united House of Israel went hand in hand with their cherished aspiration for a strong and free Israelite nation. Saul would have lost no time in recruiting the warrior elite of Judah into his standing regiment.[2]

It is therefore another in the long list of ironies that besets the early history of the Israelite kingdom that, as a direct result of Saul's greatest diplomatic coup, he unwittingly made his fatal mistake. For this achievement exposed the king to a young man perfectly equipped to exploit all his weaknesses. The new recruit was everything that Saul was not. He was a master manipulator of men and a consummate politician, as well as an egotist of huge ambition. Inadvertently, Saul had invited his future usurper, David, into the bosom of his court.[3]

The reader of 1 Samuel encounters David first as a young shepherd boy.

1 Sam. 15:34-16:13: Samuel returned to Ramah to mourn over the fate of Saul, but God chastised him and sent him to the home of Jesse of Bethlehem in Judah, where he was to anoint one of Jesse's sons as the new king. Samuel was reluctant to do so, because of his fear of Saul.

Hence, to disguise his intent, the prophet set up a sacrifice in Bethle-hem, where, among the town elders, he met Jesse and informed him of God's intentions. After eliminating the seven older sons from considera-tion, Samuel had the youngest, David, summoned from his shepherding. It was he whom the Lord revealed to be His choice for king. Before an audience consisting only of David's father and brothers, Samuel sum-marily anointed him with oil. David was infused with the 'Holy Spirit' from that day forth.

The picturesque description of the secret anointing of young David is rich in classic biblical imagery: the white-haired old man with his horn of holy oil anointing the 'ruddy' and 'beautiful' youngest son, a shepherd boy, as the future great shepherd of his entire nation. So powerful is the image of this particular anointing that, in the minds of pious Jews and Christians, it is held to be the very stuff of messianic destiny. Together with the subsequent tale of the newly anointed boy-king slaying Goliath, it forms the crux of the Davidic tradition. The lad thus described personifies the archetype of innocence, courage, and brilliance, burning with faith in God and selfless devotion to king and country. To the pious mind, the flawless child of these two stories is the ideal to which we should all aspire and is the blueprint for all our saviours: 'God was with him'.[4]

However, in all probability the anointing story is merely a skilful piece of propaganda, which succeeded brilliantly in engendering the personality cult of David. In historical terms, it is – like the Goliath story – almost entirely fictitious.

Bearing this in mind, we should now consider the following facts:
- Samuel was from the territory of Ephraim, and was a patriot whose prime objective was the unity and liberty of All Israel.[5]
- Samuel knew that neither the tribe of Judah nor Ephraim would willingly follow a prince from the other.
- Samuel therefore anointed a 'neutral' Benjaminite as nagid (and then king).
- Benjamin was not only the smallest of all the primary tribes but it also sat between its two mighty brothers, Judah and Ephraim.
- Even so, Benjamin was still a Rachelite tribe, and it was only after Saul had won stunning victories – some possibly in the service of Judah itself – that the Leahite Judah joined the kingdom.

It is reasonable to assume that as part of his courtship of Judah, Saul recruited young Judahite nobles to key positions in his court and his army. Moreover, knowing the reverence with which Samuel – whose sons, it should not be forgotten, were established in Judah – was held throughout all Israel (1 Sam. 16:4-5), Saul must inevitably have turned to the prophet when he needed an envoy to establish good relations with the elders of Judah's princely families. Once in that role, Samuel will have presented himself to the influential House of Jesse as a matter of course.

However, any such visit was only in the interests of strengthening Saul's kingdom. The idea that the Ephraim-rooted Samuel could have anointed a prince of Judah to replace his own Benjaminite appointee defies logic. To have done so would have sown the seeds of destruction of the very kingdom he had done so much to establish.

By the same token, if Jesse took advantage of the rare visit of the revered Samuel, to have him 'sanctify' and perhaps anoint his sons as princes of Judah (1 Sam. 16:5), he was merely conforming to custom, just as Kish had done with his own son – Saul – years earlier. Any wealthy family head and tribal prince would have acted in the same way, rather as a contemporary Roman Catholic might request a blessing upon his/her house during a visit by the Pope. Likewise, if Samuel was impressed with David and his brothers, it would only have been to the extent that he saw their potential usefulness in the service of King Saul and the cause of All-Israel.

With hindsight, we can see the propaganda value of such an event to a later Davidic author attempting to promote a king and/or a royal house to a largely sceptical people who were mourning the loss of the one and only royal-anointed of Samuel.

Conclusion 16
What was in reality a common, everyday event was distorted by the propagandist into a royal anointing.[6]

David as Healer (First Introduction of David to Saul)
In all that precedes the introduction of David into the story, there is not a hint of Saul's dark side. Now, according to the text, Saul undergoes a profound psychological change:

1 Sam. 16:14: Just when the spirit of God entered David, it departed from Saul, to be replaced by an evil spirit that subjected him to bouts of terrible depression.

In the context of our reassessment, it would be tempting to dismiss the concept of a dark side as just another Davidic creation, but this is, after all, a re-examination and not a reinvention. It is both probable and understandable that this most reluctant of kings found the responsibility of being the Lord's anointed ever more onerous. His innate sense of duty towards his people and his overwhelming awe at their having anointed him must have led to episodes of self-doubt, confusion, and possibly depression.

It is quite believable that, around the time of David's recruitment, Saul was genuinely downcast. Yet, that is quite different from the Jekyll and Hyde scenario presented by the authors of 1 Samuel.

1 Sam. 16:15-23: *A palliative suggested for the afflicted king was music, and one of his servants recommended David. 'I have observed a son of Jesse the Bethlehemite, who is skilled in music, he is a stalwart fellow and a warrior, sensible in speech and handsome in appearance, and the Lord is with him.'*

David was summoned to Gibeah, where he quickly became a royal favourite and was appointed armour bearer and musician to the king, whose bad moods he succeeded in alleviating.

Goliath
We now find ourselves on the battlefield of Elah, in the Shephela[7] – the territory that divided Judah from the land of the Philistines:

1 Sam. 17:1-31: *A while later, the Philistines invaded Judah and confronted the army of Saul in the valley of Elah. A long stalemate ensued. Every day the enemy sent out their champion, Goliath, a giant who challenged the Hebrews with taunts and insults. No Israelite dared to face him.*

David, the youngest of Jesse's eight sons, was sent by his father with provisions for three of his brothers serving in Saul's army. By the time he arrived at camp, Goliath's challenge had gone unanswered for forty days, and the morale of the Hebrew troops was suffering. Saul sent out word that whoever succeeded in slaying Goliath would receive his daughter's hand in marriage, and the hero's family would be awarded the freedom of Israel. The taunts of the Philistine, incensed David and he voiced his rage to those around him.

The things David said were overheard and were reported to Saul who had him brought over.

Looking the Giant in the Eye (David's Second Introduction to Saul)
Thus the 'mighty and brave warrior' – the king's armour bearer – of 1 Sam.16: 18 has metamorphosed into a callow youth.

1 Sam. 17:32-54: *Upon meeting Saul, David volunteered to take on Goliath. He allayed the king's doubts about his fitness for the task by relating how he had protected his father's flocks from lions and bears.*

After an abortive attempt at fitting him into the royal armour, David went out armed with only his slingshot to confront the giant. The combatants advanced towards each other. As Goliath approached, David shot a stone into the Philistine's forehead, toppling him. Then, using Goliath's own sword, David decapitated his sprawled enemy. At the sight of this, the jubilant Israelite army charged the dismayed Philistines and utterly routed them. Afterwards, David took Goliath's head to Jerusalem, having first put the captured weapons into his own tent.

David's Gift to Saul (David's third introduction to Saul)
Not only has David apparently undergone a complete physical transformation, he also seems to have access to the (as yet) unconquered Jerusalem – a Jebusite city until the seventh year of King David's reign (2 Sam.5: 5). Moreover, he seems to have the additional gift of super-human speed – one second in Elah, the next minute in Jerusalem and then an instant later he's back at Elah again (a combined distance of some twenty miles as the crow flies, all the while encumbered by Goliath's massive head). It's not surprising that Saul seems so confused regarding David's – his own armour bearer's – identity! This appears not so much a biblical narrative as a particularly convoluted episode of Star Trek – what with altering personalities, some ancient version of 'transportation' and sudden shifts in the 'time-line continuum'.[8]

1 Sam. 17:55-58: *After David's slaying of Goliath, Saul expressed curiosity to Abner about David's parentage. Abner then brought David – still carrying Goliath's head – before the king.*
   Saul said to him, "Whose son are you, my boy?" And David answered, "The son of your servant Jesse the Bethlehemite.'

Humorous observations notwithstanding, we now need to determine which of the three introductions of David to the royal court is likely to be authentic.

If David was not the true slayer of Goliath (as was suggested in the introduction), it follows that the second and third accounts of his introduction to the king are fictitious. The less lurid first account has the ring of truth, especially since Saul habitually recruited Judahite warriors.

The author's attempt to harmonise the two narratives, by asserting (in 1 Sam. 17:15) that David had returned from Saul's court to look after his father's sheep, fails to explain why he was unknown to the king on his return. Moreover, the idea that the king's young armour bearer would have reverted to the life of a shepherd is nonsensical on its face. But this concoction was necessary to 'explain' the anomaly. To have had an armour bearer, a bodyguard, 'a mighty and brave warrior' (1 Sam. 16:18) go out to confront Goliath would have conveyed merely the bravery expected of a king's champion. It was essential to make his courage superhuman. He is therefore presented as a shepherd boy armed only with his slingshot and his unswerving faith in God.[9] The imperative that David's courage be greater than that of his comrades – especially that of the king – has a strong messianic resonance. The ideal of unmatched, selfless bravery for the sake of his brothers-in-arms was part of David's alleged messianic heritage. In reality, he was merely the accomplished warrior described to Saul by 'the servant' in the first (and original) introduction. Somehow, the two 'parallel' Davids became juxtaposed rather than blended.

The peculiarly poor editing of the three David introductions, and the messianic texture of the Elah episode, indicate a late insertion of the Goliath story into the general narrative. An objective reading of the passage reveals, even in translation, how 'David and Goliath' seems to interrupt – however charmingly – the flow of the overall narrative. Indeed, if one edits out the episode, it is not missed at all, and in many ways assists, in respect of continuity.

All of which still leaves us wondering how the three introductions made their way into the text. There appears to be no rational answer. One has to fall back on the hypothesis that the more faithful tradition of David's early rise to fame was so well known that the later propagandist addition could not involve any tampering with the original. Thus in 1 Samuel in general, and especially in this episode, we are left to disentangle a veritable spaghetti of what most commentators are pleased to term 'parallel strands'. It was as if all that mattered was the propagation of the David myth – even at the price of editorial chaos. Such reliance on pious gullibility has proven to be well founded. The scribes were precursors of our tabloid newspaper editors who know that, true or false, a good story will be believed and that glory – however undeserved – sticks just as well as mud.

> ### Conclusion 17
> The true history of David's recruitment is reflected in the first version of his introduction to King Saul, when he entered court as an accomplished warrior and musician.[10]

David, Courtier and National Hero

The text continues, and at long last Saul seems to have at least grasped the name of his armour bearer. Unfortunately, it now appears that the King of Israel's emotionally unbalanced state has had a disastrous effect upon his powers of character judgement:

1 Sam. 18:1-4: *David was invited to join Saul's court partly as a result of Jonathan's instant infatuation with him. The two young men became close friends, and they made a solemn compact. Jonathan even dressed David in his own clothes and allowed him the use of his bow.*

. . . Jonathan's soul became bound up with the soul of David, and Jonathan loved David as himself.

Samuel presents an idealised picture of a youth, beautiful both in spirit and in body, whose motives were as pure as his ambition was noble, dutiful, and divinely inspired. He is the second Lord's anointed devoted to the service of the first (a divine paradox if ever there was one). David can do no wrong. His seduction of the House of Saul is merely a natural and innocent consequence of his sterling qualities. By contrast, Saul is presented in an unflattering light. Whereas the knightly Jonathan graciously accepts the implications of divine fickleness, his father apparently descends into paranoia.[11]

A more accurate, yet more complex, picture of this cast of characters begins to emerge when we see through the hypnotic influence of the Davidic agenda.

An early chink in David's armour of flawlessness is glimpsed in a brief remark ascribed to his eldest brother (in 1 Sam. 17:28) – ironically within the otherwise all-but-fantastical Goliath narrative: 'Eliab became angry with David and said . . . "I know your pride your wickedness of heart. . . ."'[12]

If 1 Samuel were a modern work of literature, one might regard Eliab's comment as merely vituperative – a typical display of an elder sibling's irritation with a younger brother, and this is certainly the way pious commentators view it.[13] However, this is a literary convention which was alien to the compiler(s) of the Tanakh. Each and every remark – however historical, apocryphal, or confused – had a contextual purpose. A remark is never simply slipped into the prose for the sake of added colour.

In the context of the most pro-David narrative in either of the books of Samuel, Eliab's denunciation is astonishing. The only thing more astonishing in fact, is the almost universal silence of the commentators – including anti-Davidic scholars (such as Halpern and Brookes) – on the subject.

The compiler of the narrative could not have agreed with Eliab's allegation that David was 'proud and wicked' – yet he retained it within the text. It must be, therefore, that in the Davidic hagiography, Eliab's reprimand represents the blindness that cannot perceive the saint's virtues. It might also reflect a later tension from the time when David was king, between the monarch, and his oldest brother – and natural heir to the prince-ship of Jesse – who might have regarded himself as having been usurped vis-à-vis his tribal status. In any case, to the author(s) of the Goliath story, Eliab is a contemptible slanderer. Eliab's description of David, however, was as accurate as an X-ray.

David may have been an attractive and charismatic young man. It is even probable that his ambition developed only after he had joined Saul's household. Yet, once the ambition had taken hold, David's 'proud and wicked' character provided fertile soil in which it could flourish. Saul, perhaps distracted by events and possibly socially unsophisticated, became aware of David's ambitions only when matters had progressed too far.

1 Sam. 18:5-30: David's military career was so successful that he soon became a national hero. The women of Israel were more enthusiastic in their praise of the courtier than of the king, who became jealous of his protégé. During a bout of depression, Saul's envy got the better of him. In a rage, he hurled a spear at the young musician as the latter was playing for him. It missed, but the king, now fully aware that David was the Lord's anointed, sought other ways to be rid of him. He gave David a field command, but the son of Jesse enjoyed one victory after another and his enhanced popularity only further fuelled the jealousy of the king.

Saul's next ploy was to promise David the hand of his eldest daughter Merab, on condition that he perform even more valiantly in battle. Feeling unworthy of becoming the king's son-in-law, David hesitated to take up the challenge. But in the event, Saul reneged on their agreement and betrothed Merab to another.

When Michal, the king's younger daughter, fell in love with David, Saul saw a new opportunity to rid himself of the Bethlehemite. He told all his courtiers that he would favour the match should David succeed in bringing him the foreskins of one hundred Philistines. Spurred by the new challenge, David immediately went out to do battle, returning with the foreskins of two hundred slain warriors. Saul was now compelled to give Michal to David in marriage.

The account of David's time at court is particularly difficult to verify and is unlikely to have been common knowledge at the time.[14] Many of the scenes involve only the main protagonists and have no corroborating witnesses. Here, more than at almost any other point in the narrative, we must rely on reason. If, for example, David did wed Michal, it would be more in keeping with our knowledge of dynastic marriage that he did so by virtue of his position as a prince of Judah than because of any heroics he might have performed. Indeed, given the mounting evidence of an embroidered biography, we have good reason to regard the claim for any such battlefield exploits with a degree of scepticism. Yet, even supposing he was the prodigious collector of Philistine foreskins, would this alone have earned David a princess? All we know of the inter-tribal and international royal weddings of this era point to a more prosaic and expedient probability. If the marriage took place at all, it would have been arranged by Saul in order to cement the unity of Benjamin and Judah. For all we know, the marriage may even have been an original condition of unification set by Samuel or Saul and the princes of Judah – but alas, we can only surmise. (In this regard, it would be interesting to discover the locations of Meholath and Gallim – respectively, the towns from which Saul's other sons-in-law, Adriel and Phalti, came.)[15]

Meanwhile, the narrative continues with Saul's obsessive need to do away with David:

1 Sam. 19:1-7: *Saul instructed Jonathan and his court that David should be killed. Jonathan then informed David that he was in peril and instructed him to hide somewhere safe. The crown prince then brought his father to the field where David was hiding, and they engaged in a frank discussion. Jonathan managed to calm Saul and get him to see reason. As a result, David regained Saul's favour.*

Whatever the exact truth, even the most philo-Davidic commentators admit that Saul did have good cause to be at least perturbed by the rise of David.[16] Whether one adheres to the literal description of David's time at Gibeah or a sceptical alternative reading, Saul's predicament is clear.

According to the narrative, the son-in-law he was forced to accept, by virtue of his own dare, was the new 'Lord's anointed' – a paragon of virtue and military prowess who had mesmerised Jonathan and Michal and become a hero to the nation. David was a usurper in waiting.

Even if one takes the more radical view that David coveted Michal and was the unashamed pretender to Jonathan's future kingdom, the consequences for Saul would have been the same.

1 Sam. 19:8-17: *Saul was aggravated further by David's ever-greater military successes and his soaring reputation in the eyes of Saul's own men. Following one particularly spectacular victory, Saul, was once more overcome with anger, threw a spear at his musician and once more he missed. Taking refuge in his own house, David was warned by Michal that he was about to be killed, and with her help he fled. When asked by her father, the king, why she had helped David, Michal claimed that her husband had threatened to kill her if she did not.*

David and Samuel

Having, believed – somewhat naively – that he was safe from the enraged King of Israel within the confines of his house, the narrative now stretches our credulity even further. Presumably, in some form of blind panic, the matchless hero now flees north from Gibeah – away from his native (and equally close by) territory of Judah and seeks refuge with Samuel.

1 Sam. 19:18-24: David made straight for Ramah, where he sought the protection of Samuel, and both men then went on to Naioth.[17] *All Saul's attempts to capture David from Samuel failed. One posse after another, when confronted by the judge and his followers, was overcome with prophetic rapture. When the king himself appeared at the scene, the same thing happened to him – he stripped off his clothes, then writhed around on the ground in an ecstatic trance.*

If David was far less innocent during his career at the Gibeah court than is normally assumed, and if his excuse for fleeing Saul is thus undermined, the idea that he would seek refuge with the Samuel of our thesis seems improbable. Samuel, for all his possible problems with Saul, was unlikely to support an opponent of the king he had anointed.[18]

As for the narrative's version of Samuel anointing David behind Saul's back – he surely would have been terrified of Saul in his own right (1 Sam. 16:2) and hardly in a position to ward off a rampaging king.

Alternatively, one could argue that in desperation, David turned to the great religious leader for sanctuary, perhaps gambling that he could rely on the protection of Samuel, not as a personal favour but because the judge would do all he could to avoid friction within the kingdom. If Saul succeeded in killing David, whatever his crimes, the realm could be split asunder.

However, the most informative part of the story is the subsequent meeting between Saul and Samuel, for, according to 1 Sam.15:35, they never set eyes on each other again following the victory over Amalek. Yet here they are, a short while later, enjoying a moment of shared ecstasy.

The puzzle created by contradictory statements about the meetings of Saul and Samuel is resolved by a reasoned adjustment of chronology. As we shall see, the historical war with Amalek was yet to take place at the time of David's flight from Saul, and the Judahite prince was far from being without blemish when it did.

As for the idea that David sought refuge with the undoubted anointer of King Saul, it is most probably another propagandist fantasy – a fairy tale intended to confirm the linkage between the ultimate anointer of Israelite kings and the son of Jesse. In terms of historicity, it belongs with stories of David's anointing, and his battles with giants and wild beasts.

Unfaithful Wives and Unreliable Sons

According to the narrative, a fateful new moon banquet occurs at this time:

1 Sam. 20:1-33: David later met up with Jonathan, who tried to reassure his friend that Saul's evil intentions against him had dissipated. They contrived a plan whereby David would fail to attend the new moon feast on the following day. If Saul's reaction was sanguine, the coast was clear for his return to court. If, however, his absence aroused the king's ire, Jonathan would warn him off.

At the new moon banquet, Jonathan attempted to excuse the absent David, but Saul fell into a rage.

Saul flew into a rage against Jonathan, "you son of a perverse and rebellious, woman!" he shouted. "I know that you side with the son of Jesse – to your shame and the shame of yours mother's nakedness."

Ultimately, Jonathan became the new target of his father's wrath.

At that, Saul threw his spear at him to strike him down; and Jonathan knew that his father was determined to do away with David.

We will return to this scene shortly, when it will have been placed in its correct chronological position. For now it is interesting to ponder an amazing inference contained within the verse – that Ahinoam, Saul's wife, shared in his denouncement of Jonathan, her son. Due mostly to inaccurate translations, especially in authorized bibles, the extreme and explicit accusation against Ahinoam is lost in the drama surrounding Jonathan and her husband.[19]

However, the clue to the cause of Saul's vitriol may lie in an otherwise obscure verse from a little later in the narrative when it gives a list of his women: 'Now David took Ahinoam of Jezreel [in addition to Abigail]; so both of them became his wives' (1 Sam. 25:43).

At this time – well into the future – David was an established warlord. Unless Ahinoam was a very common name in this era – and bearing in mind that few proper names (i.e. non-titular) are ever repeated in the Bible texts (especially within a single narrative) it seems that Saul's queen had either run off with, or been abducted by David! Perhaps, even more incredible, is that this revelation has been all but totally ignored, or missed, by generations of scholarship.

Indeed, those few scholars who bother to mention the odd textual juxtaposition of the 'two Ahinoams' within a single narrative, normally regard it as nothing more than a 'mistake' or a 'coincidence'. The one or two conventional commentators who do at least acknowledge the 'possibility' of a single Ahinoam – with all the accompanying implications

– typically dismiss the idea anyway. The methods employed for sub-stantiating this dismissal are generally so convoluted as to be worthy of those used by the most imaginative of revisionists![20]

This instinct to protect the reputation of David notwithstanding, the 'single Ahinoam' hypothesis seems to be confirmed in a comment attributed to Nathan – his very own prophet – who was obviously fully aware of the son of Jesse's predilection for the womenfolk of King Saul. When chastising the then King David for causing the death of Uriah the Hittite (in order to possess his beautiful wife – Bathsheba), the holy man quotes God with these telling words:

> 'I gave you your master's house [i.e. Saul's] and possession of your master's wives . . . ' (2 Sam. 12:8)[21]

Whatever one's original perspective regarding Saul's alleged behaviour towards Jonathan and David, this 'new' information in isolation would be sufficient to explain his apparent rage. Taken in context with David's pretensions to the throne with the tacit support of Jonathan, Saul would have had every cause to feel extreme anger. Though, whether he was so enraged as to attempt to kill his own son and heir is another question.

The Poor Aim of King Saul

King Saul of Israel and Judah ruled a spiritually diverse kingdom held together, in the main, by popular loyalty to his own person and a widespread fear of a common enemy. In such circumstances, Saul's two previous alleged attempts on the life of the Judahite David would have been as stupid as they were obviously inept. Nearly as stupid, indeed, as the supposed behaviour of David in continuing to put himself in harm's way even after Saul's murderous intentions had been demonstrated: '. . . Saul threw the spear thinking to pin David to the wall' (1 Sam. 18:11); 'Saul tried to pin David to the wall with the spear. . . .' (1 Sam. 19:10) It is his third attempt at murder, however, in which his son and heir was the target, that – on the face of it – makes Saul appear especially deranged.

While there is no reason to doubt that there was antagonism between the king and the pretender, and tension between the father and his son, it cannot be taken for granted that these stresses resulted in the three spear throwing episodes as reported in the text. In the light of our hypothesis, it seems far more probable that Saul's three failures with the spear are fictions intended to portray him as irrational and therefore unfit to rule. In this, they were successful.[22]

We have already seen graphic examples of how an editorial agenda has infected and corrupted the story. The three spear throwing events are further illustrations of the cynical editing which permeates the entire description of David's career at the court of Saul. If one requires proof that the pro-David scribes sought to cloud the eyes of their readers by employing vivid anecdotal imagery, one need look no further than these pages from the First Book of Samuel.

The facts as presented in 1 Samuel are these:

- Saul, (possibly his wife, Ahinoam) his heir Jonathan, his daughter Michal, his entire court, and all the people of Israel and Judah are infatuated with the young hero David;
- With each of David's military successes, however, Saul becomes increasingly jealous. From then on the ambivalence of his feelings towards the son of Jesse results in increasingly frequent bouts of irrational behaviour, including incidents of homicidal violence;
- Meanwhile, David's star continues to rise inexorably. He befriends Jonathan, who consequently swears allegiance to the Bethlehemite;
- The more Saul devises ways to endanger him, the more success David enjoys, until he ultimately wins the hand of Michal and becomes the royal son-in-law;
- Eventually, Saul's paranoid reactions extend beyond David and begin to threaten the safety of Jonathan too;
- David, in fear for his life, runs away a second time;
- Throughout this period, despite hurt and indignation, David's behaviour remains faultless and his loyalty to the erratic king never wavers. Saul, on the other hand, has succumbed to evil spirits – his conduct towards the most loyal of his subjects is mad and bad.

In countless commentaries, Saul's fears and actions are assessed as being quite reasonable given that he is knowingly harbouring his own usurper within his court.[23] But if the story of David's time at Gibeah contains even a fraction of the truth, most of Saul's behaviour deserves to be remembered not for its reasonableness but for its heroic self-sacrifice. After all, we are asked to believe that the king, following his own rejection by God – presumably out of post-Amalek pious contrition – willingly nurtured at his court the very person he knew was destined to take over his kingdom. Furthermore, Saul merely looked on while David both entered into a compromising relationship with Jonathan and had intimate relations with Ahinoam. To complete this chronicle of abjection and self-immolation, Saul is crass enough to elevate David to the status of royal son-in-law!

Who, following such a cascade of self-inflicted humiliations, would not occasionally slip into fits of rage? The only wonder is that he was so inept in his attempts at murder. If the story as presented is even partly true, rage was by no means Saul's sole failing – he was also a pathological fool.

All this makes for good theatre, but it is obviously nonsense. The story of David and his adventures at the court of Saul is redolent with fairy tale imagery – Saul is the grumpy, jealous and wicked old king, while David is the faithful, flawless and chivalrous knight. Michal is the beautiful and unattainable princess, and in place of the dragon, we have a monstrous giant in the shape of Goliath. The entire episode seems to presage the Arthurian legends of Britain, complete with a fiery, cantankerous Merlin-like old wizard in the form of Samuel and a mysterious Morgan le Fay-like witch, in the person of the woman of En-dor (whom we shall encounter presently).

Indeed, the parallels are legion, and would make the subject of another book in their own right. [24] So far as this study is concerned, it seems clear that the depiction of David's career as a servant of Saul is fanciful, propaganda at best. The main elements of David's career at Gibeah were cobbled together by a Davidic Mallory, intent on transforming – what was in all probability – a tale of ambition, lust, intrigue and treachery, into a portrait of heroic, selfless devotion. The elements of truth – as with the fifteenth century Arthurian romance – are so shrouded in myth that they are very hard to disseminate.

To build a plausible picture of David's time at Gibeah, there are several factors that must be considered. Saul would have been desperate to preserve the newly established unity of the kingdom – a disposition that must have made him particularly vulnerable to any over-ambitious young princes of Judah within his court. Similarly, such a prince with cunning to match his ambition would have found many opportunities for self-advancement – including seduction of royal women, ingratiating himself with Jonathan, and exploitation of any pre-existing domestic tensions. Once Saul realized what was going on, his options would have been limited. Dangerous military assignments for the young Judahite would have been the one possible choice for the king – there may therefore be truth in the basic fabric of this part of the story. it seems unlikely, however, that Saul would have married his daughter to David once he comprehended the far-reaching ambition of the man. As was suggested earlier, if he did allow the union it would have been early in David's career when Saul was establishing the initial ties between his house and Judah and before David had revealed himself as an adversary.

Sending David out to die in battle begins to seem a perfectly plausible method by which Saul could get rid of his domestic troublemaker. Paradoxically, this was the same method that David would allegedly use many years later – when he was king – to rid himself of Uriah (2 Sam.

11.) The main differences being that King David's action was blatantly murderous and driven by lust, while Saul's action was merely an act of desperation, driven by political expediency.

When attempting to construct a true portrait of David, it is vital to study his personality as revealed in the more historical second book of Samuel. Here David is presented as the perpetrator of multiple misdeeds, in addition to his role in the death of Uriah. Amongst these are his infamous taking of the census (2 Sam. 24), and his appalling record in managing his family affairs – especially with respect to his son Absalom (2 Sam. 13-19) and the matter of the succession (1 K. 1/2).

If the stories of Saul's spear attacks contain any truth, it is to the final incident that we should turn for the likely historical source. The king's despair at the overly close relationship between Jonathan and David, and its disastrous implications for the future of the royal line, could have caused a fundamentally noble man such as Saul to threaten his son's life.

In fact, the pro-David scribe took what was then a commonly known incident concerning Saul and a spear and wove it into the fantasy of a wronged David. This achieved two objectives: first, it gave David honourable cause to flee from Gibeah; and second, it made Saul look all the more despotic and crazed.

It is likely that the first two attack stories – which constitute another 1 Samuel doublet – stem from actual arguments between Saul and David. Given the possible subject matter of those disputes, and the potential for passionate accusation and denial, verbal and/or physical violence may well have occurred. However, since there were no third-party witnesses to either of the alleged incidents, and the accounts come from a pro-David author, our credulity is severely strained. More specifically, as we stated earlier, the notions that the wily David would have offered himself up as a target and that Saul would have missed at close range on consecutive occasions are highly implausible.

In stark contrast, the third incident, at the new-moon banquet, was witnessed by numerous court members and offers the rational Saul we have been describing a legitimate reason for losing his composure.

For the sake of the pro-David narrative, it was expedient to place the new-moon incident at the very start of David's exile. This placement reinforces the image of David's undeserved persecution at the hands of a maniac. It is a powerful, lyrically drawn image but, as we are learning, one that fails to stand up to scrutiny.

In the reinterpretation offered here, David either fled or was expelled from Gibeah because he was known to be plotting or even initiating a rebellion against the throne. In this context, the idea that David would have risked staying within the confines of the city, let alone return to court, is preposterous – Jonathan's support notwithstanding. Furthermore, for the narrative to be taken at face value, we are required to believe that David wanted to return to the side of a king who had twice attempted to murder him – in other words, that David was an imbecile. Whatever else he may have been, he certainly was not that.

Conclusion 18
The three accounts of Saul's spear throwing are apocryphal, pro-David distortions of the actual tensions which existed between the king, his heir, and the would-be usurper.[25]

Meanwhile, the traumatised crown prince has to tell the bad news to his beloved friend:

1 Sam. 20:34-42: *Jonathan, angry and humiliated by his father's actions, left the banquet and went to tell David the bad news. Following emotional pledges of mutual loyalty, the prince sent his friend away to live as a fugitive.*

Jonathan said to David, 'Go in peace! For we two have sworn to each other in the name of the Lord: 'May the Lord be witness between you and me, and between your offspring and mine forever.'"

The narrative would further have us believe friendship was innocent in its ideals, consistent with divinely ordained fate, and an icon of true friendship for all time. Yet our growing awareness of the real David leads us to a very different understanding of the relationship, and in particular, of his motives in sustaining it.

Jonathan

Unlike the other major players in the drama of 1 Samuel, Jonathan is not significantly affected by any major narrative anomalies. Though one or two of his encounters with David have a feeling of duplication about them, this is merely a by-product of the editorial manipulation with which we are now familiar. For example, if the two accounts of David's fleeing from Saul are versions of the same event, it is hardly surprising that Jonathan and David's emotional discussion is duplicated too. Similarly, Jonathan's victories in earlier years are chronologically misaligned because the editorial imperative demanded that Saul's campaign at Michmash be shifted in time. In the pro-David narrative of 1 Samuel, the royal heir is peripheral. Whereas in a hypothetical 'Book of Saul' Jonathan would be a central character around whom many events would revolve, in the de facto 'Book of David' (i.e. Samuel) his only importance is in relation to David's claim to the throne. This must be borne in mind when assessing the nature of the historical Jonathan.[26]

In the days before David arrived on the scene, Jonathan operated almost independently of Saul. According to 1 Samuel he had his own regiment and fought his own battles from the outset of the resistance against the Philistines.[27] If this merely shows that father and son were fighting on a broad front, the record of their joint efforts suggests a disharmony of leadership and disunity of purpose. The story of Jonathan's unilateral assault on the Philistine camp at Michmash and of Saul's wrath at his subsequent eating of honey hints at an undercurrent of general tension between the king and his heir (1 Sam. 14:27-30).

Furthermore, it is worth noting, that some commentators view this incident as merely a symbolic (and certainly fictitious) constituent part of the "tripartite kingship ritual", whereby the king-elect, i.e. Jonathan, undergoes a sort of three-stage test or proving:

1. designation;
2. military deed, and;
3. coronation.

However, whereas Saul (designation by Samuel; battle of Jabesh; Gilgal coronation) and David (designation by Samuel; defeating Goliath; Hebron coronation) passed through the process with flying colours, Jonathan's tasting of the honey represents his failure of the test at the second stage. All of which was very convenient for David and more importantly, for both his and later scribes and redactors, left with the problem of explaining the reason for Jonathan never succeeding his father as king.[28]

The reliability of the historicity of Saul's alleged inferior military record vis-à-vis Jonathan's notwithstanding, it is quite plausible that the two men had their problems independent of David.

But, whatever the state of their relationship prior to David's arrival on the scene, it seems undeniable that it was David's presence at Gibeah which proved the catalyst for the most significant and fateful rift between Saul and Jonathan. We shall see shortly how the succession of one of Saul's hitherto obscure offspring – his second-born son, Ishboshet – was not due merely to a quirk of fate but actually formed part of a contingency plan drawn up the king himself. Furthermore, it will be demonstrated how Jonathan's death at the Battle of Gilboa was a direct consequence of his 'divided loyalties'.

The friction between father and son had profound and fateful consequences for the House of Saul.

Othodox Sequence	Major Variants

1 Sam. 16: God sends Samuel to anoint David, son of Jesse, in Bethlehem; 'The Spirit of the Lord' enters David.

Samuel's diplomatic visit to Jesse and the other elders of Judah on behalf of Saul took place about ten years earlier, when Saul was King of Israel only.

At that time, he may have anointed David, and many other princes of Judah, as part of his recruiting drive for Saul. Thus, David and his brothers probably entered the service of Saul, with Jesse's permission, before the uniting of the kingdom.

An 'evil spirit' enters Saul; the valiant warrior David, is appointed court musician to soothe the troubled soul of the king; Saul makes David his armour bearer.

1 Sam. 17: Battle of Elah.

The Philistines send out their giant champion, Goliath, to challenge the Israelites; in spite of his goading, no Hebrew dares to face him.

The battle of Elah probably dates from shortly before the uniting of Judah and Israel. A possible treaty of co-operation between the two halves of Israel could have provoked the Philistines to enter the Shephela – which may in turn have resulted in an outbreak of hostilities between Judah and the Philistine confederation.

Saul allows the boy David to be his champion; David slays Goliath; Israel is victorious in the ensuing battle; David takes the severed head to Jerusalem; he then presents it to King Saul; both Saul and Abner are ignorant as to David's identity.

By the time of the battle of Elah, David and his brothers were established members of Saul's elite corps of 3,000.

The Goliath episode belongs to a much later conflict, during *King* David's own war against the Philistines. Elhanan, David's champion, slew Goliath, then presented the severed head to David, who took it back in triumph to his new capital of Jerusalem.

1 Sam. 18: Jonathan becomes infatuated with David; David becomes a royal courtier; David's military successes make him a national hero; Saul becomes jealous of David and attempts to murder him; He gives David a dangerous military command; David flourishes; Saul offers David the hand of his eldest

The entire 'David at Gibeah' episode with all its intrigues takes place during the early part of Saul's ten-year reign over All Israel – well before the Amalek war.

daughter, Merab, if he achieves more victories; David is victorious again; Saul then reneges on his promise, and gives Merab to Adriel.

Saul's youngest daughter Michal falls in love with David; David wins the hand of Michal by slaying 200 Philistine warriors and presenting Saul with their foreskins; David's star rises ever higher and Saul becomes ever more envious.

1 Sam. 19: Saul attempts to murder David; David escapes, assisted by Michal; David takes refuge with Samuel at Ramah; Samuel uses prophecy to help David evade the pursuing Saul.

1 Sam. 20: Jonathan's attempts to reunite Saul and David fail; Saul attempts to kill Jonathan; Jonathan sends David away.

Jonathan and David

7
David
'Enemy of the State'

David went to the priest Ahimelech at Nob . . .¹ (1 Sam. 21:2)

A Rebel Army
Since his first flight from Gibeah – having originally headed north to Ramah and then doubled back to Gibeah for his tryst with Jonathan – David now turns up in Nob, south of Saul's capital, in the region of Jerusalem. At this point, the narrative seems to be describing a man in the throes of a particularly extreme form of panic, rather than a fearless prince of Judah:

1 Sam. 21:1-9: *Following his parting from Jonathan, David sought refuge among the priestly community at Nob. He told Ahimelech, the high priest, that he was on a royal errand, and asked for bread and a sword. Ahimelech gave him the sword of Goliath.*
This entire scene was witnessed by Doeg, Saul's Edomite herdsman.

The two stories of David fleeing the wrath of Saul have the following elements in common:
· Each episode is initiated by a spear-throwing event.
· Each escape is facilitated by one of Saul's children.
· In each case, David's first port of call is to holy men.
The similarities would seem to suggest that David fled only once from the wrath of Saul. Nevertheless, this is not to dismiss all the individual components as pure fiction. Rather, the inference to be drawn is that, once again, a series of actual events was scrambled by multiple and biased authors and eventually remixed in the form of yet another 1 Samuel replication.

If the previous episode involving Samuel is – as we suspect – a propagandist fantasy, it would, nevertheless have been logical for the desperate and ambitious David to approach other important clerics. Especially so, if those same clerics were empathetic, and shared his animus towards Saul. However, the precise details of David's encounter with Ahimelech remain elusive. Certainly, he could not have been given Goliath's sword, since the Philistine would not be felled by Elhanan until some years later.

David's desperate search for sanctuary now takes him to the greatest enemy of his people:

1 Sam. 21:10-22-5: David then fled to Achish,[2] the Philistine King of Gath. But his prospective hosts were wary, knowing him to be the lauded warrior of Israel. He realized he was in danger and feigned madness in order to escape.

David found refuge in the cave of Adullam,[3] where he was joined by four hundred fellow fugitives. He then took his family across the Jordan and placed them under the protection of the King of Moab so that they were safe from Saul, while he, following the instructions of the prophet Gad, moved his small army into eastern Judah and the forest of Hareth.[4]

Here the narrative admits that David was leading a private army shortly after the commencement of his exile. Even if he was alone at the moment of leaving Gibeah, it could not have been long – perhaps as early as Ramah or Nob – before family and friends joined him.

We can extract the following facts from this chaotic episode:
  · that David's initial instinct was to seek help from the clergy;
  · that his alleged next ports of call, Gath and Moab, were enemies of Israel and Judah.

Given Saul's apparent antipathy towards and sidelining of the established priesthood, and his wars with the Philistines and Moab, these are telling moves. Furthermore, David was forced to take sanctuary in the wilderness, finding no refuge within his own tribe. Allowing for the certainty that a few fellow malcontents from Saul's court – Joab and his brother Abishai, for example – joined him, his main source of companionship was the ranks of fellow fugitives.[5]

Hence, instead of the wronged hero of the superficial story, we are confronted with an ambitious and cunning maverick, whose first instinct was to ally himself with all those who bore a grudge against, or had reason to fear, Saul: the clergy, the Philistines, Moab, and a small army of misfits.

Slaughter of the *not so* Innocents?

The last time we encountered Saul in the narrative, we were privileged to observe his full repertoire of lunatic behaviour and abject ineptitude:
  · his second attempt on the life of David;
  · his crazed naked frenzy in the countryside near Ramah;

· his subsequent bizarre puzzlement at David's absence from the new
  moon feast;
· his attempt on the life of his son, Jonathan.

Small wonder, that when we next meet Saul, he is taking a much needed
rest, well out of the sun, seated under the dense shade of a leafy tamarisk
tree at Gibeah – no doubt due to strict medical advice. However, the
brooding maniacal and paranoid side of the king's personality is never
far from the surface, and before long he is once again obsessing on the
innocent and maligned David:

1 Sam. 22:6-23: *Meanwhile, Saul reprimanded his fellow Benjaminites
and warned them that they had a bleak future in store should the Judahite
David become king. He accused them all, and especially Jonathan, of
conspiring against him and of being in league with the son of Jesse.*

*At that moment, Doeg came forward and informed the king of what he
had witnessed between David and the priests of Nob. Saul immediately
summoned Ahimelech and his people to answer a charge of treason.
Not believing their protestations of innocence, the king ordered Doeg to
execute the entire community, women and children included. Abiathar,
the son of Ahimelech, managed to escape the carnage and fled to David,
who, on hearing of the atrocity, was racked with guilt.*

Ahimelech was the son of Ahitub and thus Eli's great-grandson. He is
almost certainly one and the same as Ahia, the high priest of Saul at
the battle of Michmash (1 Sam. 14:3).[6] The name change is probably a
posthumous promotion by a grateful King David. (The melech component
of 'Ahimelech' means 'king.' Ahi or Achi means either 'brother of,'
producing 'brother-of the-king', or 'my brother is', producing 'my-brother
is [the] king'.)

The fact that Ahia/Ahimelech is now to be found living in Nob when
presumably, as high priest, his place was beside the Ark at Gibeah
suggests a possible breakdown in relations between him and Saul. The
origins of this rift are alluded to in an earlier story set just prior to the
battle of Michmash, when Saul was still a nagid. It seems that Saul had
summoned the Ark, initially intending that it either be carried into battle
or included in some pre-battle rite. He changed his mind, however,
demanding that the priest 'stay his hand' (1 Sam. 14:18-19). Could
this hugely important yet strangely understated episode be alluding to
a catastrophic confrontation between the then nagid, Saul, and the high
priest, Ahia/Ahimelech?[7]

Bearing in mind that Ahia/Ahimelech's grandfather was the discredited
Phinehas who had 'lost the Ark' less than a year before, at Aphek, the

new high priest may have had a keen desire to re-establish the authority of the House of Eli as soon as possible. Leading the Ark into battle and to victory would have been a powerful way for him to effect a swift reversal of his family's declining status in the ruling hierarchy of Israel.

It should be noted that some commentators agree with the Septuagint's version here, which reads ephod rather than Ark.[8] This discrepancy originates from the information in 1 Sam. 7: 1-2, which is often taken to mean that the Ark never left the house – i.e. physical structure – of Abinadab until David moved it to Jerusalem. These commentators also maintain that the seemingly anomalous Gibeah (2 Sam. 6: 2-3) from which it was removed by David was a hill within Kiryath-jearim upon which Abinadab's house was built, rather than Gibeah of Saul. However, if one accepts that the Hebrew versions of both episodes are merely confusions resulting from wilful pro-David redactions, and then simply fill in the obvious gaps, it seems reasonable and logical to assume that the *men of Kiryath-jearim* – to whom the Ark had been returned by the Philistines – handed it over to the priestly *Benjaminite* clan of *Abinadab of Gibeah* for safe keeping; all of which is consistent with Saul already being a prominent resistance leader and a natural choice for the job of protecting the Ark of God. This hypothesis also explains what the Ark was doing at Gibeah prior to the Michmash battle and casts further light upon why Saul was so reluctant to permit Ahia, from a rival non-Benjaminite priestly clan lead it into battle.

It is also plausible that Saul might simply have had second thoughts about risking the Ark again so soon after its return from capture. Or it might have occurred to him that the presence of the high priest and the Ark in battle would compromise his own authority in front of the troops. In either case, the incident represented a slapping down of the high priest by the captain of the army, and is therefore highly relevant when we attempt to understand the relationship of the two men.

How might Samuel have regarded this apparent tension between priesthood and army?

At the time of the Ark's return from Philistine captivity, before the outbreak of the war of liberation, Samuel was probably the de-facto leader of Israel, his appointment of nagid Saul notwithstanding. Thus, presumably it was he who at that time entrusted the guardianship of the Ark to the clan of Abinadab (1 Sam. 6:21). If so, the process of 'demoting' the House of Eli was begun by Samuel, not Saul. Indeed, Samuel may even have held Eli and his sons directly responsible for the calamity of defeat.

Whatever strains may have existed between Samuel and his anointed

general, in any dispute between Ahia and Saul, Samuel would undoubtedly
have thrown his weight behind the latter. Whereas the House of Eli was
tainted by association with defeat, the House of Kish symbolised hope.
And as Saul's victories mounted and Israel was redeemed, Samuel's
support for his captain and future king was vindicated, with the result that
Ahia and his clan must surely have become ever more marginalized.

We may speculate further that, once crowned, Saul demoted the
high priest and appointed another who was more to his liking (i.e.
the Benjaminite Gibeah priesthood), resulting in the tradition that the
House of Eli was destined to lose its position as guardian of the Ark and
the sanctuary. We can now see why David's supposedly innocent and
desperate visit to Eli's descendants at Nob might have seemed altogether
more sinister to King Saul.[9]

Nob was perhaps a town of refuge and exile for the House of Eli. The
highly symbolic insertion regarding Goliath's sword and it being handed
to David is resonant of a passing of the baton from one king to another.
It was also, quite possibly, an editorial attempt to cover up the fact that
David and his band of men received significant supplies of arms and food
from Ahimelech. Otherwise, we have to trust the text when it tells us that
Ahimelech accepted at face value David's improbable story that he was
unarmed and starving while on a secret mission for the king and safely
within the borders of Israel.[10]

We can now see events through the eyes of Saul. From his point of view
and that of his subjects, the truth was that the priests of Nob colluded with
the pretender to the throne of the Lord's anointed. The assistance given
to David had to be regarded for what it was – treason.

Tyrant or Merciful King?
Aside from claims of Saul's spear-throwing, demonic possession, and
dogged pursuit of the fugitive David, there is no evidence of tyranny
during his reign. His later massacre of the Amalekites, for all its
gruesomeness, was nothing remarkable in its day, merely an accepted
and expected act of war.

In essence, the image of an evil Saul is a manifestation of David's
personal fear, which is so eloquently transmitted to us through the pages
of Samuel and several of the Psalms accredited to the son of Jesse. '. . .
deliver me from all my pursuers, and save me, lest, like a lion, they tear
me apart, rending in pieces . . .' (Pss. 7:2-3); '. . . I lie down among man-
eating lions whose teeth are spears and arrows, whose tongue is a sharp
sword' (Pss. 57:5)

The portrayal of the wicked Saul and his henchmen as a pride of ferocious, blood-hungry lions stalking God's anointed is firmly fixed within our collective consciousness, yet by the standards of his day Saul was just and merciful, almost to a fault. The false picture of a raving Saul is another masterstroke of the pro-David propagandist. The irony is that the allegations levelled against Saul are a perfect fit for David, whose long reign was marked by successive bouts of cruelty and murder. By contrast, there is no record, even within the pages of a text heavily weighted against him, of Saul having committed any act – with the possible exception of Nob[11] and his alleged persecution of the Gibeonites (2 Sam. 21)[12] – that an objective modern-day observer would regard as an abuse of autocratic power.

The Keilah Clue

Despite the fact that David had recently approached Achish – the Philistine seran or lord – and was no longer trying to win the hands of fair maidens; he had not – according to 1 Samuel – lost his touch as a smasher of Philistines:

1 Sam. 23:1-6: David liberated the town of Keilah[13] from Philistine harassment, in spite of his men's reluctance to stir up more enmity. At this point, Abiathar made good his escape from Saul and joined David, bringing with him an ephod, one of the ritual vestments of the high priest.[14]

Abiathar was the son of Ahimelech and the sole survivor of the massacre of his people. His coming to David is described twice: '. . . one son of Ahimelech son of Ahitub escaped – his name was Abiathar – and he fled to David.' (1 Sam. 22:20); 'When Abiathar the son of Ahimelech fled to David at Keilah . . .' (1 Sam. 23:6)

Both versions tell us that the liberation of Keilah followed closely after the slaughter at Nob. This is very odd because, according to 1 Samuel, several major events occurred between David's flight to Ahimelech and his liberation of Keilah. These were, sequentially:

· His visit to Achish of Gath;
· The setting up of his mini-army in Adullam of Judah;
· His dispatching of his family to the King of Moab.

In addition to all of the above there is a possible fourth port of call to which David made a visit during this time. Its identity and that of its king is alluded to in yet another commonly ignored verse in the second book of Samuel. Placing it in the context of this episode, it makes for telling reading: 'David said, "I will show kindness[15] to Hanun son of Nahash, just as his father showed kindness to me . . ." (2 Sam. 10:2).

Unfortunately, the text does not describe the exact nature of this act of 'kindness'. Whether it relates to the period we are dealing with in this chapter, or perhaps to some military assistance Nahash may have given David later during the civil war – between David's Judah and Ishboshet's (Saul's son and successor, and their common enemy) Israel – is impossible to determine. However, Nahash is the only name missing from the bevy of anti-Saul characters in David's list of allies. It seems highly plausible, that the wily son of Jesse chose this time to establish a useful link with someone who had more reason to loath Saul than anyone else.[16]

Visits to Ammon notwithstanding, it would have taken several weeks, if not months, for all this to occur. Therefore, either Saul did not find out about the Nob encounter until long after it happened or he somehow managed to contain his wrath for a lengthy period.

Given the violence of his reaction, it is safe to assume that once Saul found out about the liaison at Nob, he acted with extreme urgency. Moreover, it is illogical to assume that Doeg, a servant of the king, would have concealed his knowledge beyond the time it took for him to return to Gibeah from Nob. In all probability, Saul learnt of the encounter within a day or two at most and more likely within hours of its occurrence.

This in turn means that David's visit to Achish, his raising of a small regiment and the dispatching of his parents in Moab occurred prior to his meeting with Ahimelech at Nob. The unavoidable conclusion to this line of argument is astonishing – David's departure from Gibeah was the first step of a carefully planned rebellion against Saul, and not merely an impromptu flight that escalated into a noble resistance. In contrast to the innocent portrait set before us by the biblical author, we now see how the historical David:

· Raised a private rebel army;
· Established ties with the Philistines;
· Took his family to the safety of Moab where he established ties with the king;
· Established ties with Nahash of Ammon;
· Arranged for Nob to be his arms and supplies depot;

Conclusion 19

David's taking of Keilah was part of a planned rebellion against Saul in which the House of Eli and the four hundred malcontents were co-conspirators.

There are other implications to be drawn from this scenario, to which we will soon turn.

Jonathan – the Mediator

God – presumably suffering from a bout of typical '1 Samuel fickleness ' – having 'instructed' David and his men ('against their will') to take Keilah, now changed his tune and ordered them to leave immediately:

1 Sam. 23:7-18: *After learning of David's relief of Keilah, the King prepared to march on the town. But God told David that the townsfolk were loyal to their king and that they would betray him, whereupon he left Keilah with an enlarged force of six hundred men while Saul remained at Gibeah.*

David next hid in the wilderness of Ziph,[17] where he and Jonathan had a secret meeting. The crown prince swore an oath of allegiance to his friend, ceding the succession to the Bethlehemite.

If Jonathan mediated between his father and his friend in occasional times of crisis, it is now easy to see how these negotiations became distorted by the pro-David author, who sought to legitimise David's succession. Hence, all accounts of private conversations reported in 1 Samuel must be treated with caution. Jonathan's ceding of his future kingdom to David stretches our credulity both because of its incontrovertibility and because it supplies a convenient justification for David's later rule over Israel (1 Sam. 20:13-17&23:16-18).[18] Nevertheless, we have learnt that in all likelihood Jonathan was more than open to some kind of power-sharing arrangement with his friend once his father, the king, was dead. Whether or not David would have settled for such an arrangement is open to speculation.

According to 1 Samuel, Jonathan affirms his recognition of David's royal supremacy on two occasions. The first was outside Gibeah at the time of the new moon festival, before David's flight: 'Nor shall you fail to show me the Lord's faithfulness, while I am alive; nor when I am dead, shall ever cease your faithfulness to my house . . .' (1 Sam. 20:14-15).

The second was in the wood of Ziph, when David was an established chieftain living in the wilderness of Judah: 'He said to him, "Do not be afraid, because the hand of my father Saul will never touch .You are going to be king over Israel, and I shall be second to you . . ." ' (1 Sam. 23:17).

An interesting fact to note is that Jonathan is not mentioned again until the moment of his death on Mount Gilboa. He apparently disappears from public life. A search for the reason will take us back to the dramatic new moon dinner, which we are now close to placing at its correct point in history.

As we have seen, the tension between Saul and his heir had developed over a long period, but something happened, probably in the wood of Ziph, that led to the dramatic climax at Gibeah. The problem is that we only have David's version of events; what better warrant for his succession to the throne of Israel could he have presented to his future subjects than the direct bequest of the kingdom by the noble Jonathan? And even if David's account is an exaggeration, it is not impossible that the two friends may have come up with some kind of arrangement.

Jonathan might have looked forward to a time after Saul's death when he could share the kingdom with David, perhaps by making him his deputy or even King of Judah. Some such pact may have been drawn up at Ziph, in an attempt by Jonathan to keep both his father and his friend happy. For such a reward, David may have agreed to retreat into the wilderness and lay low. The friends may then have planned encounters between Saul and David so that the principal parties could shake hands on the deal. If this is what happened, it would indicate that Jonathan had no understanding of the depth of his father's concerns over David, and was allowing hope to triumph over experience. It would confirm that Jonathan was blinded by his affection for his friend.

If the new moon banquet is placed around the time of the Ziph assignation, the verbal and physical reactions of Saul make complete sense. A unilateral deal offered by Jonathan to his friend would have incensed the king. However, would he have been angry enough to throw a spear at his son, or is this an over dramatised account of a bitter quarrel? The answer may lie within the text itself when it suggests that:

. . . Jonathan realised that his father was determined to do away with David. (1 Sam. 20:33)

Worrying about a person who is not in the room seems an odd initial reaction for someone who has just escaped death. Unless that is, Jonathan's love for David had reached insane proportions – which would at least make his personality consistent with those of all the other eccentrics who inhabit the pages of 1 Samuel.

However, it can be read in quite a different way if one recalls that a place was reserved for David at the banquet (1 Sam. 20:25). Considering that some time had passed since David's final departure, the vacant place may have been retained as a perpetual reminder to all the king's company of David's ambition and treachery. Hence the possibility that Saul, in his rage, threw the spear towards the empty place where David would have sat, next to Jonathan, striking the wall behind. Such a deliberate act could explain all three accounts of a seemingly incompetent spearman. Far from aiming at Jonathan, Saul was directing his spear at the absent David. In any event, it resulted in Jonathan's retirement from the scene.

The Bible tells us that Jonathan felt 'humiliated'[19] – or in some translations 'shamed' – by his father's words and actions, but is it not equally likely that he was in truth 'ashamed'? As told by the author of 1 Samuel, Saul had done wrong by shaming his son, yet the actions of Jonathan as we have reconstructed them verged on the treasonable. The historical Jonathan, so it seems, 'deserved' his public shaming, and his ultimate display of loyalty to Saul on the battlefield – in the forthcoming battle of Gilboa – suggests he may have been profoundly ashamed and contrite.

The rift with his son was a genuinely tragic development in the reign of Saul. If the Crown Prince of Israel was as popular and militarily adept as 1 Samuel asserts, his disappearance from his father's side could only have damaged the king. Although not catastrophic, it symbolised the fragility of Saul's rule over All Israel and marked the start of his decline.

Conclusion 20

The falling out between Saul and Jonathan at the new moon banquet occurred as a direct result of the meeting at Ziph between David and the heir to the throne, when Jonathan pledged a significant part of his future power to David.[20]

An Unpopular Rebellion

By now, David is finding it hard to settle anywhere within Saul's realm:

1 Sam. 23:19-29: The local Ziphites betrayed David's location to Saul, who then set off in pursuit. When David learnt of the king's approach, he fled into the wilderness of Maon. Before Saul could close in for the kill, he was distracted by news of a Philistine incursion, which forced him to abandon the chase. David then moved his force to the caves of En-gedi.

The narrative here informs us that the charismatic prince of Judah, anointed by Samuel, is compelled to live in desert caves with his brave and loyal band of desperados. Furthermore, both the Keilahites and then the Ziphites – peoples of Judah – show loyalty to Saul in preference to David.[21]

The text suggests that these displays of loyalty towards Saul were acts of betrayal against David, induced by fear of the tyrant king. Whereas, most probably Judah remained committed to Saul because the tribe perceived the Benjaminite king as their genuine hero, saviour, and protector – the true Lord's anointed. David, in stark contrast, was regarded as a freebooter and a bully who, with his band of cutthroats, terrorised the countryside, stealing food, livestock, and even men's wives if they took his fancy (1 Sam. 25).[22] That his crimes were perpetrated in God's name and sanctioned by rebel priests (Abiathar and Ahimelech: 1 Sam. 21; 23: 6) and prophets (Gad: 1 Sam. 22: 5) must have seemed sacrilegious to the Israelite people as a whole.

Yet, David was more than a mere bandit. With a following of four to six hundred armed men, he was a formidable warlord. From his earliest days on the run, he displayed an astute political awareness. In seeking alliances with Moab, Ammon and the Philistines, he demonstrated a single-minded ruthlessness, a lack of sentiment, and, above all, vast ambition.

In this context, it would be enlightening to know the exact sequence of events from the day David fled from Gibeah until his enrolment as a Philistine mercenary in the pay of Achish of Gath. According to 1 Samuel, the sequence is as follows:

- David fled to Samuel and then, at the time of the new moon feast and following an aborted return to Gibeah, he went to Nob, followed by a short stay in Gath as the guest of Achish;
- He fled again to Adullam, where his family and the four hundred fugitives joined him;
- His next stop was as a guest of the King of Moab, where he deposited his family;
- He then spent a while in hiding until ordered by the prophet Gad to move to Judah and to the forest of Hareth;
- At this juncture, we are informed that Saul massacred the priests of Nob, and that Abiathar escaped and sought out David.
- David then liberated the town of Keilah from the Philistines, and Abiathar joined him there. Employing the runic qualities of the ephod, the priest warned David that the people of the town would betray him to Saul if he remained, so he departed and returned to the wilderness. By now, his army had swelled to six hundred.

However, if our theory that David went more or less directly from Nob to Keilah is correct, the textual sequence of events is fatally compromised. (A historically more plausible rearrangement is proposed in the 'Book of Saul' conclusion, see pp. 178-179.) The entire story of David's flight from Saul may be apocryphal, the likely cause of their conflict being David's formation of alliances well before the final rift. As has already been suggested, it may have been Saul's discovery of such seditious manoeuvres that resulted in open hostility.

It was probably not the initial intention of David's rebellion to overthrow Saul himself. This may have been part of his ultimate goal, but from what we can glean from this section of 1 Samuel, it seems he was merely attempting to take control of Judah. When he 'raised his standard' over Keilah, he must have believed that thousands of his compatriots would flock to his banner.[23] It was to this end that he had approached Achish of Gath, hoping that he could secure the seran's support at the outbreak of war between Judah and Israel.

In the event, things developed very differently from the way David had expected. His fellow Judahites had no stomach for a civil war against their king, whom they had jointly anointed with Israel at Gilgal. Seeing this, the Philistines stayed at home, singularly unimpressed with this firebrand and his misbegotten scheme.

Thus, David's intended takeover of Judah came to nothing, and he was forced to retreat into the wilderness. His rebellion had failed before it had begun. Ambition and perhaps an overestimation of his own charisma had fooled David into believing he could lead a successful rebellion against King Saul. This mistake forced him – in the next phase of his career – to rely on his other great trait: cunning.

Conclusion 21
Behind the confused narrative of David's initial time 'on the run' from Saul lies the history of a failed insurrection by an unpopular pretender against a popular king.[24]

The First Sparing of Saul's Life
Nevertheless, David was an aristocrat of his tribe, and for that reason alone he could have counted on tacit support from an influential minority of the Judahite population. Moreover, from early on, he could rely on the overt encouragement of an important section of the clergy, not to mention budding alliances with three of Saul's most dangerous enemies, the Philistine confederacy, Moab and Ammon. This combination of circumstances could explain Saul's apparent restraint in the face of the provocations of the pretender.

1 Sam. 24:1-25:1: After dealing with the Philistine incursion, Saul resumed the chase to En-gedi, where he and his soldiers made camp, unaware of David's proximity. Saul then relieved himself in the very cave where the Judahites were hiding, unwittingly placing himself at the mercy of his intended quarry. David could not summon the will to harm the Lord's anointed, and instead cut off a piece of Saul's cloak. He then made himself known to Saul outside the cave, showing him the piece of cloak as proof that he had spared his life. David professed his innocence and his loyalty to the king, and pointed out that their fate was ultimately in the hands of God. Humbled, Saul realised the magnitude of his sin, acknowledged David's virtues, and recognised his right to succeed him to the throne. Before they parted, David swore that he would spare Saul's descendants.

At this point in the story, Samuel dies and 'Israel' mourns him for seven days.

Thus, we have reached the point in the narrative of 1 Samuel at which its ostensible eponymous author passes away. By biblical standards, the description of the death of this great prophet of Israel is a non-event. In chapter nine, we will learn the reason for this apparent textual indifference.

Nabal and Abigail – A Sign of things to come

1 Samuel now gives us a rare insight into the methods David used to establish himself in southern Judah:

1 Sam. 25: In Carmel of Maon,[25] in Judah, David sent messengers to Nabal, a local sheep baron, requesting a reward for having protected Nabal's flocks. But Nabal spurned David, who immediately set off with a hundred men to exact mortal revenge. However, Abigail, Nabal's beautiful and resourceful wife, apprised of the situation, intercepted them. After humbling herself and presenting gifts of food, she convinced them not to stain their swords with the worthless blood of her husband. Abigail then asked David to remember her fondly, which he enthusiastically agreed to do, and he thanked her for having spared him from shedding much innocent blood.

Abigail returned home to discover Nabal enjoying a feast to celebrate his escape from David's wrath. However, the next day, when Abigail told her husband of all that had transpired between David and herself, Nabal suffered a seizure and collapsed. After lying in a coma for ten days, Nabal died, and David, hearing the news, returned and proposed to Abigail, who eagerly assented and became his third wife in addition to Michal and Ahinoam. In the meantime, Saul had given Michal to another man.

Even a cursory review of the Nabal episode reveals a classic gangster's protection racket at work, complete with conniving moll and a suspiciously convenient death. The story is so shocking that it makes for awkward reading even in pious milieus.[26]

However, the Nabal story is presented in a different way from the equally disturbing later story of Uriah's death (2 Sam. 11). Whereas David's transgressions in that episode are seen for what they are, in the Nabal tale his wrongdoings are glossed over. There is a reason for this disparity in treatment. The Nabal story, unlike that of Uriah, is contemporary with the reign of Saul; therefore, the maintenance of a flawless David is imperative. Nabal is depicted as somehow deserving of his fate, to preserve the perfection of David. He stands in stark contrast to Uriah, whose honour and virtues remain untarnished as he falls victim to his king's machinations. As for David, he gets the girl on both occasions.

In fact – as we discussed earlier, in chapter six – it seems that David was solely attracted to the wives of other men. This fact is confirmed when we consider his first three main wives, the manner by which he acquired them and the rich rewards vis-à-vis his usurpation of Saul which accrued.

1. Ahinoam, wife of Saul – circumstances unknown; the king's harem and with it the symbolic ownership of Saul's power;

2. Abigail, wife of Nabal – husband possibly murdered – wife seized; the supremacy of his Boaz clan over the Calebites, and supremacy in Judah;

3. Michal, wife of Phalti – simply appropriated (ostensibly 'reclaimed'); membership of the Saulide royal family;

The evidence of the list is compelling.

The Second Sparing of Saul's Life

According to 1 Samuel, Saul, Samuel and Jonathan (and even God) all displayed varying degrees of emotional and psychological handicaps – dementia, paranoia, unstable personality and chronic inability to sustain relationships – whereas David's main problem seemed to have been a total failure to appreciate when and where he wasn't wanted. This life-threatening condition – probably originating from his extreme vanity – manifested itself most notably with his repeated returns to Gibeah, where he obviously enjoyed dodging Saul's javelins. This syndrome now reappears in the narrative, with David making another visit to Ziph:

1 Sam. 26:1-25: The Ziphites betrayed David's exact location to Saul a second time, whereupon the king, with his cousin Abner and a thousand men set off in pursuit. Once more, however, Saul unwittingly placed himself at the mercy of David, who again decided to spare the Lord's anointed.

But David said to Abishai, "Don't do him violence! No one can lay hands on Lord's anointed with impunity"

David removed the king's spear from where he slept, as proof of his mercy. Then, from the safety of a distant hilltop, David called out to Abner and rebuked him for failing to guard his king. When Saul responded to his voice, David made complaints similar to those he had uttered earlier at En-gedi, about the unfairness of his persecution and his status as a fugitive. Saul was once more overcome with regret and remorse and again the two men went their separate ways.

It is impossible to determine how long David remained in southern Judah or the real nature of Saul's persecution of him. It is also difficult to verify the details of David's alleged sparing of Saul's life, though these traditions probably reflect at least one historical encounter.[27]

Among the parallel episodes examined previously, some were shown to be descriptions of similar though distinct events and others were revealed as duplications of the same event. The two instances of David's mercy are examples of the latter, with the addition of an identical distortion woven into each narrative.

Apart from the identical central theme of each episode, both the structure and the language of each narrative contain sharp similarities. Both stories open with Saul being told of David's location in the Judahite wilderness and then his marching off in pursuit. This is followed by the king unknowingly falling into the hands of David, who then spares Saul's life after having first secured physical 'evidence' of his mercy and in-so-doing acquired symbols of kingship – the royal cloak and spear. The climax of both texts is an encounter between the antagonists, with David protesting his innocence and affirming his loyalty, and Saul seeing the terrible error of his ways.

The dialogue in each encounter is similar.

At the opening of the first episode in 1 Sam. 24:6, with Saul at his mercy, David refrains from harming him with these words – remarkably similar to those he uttered to Abishai, quoted above: 'The Lord forbid that I should do such a thing to my lord – the Lord's anointed – that I should raise my hand against him; for he is the Lord's anointed.'

During their first encounter as described in 1 Sam. 24:15, David protests to Saul in these words: "Against whom has the King of Israel come out? Whom are you pursuing? A dead dog? A single flea?"[28] He uses the identical metaphor at their 'second' encounter in 1 Sam. 26:20: ". . . For the King of Israel has come out to seek a single flea . . ." For his part, in the first story in 1 Sam. 24:17, the remorseful Saul asks David: "Is that your voice, my son David?" Two chapters late in 1 Sam. 26:17, he asks the identical question: "Is that your voice, my son David?" Both episodes end with the king acknowledging David's approaching supremacy – firstly, in 1 Sam. 24:21: "I know now that you will become king, and that the kingship of Israel will remain in your hands." Then secondly in 1 Sam. 26:25: ". . . May you be blessed, my son David. You will achieve, and you will prevail." The two versions of the single encounter may be abstractions of an actual negotiation and treaty between David and Saul. The clue to the genuine nature, background, and result of such an encounter may lie in the second version, when David utters these words as stated in 1 Sam. 26:19: "For they have driven me out today [i.e. Saul and his henchmen], so that I cannot have a share in Lord's possession, but am told, 'Go and worship other gods.'"

According to the narrative, it was immediately following David's second encounter with Saul that he went to work for Achish of Gath as a mercenary. Hence this verse must be a reference, albeit an allusive one, to that historical fact.[29]

It is not easy to ascertain why two versions of the same event eluded the editorial censors. Conventional scholarship would seek to solve the dilemma by pointing to a 'dual tradition' or 'strand'. However, the near-identical nature of the two texts makes this explanation unconvincing. Whereas a dual tradition may reasonably be invoked to account for two mutually exclusive Samuels or the two contradictory accounts of Goliath's slaying, it fails to explain passages that, textually and structurally, are virtual clones.

To understand how the same episode can appear twice in the narrative, we would do well to consider its theme and intended message.

While much of the obsequiousness and the imagery of the alleged dialogue reflect the formalities of the time, the narrative is designed to display David's righteous indignation in contrast to the pathetic contrition of the broken-spirited Saul. In effect, the propaganda presents the son of Jesse behaving like a true king, dispensing mercy upon a remorseful subject.

When David eventually became ruler of the Kingdom of Saul and Jonathan, he had the difficult job of justifying his accession to the majority of his unwilling northern subjects. It was undoubtedly common knowledge that Saul had forced him out of Israel and that he had enrolled in the service of Achish of Gath. The author therefore faced the challenge of presenting David in a more sympathetic light. He could not, however, stray too far from the basic facts, so he merely twisted the truth to David's advantage. Rather like an industrial dispute today, when both sides emerge with polarised summations of the same negotiation. In reality, David's encounter with Saul had probably been a humiliating experience – his life being spared under certain strict conditions. The author simply turned the story on its head, portraying David as the initiator of events and master of ceremonies. This alternative picture was made more vivid by use of lyrical and poetic imagery. Of course, the stratagem worked: if not in his own day, eventually the pro-David version of events was accepted, becoming ever more incontrovertible with the passage of time.

That Saul could not have ignored the presence of an active and ambitious warlord on the southern periphery of his kingdom goes without saying. Yet, as suggested earlier, it is doubtful that he would have risked the unity of his realm by killing David except as a last resort. Similarly, it seems safe to assume that David in his turn would not have wanted to be seen as the slayer of King Saul, the Lord's anointed. Thus all the drama, actual and fanciful, seems to have stemmed from a situation determined by a mutual antipathetic toleration.

The episode presents us with our next chronological key by placing the encounter immediately before David's sixteen-month exile.

The salient points which arise from what we now see as a single event, and from the general depiction of David's time on the run, are these:
- David and his men were vulnerable as long as they remained anywhere within Saul's kingdom;
- The hostility they faced necessitated their resorting to ruthless banditry against their compatriots, even to the point of extortion, wife stealing, and murder;
- Saul, despite having slaughtered the priests of Nob, retained the loyalty of nearly all his subjects, Israelite and otherwise, including many within Judah;

Thus, there seems little doubt that if the mighty King of Israel had wanted to wipe David and his band from the face of the earth, he could have done so. It would have been a messy business, costly in time and men, but it could have been eminently achievable, given his record of success on the battlefield. The fact that Saul chose not to exercise this option can be adequately explained only by considerations of political expedience: he dared not swat the wasp for fear of incurring the wrath of the swarm, namely, David's foreign and remaining Judahite allies.

On the other hand, if Saul took no action at all, he ran the risk of David emerging as a de facto rival, ruling over the southern part of his kingdom. His solution might have been to compel David to swear an oath of non-belligerence.

Conclusion 22
The two descriptions of the sparing of Saul's life are pro-David myths, created to mask a meeting which resulted in David's banishment from Israel.

By putting an end to his banditry, such an oath would effectively have removed David's ability to supply and fund his army and his community. Thus, compelled by circumstance as much as by King Saul, he went in search of fresh pastures, rich in booty.

Any relief Saul may have felt at David's removal was very short-lived, for David's exile in Gath proved to be just another, inevitable nail in the coffin of the first King of Israel.

Orthodox Sequence

1 Sam. 21: David tricks the priests of Nob into giving him bread and Goliath's sword; the scene is witnessed by Doeg, Saul's Edomite chief herdsman. David flees to Achish, King of Gath; the Philistines are suspicious of him; David escapes by feigning madness.

1 Sam. 22: David flees to the cave of Adullam in Judea; There, he is joined by his family and four hundred fellow fugitives.

David places his family under protection of the King of Moab in Mizpeh.

Saul orders Doeg to slaughter the priests of Nob; Abiathar, the son of Ahimelech, escapes to David with the sacred ephod (a priestly vestment).

1 Sam. 23: David liberates Keilah from Philistine raiders; He is joined

Major Variants

Goliath's sword would not become an Israelite possession till many years later, when David ruled from Jerusalem. Both it and the breads mentioned here represent an attempt by the Davidic author to disguise the fact that Nob was a secret food and weapons dump for David's planned rebellion against Saul.

Similarly, David's 'flight' to Achish was no such thing. He was probably testing the views of Saul's primary enemies well before he fled from Gibeah. His contacts with Achish, King of Moab (Ch. 22), and his friendship with Nahash, king of Ammon, mentioned in 2 Sam's Sam. 10 were possibly all initiated while he was still at Gibeah.

there by Abiathar with the ephod; the Keilahites remain loyal to Saul; David leaves Keilah with an additional 200 men; David flees to the wilderness of Ziph; Jonathan cedes his succession to David at a secret meeting in the wood of Ziph; the Ziphites betray David to Saul; Saul sets out in pursuit; David moves to Maon; Saul and his men encircle David but are forced to withdraw when news arrives of a Philistine incursion; David moves to Ein-gedi.

1 Sam. 24: Saul pursues David to Ein-gedi, and falls unwittingly into David's hands; David spares Saul's life.

1 Sam. 25: Samuel dies.

Samuel was alive at the time of Gilboa (see pp. 127-128).

David moves to wilderness of Paran; Nabal, a local sheep baron, refuses David's offer to protect his sheep; Outraged, David decides to kill Nabal, but is persuaded to stay his hand by Abigail, Nabal's wife; Nabal holds a feast to celebrate the withdrawal of David, but is taken ill, falls into a coma and then dies; David marries Abigail.

1 Sam. 26: The Ziphites betray David to Saul; Saul pursues David into Ziph; Saul again falls into David's hands; David again spares his life.

1 Sam. 27: David leaves Judah and becomes a servant of Achish.

David Grovels at Saul's Feet

8

David

The 'Servant' of the Philistines

David thought to himself, "Some day I shall certainly perish at the hands of Saul. The best thing for me to do is to flee to the land of the Philistines; Saul will give up hunting me throughout the territory of Israel, and I will escape him." (1 Sam. 27:1)

David's wooing of Judah

Having escaped from the clutches of King Saul, David now sought pastures new under the protection of the powerful Philistine chieftain, Achish – Lord, or Seran, of Gath.

1 Sam. 27:1-4: *David felt that his luck with Saul was running out, so he and his small army went and offered their services to Achish, Lord of Gath who now willingly accepted the Judahite's offer. Once Saul heard of this, he called off his search for David.*

David's second arrival at Gath was a very different affair from the first (1 Sam. 21:11-15). By now, his company had grown to some six hundred men, who, together with their chattels and accoutrements, resembled an army. Furthermore, he and his men had by now a proven record of sustained hostility towards Achish's sworn enemy, Saul. Thus, despite his or his advisors' possible reservations, the Seran of Gath welcomed David with open arms, and from that day, sixteen months before the Battle of Gilboa, the young rebel became a mercenary in the pay of Israel's deadliest foe.

The Bible describes David's work for Achish with brutal frankness. It seems that his task was to gather as much loot for his master as possible. To do this, he simply continued where he had left off in Judah, but on a much grander and bloodier scale. His newfound security made him bolder than ever.[1]

1 Sam. 27:5-12: David did so well for his new Philistine master that he was given the town of Ziklag² as a home and a military base. David dwelt in the land of the Philistines for sixteen months.

David and his men went up and raided the Geshurites, and the Gezerites and the Amalekites – who were the inhabitants of the region of Olam, all the way to Shur and the land of Egypt.

[Moreover] When David attacked a region, he would leave no man nor woman alive. . . .

David took away only booty, pretending to Achish that it was the proceeds of raids on southern Judah. He presented so much loot to his master that the latter, convinced of how loathed his employee must have become among his own people, made the willing David his bodyguard for life.

[Achish] thought, "He has aroused the wrath of his own people Israel who loath him, and so he shall be my vassal forever."

This episode remains a particularly inconvenient one even for pious David supporters, for more than most it gives us a glimpse into the ruthless workings of his cunning and ambitious mind. This is hardly the David of song and legend, loyal to his liege lord Saul and the slayer of the giant Goliath, compatriot of Lord Achish of Gath.

It is unlikely that the David we have now come to understand would have refrained from raiding Judah – thereby risking the wrath of Achish – merely to honour his possible oath to Saul.[3] We learn the true reason a few chapters later, when, after the Battle of Gilboa, on David's return to Ziklag: 'He sent some of the spoil to the elders of Judah, to his friends, saying, "This is a present for you from our spoil of the enemies of the Lord" ' (1 Sam. 30:26).

While it would be consistent with the propagandist editor's agenda to show David ingratiating himself with his compatriots only after Saul had died, there is good reason to believe that he started this policy early in his mercenary career. The more we learn of David's motivations, the more we understand that he wanted to replace the king. But, as long as his own tribe remained loyal to Saul, he knew he had no hope of realising this ambition. By raiding Judah's southern neighbours – and probable antagonists – such as the Amalekites, and making gifts of the spoil to Judah, David hoped to wean his people away from their allegiance to Saul. Moreover, far from needing to conceal this policy from Achish, it is far more likely that he initiated it with the Philistine's enthusiastic consent. After all, the disintegration of the Israel-Judah alliance was of equal advantage to both master and servant. We shall discover whether this policy succeeded when we consider the other possible by-product of David's time in Ziklag: Saul's war with Amalek.

Conclusion 23
David bribed the princes of Judah to win their loyalty at
the expense of Saul. [4]

David – Agent Provocateur

Although Saul had succeeded in liberating the greater part of Israel and Judah from foreign domination, there were undoubtedly areas that remained under occupation. Trying to determine the exact borders of Saul's kingdom is a tricky business, because of the lack of certainty in archaeological circles about the identity of many biblical sites. For example, there are at least three candidates for Gibeah itself, including one that is associated with one of two possible locations of Kiryath-jearim.[5] If we then add in the factor of at least two Gebas – which may or may not be identical to one or all of the Gibeahs – or the fact that all the sites seem to lie within what had been the land of Gibeon (which is also the name of a town), the problem becomes self-evident. Yet, as this has no fundamental bearing on the central thesis presented here, an effort has been made to protect the reader from further muddying of already murky waters.

The relevant point is that we will never be certain about the exact theatre of operations of David's forces during his year or so at Ziklag. Fortunately, though, we do have a fair idea of the locations of Gath and Ziklag themselves, so we can draw at least a rough map of that part of Judah and Simeon over which the Philistines – and by implication, their vassal, David – had control.[6]

Gath was located in the low hills (close to the Shephela) abutting the border of western Judah, while Ziklag lay about twenty miles further to the southwest, on the edge of Simeon. Both towns, together with the other Philistine cities, dominated the immediate vicinity. The entire area comprised a small but significant part of what was nominally Israelite, and thus Saul's territory.

If this reconstruction is correct, Saul must have gone to war with Amalek in about the eighth or ninth year of his reign. This would imply that, for at least a decade, Israel and her perpetual enemy enjoyed some form of peace. It necessarily follows that something happened to disturb the equilibrium.[7]

The disturbing event could have been David's move to Ziklag. The sudden influx of six hundred Israelite fighters and their chattels into the volatile area that formed the apex between Israel, the Philistine confederacy and Amalekite territory would have created a catastrophic fault in the status quo.

There was certainly friction between David and the Amalekites on occasion and hostilities broke out early on in David's wilderness exile. It seems that with his establishment at Ziklag, David's prior nuisance value to the desert dwellers grew into a serious threat. If so, there can be no doubt that these apparently warlike peoples would have acted to remove the danger. As we shall soon see, according to the narrative, the Amalekites did indeed raid and sack Ziklag. However, the contention of this hypothesis is that this was not when David and his men were absent, marching northward with the Philistine army on its way to Gilboa, but over a year earlier, during his own private war with the warriors of King Agag. Yet, however personal the cause, the resulting rise in temperature in such a crucial and sensitive area would have been felt throughout the region. If the Amalekites identified David with Judah they might not have restricted their reprisal raids to his own fiefdom of Ziklag. Most probably, the Amalekites took their revenge against his growing band of allies in southern Judah/Simeon.

Such a scenario would have compelled Saul to act, against both Amalek and then later, the Philistine confederacy (and David). He would have hoped that a crushing victory against the former would restore his influence amongst those Judahites who had recently switched their allegiance to the son of Jesse. Consequently, Saul would have felt more confident about taking on the Philistines in a single, decisive campaign. Unfortunately for the King of Israel, any such calculation would fatally underestimate David's growing appeal within his own tribe.

According to one part of the narrative, David was still a shepherd boy living with his father when the army of All Israel marched south (1 Sam. 16). However, we have shown that this was unlikely to have been the case; David was by then – as implied in Samuel's first rejection of Saul (1 Sam. 13: 14) – a famous warlord and a Philistine mercenary. Once again, historical truth has been sacrificed at the altar of pious wishes. The reality of a not so young, not so innocent rebel and enemy mercenary provoking a regional war that would eventually lead to Saul's overthrow could not be countenanced.

In addition, the repositioning of the Amalek episode provides us with a vital piece of information relating to Samuel, who – according to the biblical sequence – died before David's move to the Philistines and after the war with the Amalekites. In our revised order of events, Samuel's presence before and after the battle is no longer required, the war having been prompted not by a need for a herem, but by national interest. Nevertheless, there is no reason to deny him his customary ritualistic role in the pre and post-battle ceremonials.

The ramifications of the muddle concerning Samuel's date of death will shortly become apparent.

> ## Conclusion 24
> ## David provoked Saul's war with Amalek during his time at Ziklag.

Saul's Final Victory

The identity of the Amalekite people has been the subject of prolonged academic debate. As far as our story is concerned, it is sufficient to know that they were formidable warriors who occupied the region of northern Sinai between Simeon to the north and east and Egypt to the south and west.[8]

The scale of Saul's preparations for the task of eliminating Amalek confirms the strategic importance of the campaign. For only the second time in his reign, as either nagid or king, Saul felt compelled to raise the entire levy of Israel and Judah. The enormous gathering of the army at Telaim informs us of more than just the seriousness of the operation (1 Sam. 15:4); it also tells us something about both the state of affairs within the Israelite nation itself and the strength of the Philistines.

At the mustering at Bezek, eight or nine years earlier, Saul had 'counted' three hundred thousand men of Israel and thirty thousand men of Judah. At this second mustering, at Telaim, he numbers Israel at two hundred thousand and Judah at only ten thousand.

Even allowing for a degree of exaggeration over both sets of figures, the initial conclusions to be drawn are the most obvious: that Nahash, King of Ammon, represented a more powerful foe than Agag, King of Amalek, and/ or that Saul's army was by the time of the Amalek crisis sufficiently trained and experienced to obviate the need for such a large force. Furthermore, the liberation of Gilead had extended Saul's north-eastern borders to such an extent that a significant section of the levy was required to guard and patrol them. There is also the possibility that by this time, some of Saul's Israelite men had been lured over to David's cause.

A secondary conclusion however, is perhaps more illuminative of this period of Saul's reign. Whereas at the time of the earlier campaign the Philistines posed a threat neither to Israel nor to Judah because they had been decimated by the ophlim, they were by now fully recovered. Hence, Saul was compelled to leave over a third of the levy behind to guard his western border.

The third point to consider concerns the apparent weakening in the loyalty of Judah to their king. In contrast to Israel, whose numbers were reduced by one third, the Judahite contingent had dwindled by two thirds. Whether this disproportionate number of absentees was a testament to David's policy of buying off the princes of his tribe, the effect of sedition spread through Judah by his agents, the result of an increased Philistine threat, or a combination of all three, we can only surmise. Whatever the cause, it seems that Saul had lost his grip over a substantial portion of Judahite sentiment.

As we have already seen, the accepted tradition of Samuel's role as instigator of the campaign is most likely a fantasy. His terrible instructions and his subsequent, equally lunatic, rejection of King Saul can be catalogued with the numerous other instances of editorial invention we have identified (1 Sam. 15:3). That Saul continued to honour the judge at times of national crisis need not be questioned. Neither is there reason to doubt that the complex official relationship between judge and king – despite their mutual personal respect and affection – must have led to tension and occasionally friction, especially over ritual and protocol. However, that is quite a different scenario from the one presented to us by the pro-David narrative, obsessed as it is with justifying the overthrow of the House of Saul.

Military campaigns normally commenced during the spring, so we can assume that Saul and his army set off around April in the ninth year of his reign over All Israel.[9] The Bible gives only the most limited description of the war, leaving the impression that it comprised just one battle (1 Sam. 15:6-8). However, we can be confident that Amalek held sway over a large area of land and may have controlled several encampments and strongholds. Josephus states that the campaign was a long one, involving many skirmishes, culminating in a great battle against King Agag.[10] We learn from both sources that Saul made a point of sparing the lives of the Kenites, in consideration for their kindness to his Israelite ancestors (Ex. 18).[11] As for the Amalekites, it was their dismal lot to pay the ultimate price for David's provocations, joining the long list of those vanquished by the King of Israel.

The Ingratitude of Judah

If Saul hoped that his crushing of Amalek would win back the loyalty of Judah, he underestimated the degree to which David's generosity had lured the princes of Judah.

David's position in Ziklag gave him more than just raiding opportunities; it enabled him to establish diplomatic relations between Judah and Egypt. The Bible informs us that, David's successor, Solomon, enjoyed cordial relations with the pharaohs (1 K. 9:16). His predecessor's time as lord of Ziklag might have provided an excellent opportunity to forge that Judahite-Egyptian link. In any event, the Judahite towns under his protection probably would have benefited from direct access to the markets of Egypt.

By contrast, Saul's victory, far from opening up links with the land of the pharaohs, had merely resulted in a change of gatekeeper, from Agag to David. Thus, Judah was gradually drawn away from Saul, towards the growing aura emanating from one of their own. Inadvertently, the king had empowered the pretender to his own throne.

The Enemy of Israel

The crisis for Saul was imminent, even at the moment of his victory celebrations. In a way reminiscent of King Harold of England meeting his doom at Hastings, just days after his great victory at Stamford Bridge, so it was for King Saul of Israel some two millennia earlier:

1 Sam. 28:1: *When David had served Achish for sixteen months, the Philistines mustered their forces to attack Israel.*
. . . the Philistines mustered their forces for war, to take the field against Israel. Achish said to David, "You know, of course, that you and your men must march out with my army." (1 Sam. 28:1)

In the early summer[12] of the tenth year of Saul's reign over All Israel, the Philistines gathered their combined forces at Aphek (on the coastal plain), as they had done some thirteen years earlier (1 Sam. 4:1). The time was as opportune as it would ever be for them to reaffirm their supremacy in the region. Thanks to the sterling work of David, and in spite of the recent Israelite victory over Amalek, Saul could no longer count on the military support of Judah. Furthermore, the Philistines had recovered from the ophlim disaster, and their army was back to full strength. The very fact that they initiated hostilities suggests that they felt they could not lose.[13] As for Saul, his actions before the battle, which will soon be described, reveal that he was equally aware of the long odds against his army.

Samuel Redux

Now Samuel had died, and all Israel made lament for him; and he was buried in his own town of Ramah. And Saul had forbidden [recourse to] ghosts and familiar spirits in the land.' (1 Sam. 28:3)
As we have now established that the Amalek war occurred during David's time at Ziklag, we must conclude that Samuel was still living towards the end of Saul's reign and that all prior reports of his death were exaggerated. Thus, his ghostly manifestation on the eve of the battle of Gilboa requires a re-examination.

For the moment, we should consider a few facts gleaned from the peculiarly terse description of the passing away of the last judge of Israel:

· His burial seems not to have been attended by either Saul or David;
· His mourners were anonymous Israelites;

· Samuel was second only to Moses in the pantheon of Israelite prophets, yet his passing merits no more than two lines of emotionless text without even the briefest eulogy.[14]

All of which might simply reflect Samuel's possible marginalisation by this time, to the point of virtual insignificance. But, this seems unlikely, bearing in mind the pro-David scribe's textually reckless efforts to link the great king-maker with the Davidic dynasty.[15] Behind this casually reported "death" there may lie a story of fear – Samuel's probable fear of David. The Judahite warlord's many displays of ruthlessness would have made a deep impression on those who believed themselves to be his enemies. If Samuel did not, as the narrative claims, anoint David to be King of Israel, he would have known that his continued existence represented a monumental obstacle to the Judahite's regal aspirations.[16] Moreover – despite their initial, mutual reluctance for the institution of the kingship – Samuel would by now have shared his king's zeal for wanting to preserve and ensure the continuance of the House of Saul and the integrity of the kingdom.

If Samuel felt himself to be in mortal danger and could not rely on the protection of an ever more beleaguered king, a discreet disappearance from the scene would have been a relatively simple and logical step for him to take. A sudden vanishing act on the part of such an eminent, albeit retired, personality, just as was the case with fading soviet leaders in the last century, would naturally lead to the rumour of his death.

With this in mind, it is interesting to note that Samuel's final, 'spectral' appearance was in the north of the country, well away from his habitual environs and relatively safe from the attentions of David.

Conclusion 25
Samuel was alive at the time of the battle of Gilboa.

En-Dor

Of all the episodes centred on the personality of Saul, it is his visit to the 'witch' of En-dor which is the most mysterious – both superficially and materially.

1 Sam. 28:4-25: *The Philistines camped at Shunem[17] while the army of Israel gathered on Mount Gilboa. The vastness of the enemy army, combined with God's silence, caused a terrible dread in the heart of Saul. In desperation, he asked his servants to find a spiritual medium with whom he could consult. That night, he went in disguise to the home of a woman in En-dor, who, on receiving assurances for her safety, asked him which* *spirit he wanted to meet. Samuel, he said. When the ghost of Samuel appeared, the woman realized to her horror that her client was none other than King Saul. Following his further reassurance, she continued to engage the dead prophet. Samuel, angered at being disturbed from his rest, offered no comfort to the prostrate monarch. Instead, he rebuked Saul for his disobedience and foretold imminent doom for him and his heirs. God, said the prophet, had given Saul's kingdom to David.*

The dispirited and forlorn Saul, after reluctantly accepting a meal from the woman, rejoined his troops on Gilboa.

One of the many attractions for the rational reader of 1 Samuel is the relative scarcity of miraculous events. Apart from one or two thunderstorms and a few encounters with divine auguries, supernatural occurrences are conspicuous by their absence. God is a bit player, and his minions, Samuel notwithstanding, merely the supporting cast. This has the advantage of leaving more room for the human story, however confused. The four major departures from this mood all involve Samuel:

· The first occurs when he is called to the position of God's representative in Israel as successor to Eli (1 Sam. 3);

· the second is when he is directed by God to anoint Saul as king-elect (1 Sam. 9: 15-17);

· the third is when God commands him to anoint David as king-elect (1 Sam. 16: 1-13);

· and the fourth is his own spectral appearance before Saul at En-dor[18] (1 Sam. 28: 4-19).

The common theme is the passing of the baton of power from one person to another – from Eli to Samuel, from Samuel to Saul, from Saul to David, and the conformation that Saul's dynasty is doomed, signifying the imminent kingship of David.

The hand of both the pro-David scribe and the prophetic redactor are obviously hard at work and it is tempting to dismiss the En-dor episode in particular as merely another propagandist myth. As with the scene of Saul's rejection by Samuel at Gilgal, the image of a pathetic, terrified, and desperate Saul cringing before the ghost of Samuel – in direct contravention of his own laws – creates a decidedly undignified impression. This was a man obviously unfit to wear the heavy mantle of the Lord's anointed, and, by implication, so were his descendants. Yet this picture of Saul is strikingly at variance with the figure portrayed in other sections of the narrative. The pro-David portrait of a sad, mad, and bad Saul sits uncomfortably with the information we glean about him elsewhere.

Yet, as with another myth, that of David's anointing, once the spiritualistic clutter is removed and one recognises the problem of biased and confused editing, a sharper and more realistic image emerges from the house at En-dor. And, it is even plausible to believe that, on the eve of the battle of Gilboa, Saul met not with a ghost but with the living and breathing Samuel.

The story of En-dor may be a distorted account of Saul's typical preparation for a major battle, which, as before Michmash, Mizpah, and the Amalek war, centred on the sacred rituals of Samuel the prophet. En-dor, like Mizpah and Gilgal, was merely a convenient 'high-place', and the 'woman', in all likelihood, was a fellow shaman of Samuel's, possibly the guardian of the shrine. Given the dearth of Israelite holy women and the plethora of Canaanite priestesses, it is safe to assume that the woman of En-dor was a pagan priestess and that her shrine was one of the many dotted about Israel, sacred to Canaanites and Israelites alike.[19]

The story of En-dor provides fascinating confirmation of the syncretistic ambiguity of Israelite worship and cultic ritual at the turn of the tenth century BCE – an ambiguity that enveloped even Samuel himself.

The pious attitude of the chronicler is expressed in 1 Ch. 10:13&14, 'So Saul died because of his transgression which he committed against the Lord . . . by seeking advice from a ghost . . . therefore He slew him and gave the kingdom to David. . . .'

This Passage merely confirms that by the time of the chronicler, hundreds of years later, the religious ambiguity had been resolved. So much so, that Saul's visit to En-dor was of itself sufficient justification for his being deposed and extra cause to rejoice in the succession of David.

In all probability, the ban on necromancy, as described in Samuel and Chronicles, was as fictitious as the ghost itself – an anachronistic insertion from the pen of a later pious monotheist, embarrassed by the historical association of the great prophet Samuel, and a pagan holy woman.[20]

The process of making Samuel into a ghost, which had already been started inadvertently by having him 'die' earlier in the narrative, was now advertently completed. This achieved three things for an author intent on establishing a central locus of worship for the single God of Israel in Jerusalem:

· It disassociated Samuel from a pagan act by turning him from an active participant into a passive and unwilling one;
· It depicted Saul as a violator of his own law;
· It further discredited Saul by both portraying him as a pathetic and broken man and confirming David's divine right to the throne through the voice of Samuel.

In reality, far from breaking his own law, Saul was obeying what he and his people must have regarded as a righteous imperative. Moreover, in making their pilgrimage to Samuel, Saul and his two companions would have had to travel across enemy lines – if, as is commonly accepted, the Philistine encampment lay on the route to En-dor.[21] The fact that the King of Israel felt it necessary to risk his life to receive the endorsement of Samuel is a testament to the respect he retained for the 'word' of his old colleague right up until the final moments of his reign. Moreover, far from the condemnatory message ascribed to Samuel's ghost in the myth, the old judge probably bade a warm and emotional farewell to his cherished Lord's anointed as they parted for what they might well have guessed would be the last time.

However, in addition to these 'unremarkable' reasons for Saul's visit to En-dor, there is a possible third, highly 'remarkable' cause, for the risky venture. The clue to this lies in fact that Saul had to travel 'disguised' and the fact that he was accompanied by two men.

This begs two obvious questions:

1. Why did Saul need to be disguised?
2. Who were the two men who accompanied the king?

The narrative does not provide answers to either question. The accepted 'take' is that;

1. Saul was disguised to hide his identity from the woman of En-dor and/or any Philistines whom he might have happened to run into en-route;[22]

2. A 'bodyguard' of only two men would not alert the woman's suspicions regarding her client's identity and would allow him to slip past enemy lines with greater ease.

Neither of the two answers stands up to the slightest scrutiny in the context of this study.

We now understand that King Saul had no cause to hide his identity from the woman of En-dor, who was, in all probability, a legally practicing Shaman and colleague of Samuel. Therefore, if Saul was disguised, it must have been to hide his identity from someone other than her.

For the same reason, he had no need to compromise his safety by restricting himself to only two guards. Three warriors, however formidable, would have stood little chance had they run into an enemy patrol. Thus, Saul's two companions must have been more than mere bodyguards. And, whoever they may have been, it was equally as vital for them as for their king to meet with Samuel.

In the hypothetical 'Book of Saul' at the end of this work possible reasons for Saul's disguise, the identities of the two strangers, and their reason for accompanying their king to En-dor (see p. 182) are suggested.

However, this is the point in the story where Samuel truly exits from the scene, never to be heard of again, in either human or spectral form. We can only guess as to his fate. However, a clue to where Samuel 'might *not* be buried' at least, may lie in the fact that his tomb has yet to be authoritatively identified within the borders of what constituted Israel in his day.

One of the key factors that makes the 'Holy Land' holy is the proliferation of sacred tombs. While Christians flock to the various sites postulated as the 'garden tomb' of Jesus, Jews and Moslems are drawn with equally pious fervour to the alleged sepulchres of the patriarchs and prophets.

The land that comprised ancient Israel is one great cemetery for the major and minor judges, prophets, kings and messiahs who lived during the long era of the Bible. However, there are exceptions – major personalities whose burial sites have remained unidentified and lost to history. And, amongst the most noteworthy of this group are Samuel and Saul.

This is not to say that there has never been an 'old Arab tradition' or an ancient monk or the inevitable Victorian explorer who suggested this or that piece of land as the place(s) in question. Yet, so far as serious archaeologists, and more importantly, the Israeli tourist board are concerned, the whereabouts of the tombs of Israel's most important native prophet, and first king remain as obscure as the location of the 'divinely interred' remains of Moses himself.

While one can see how Saul's tomb became 'lost' due to David's probable discouragement of the glorification of his predecessor's memory, the disappearance of Samuel's grave is far harder to explain, especially in the light of the Bible's assertion that he was buried at Ramah – an identified site (1 Sam. 25: 1).

Bearing in mind the near cult status, which Jews in particular grant the sepulchre of Abraham (in Hebron), the 'founder of the faith', one can only imagine the feelings that the tomb of the 'founder of the nation' and 'anointer of Kings' would inspire. Therefore, it seems plausible to assume, in common with his illustrious predecessor Moses, that Samuel the prophet died in anonymity beyond Israel's borders.

The one thing we can be certain of is that ,when he eventually lay on his deathbed, he must have been an exceptional sad and disillusioned old man. When the author of 1 Sam. 15:35 wrote that 'Samuel grieved over Saul', he was surely closer to the ultimate truth than he could have realised.

Conclusion 26
The En-dor narrative is a corrupt account of the last and innocent meeting between Saul and a living Samuel.

The Ziklag Alibi[23]

At this point the narrative backtracks to a point before the Philistines had reached Shunem.

1 Sam. 29: *As the Philistines and David marched to do battle with Israel, Achish's fellow city lords demanded that he send the Israelites back to Ziklag, for fear they would turn on them once the battle commenced. In spite of David's protests, he and his men returned home, leaving the Philistines to continue their advance into the Jezreel Valley.*

The text states that David marched with Achish to Aphek fully intending to fight against Saul (1 Sam. 28:1-2; 29:8). In fairness, he may have had no choice. The seran of Gath was his lord and master, whom he had to obey. Nevertheless, the image of the slayer of Goliath, collector of Philistine foreskins, and liberator of Keilah marching side by side with that very same enemy to fight Saul is remarkable.

Bearing in mind the overriding pro-David agenda of 1 Samuel, one cannot help but wonder how this episode slipped through the censor's net.

It must have been the case that David's sixteen month career as the henchman of Achish was common knowledge in his own day, and therefore impossible to sweep under the carpet. Hence, the only option was to attempt some damage limitation by presenting familiar facts embellished with distorted details. It may also be the case that David and his scribes were not so much asking that people be stupid enough as to actually believe the distortion, but merely to accept the reason behind the distortion.

While pious scholars mostly view the entire episode through Davidic tinted spectacles,[24] critical academe generally accepts the apparent exigencies of David's compromised position.[25] Fortunately, our present thesis is neither constricted by piety nor bound by academic convention. Therefore, we are free to examine the facts objectively.

The first task is to look at the details as presented in the text:

· The Philistines gathered at Aphek;
· Together with David and his troops they marched to Shunem at the north eastern corner of the Jezreel Valley, opposite the Israelite camp on Mount Gilboa;
· At some point en route between Aphek and Shunem, Achish's wary associates sent David away;

If David really was the renowned former scourge of the Philistines, one could understand why they might not have trusted him in a battle against Israel. It is the contention of this hypothesis, however, that his reputation was concocted retrospectively, in part to substantiate his claim to the throne.

In truth – by the time of Gilboa – David was a proven and trusted ally of the Philistines. Nevertheless, this does not mean that we should dismiss the story of his separating from the Philistine army in its entirety.

1 Sam. 30:1-6: Three days later, David arrived back at Ziklag to find the town sacked and all its women and children missing. His men were grief-stricken, and in their anger threatened to kill David if he refused to take immediate reprisals.

He then embarks on a campaign of retrieval that runs concurrently with the Battle of Gilboa.[26]

1 Sam. 30:7-31: Once God confirmed the orders for battle, David and his six hundred men set off in pursuit of the raiders, but when only four hundred were able to keep pace, David left the rest behind to guard the baggage.
*   With the assistance of an escaped Egyptian slave, the Israelites discovered the identity and location of their foe. They then surprised the rejoicing Amalekites and liberated their loved ones, together with all the accumulated booty the raiders had collected from several towns. Unfortunately, this led to friction when the two groups of Israelites were reunited. Some of the combatants failed to see why they should share the spoils with those who had not risked their lives. David resolved the problem by issuing a far-reaching decree that booty was henceforth to be shared equally by all his troops, combatants and non-combatants alike.*

There are three elements of this narrative which are of great historical relevance, and which will show that David, with the majority of his force did indeed continue to Gilboa – but independently of his masters.
    The first is the structure of the episode itself, in that the sacking of Ziklag and David's rescue mission run concurrently with the battle of Gilboa. While this rare biblical attempt at parallel narrative might be viewed as a laudable literary advance, its novelty suggests that something suspicious is going on. The second is the dividing of David's force into two groups, four hundred remaining with him and two hundred left behind (1 Sam. 30:9-10). Although this might be a genuine detail pertaining to an earlier event from the time of the Nabal episode (1 Sam. 25:13) or during an actual encounter with the Amalekites, it probably has much more to do with the composition of David's force before and during the battle of Gilboa. Not wishing to leave Ziklag unguarded, it would have been expedient for David to have left some troops behind, to guard his city. Moreover, if the lengthy role call of warriors – who joined him during his time at Ziklag (cited in 1 Chronicles 12:1-14) – is to be believed, his private army must have been considerably larger and more formidable

than a mere six hundred by the time of Saul's defeat.[27]

The third element, to which we have alluded on several occasions, is the distribution of booty among the towns of Judah: 'When David reached Ziklag, he sent some of the spoil to the elders of Judah, his friends, saying, "This is a present for you from our spoil of the enemies of the Lord" ' (1 Sam. 30:26). The importance of David's courting Judah to separate it from Saul is self-evident.

As far as the parallel narrative is concerned, one may again note how the pro-David author repeatedly abstracted actual events and reworked them into a new sequence to suggest a contrary conclusion or message. It is a form of narrative collage, where text is cut up, then pasted together in a configuration more supportive of the required agenda.

Covert Operator

Since no credence need be given to the story that the Philistine serans developed last-minute jitters over the presence of David in their midst as they marched from Aphek to Shunem, his splitting from the main army requires an alternative explanation. Furthermore, if we are correct in our assertion that the three-day Ziklag adventure was chronologically misplaced we still have to determine where David and his men actually went and what they did once they got there.

By now, even the most philo-Davidic reader should be able to see a much clearer, more logical, and more plausible picture emerging in our reconstruction. David, far from requiring coercion to fight Saul, was, on the contrary, chafing at the bit. With most of Judah in his pocket and the backing of his Philistine friends, his big chance had arrived at last.

The Philistines regarded David as their man. He had proven himself by serving up Israel (minus Judah) on a plate. They trusted him, and they were in his debt and he would soon extract rich rewards for his services. The first of these would be a free hand in the coming battle. The second was the governorship of Judah itself. Yet, despite his enthusiasm – and in direct contrast to the narrative version – it was certainly he and not his Philistine masters who realised that his position was untenable in the midst of their battle host. Fighting Israel's and the confederacy's common antagonists, the Amalekites – albeit in the service of Achish – had been one thing. Fighting as a Philistine mercenary against Israel itself was quite another. Thus, David's role in the unfolding drama had to be clandestine.

Conclusion 27

The sacking of Ziklag is chronologically misplaced; it occurred about a year prior to the battle of Gilboa.

Orthodox Sequence   ## Major Variants

1 Sam. 27 (cont'): Achish presents David with the town of Ziklag as a gift; David slaughters many non-Israelite communities; he presents Achish with large quantities of loot.

It was at this stage, over a year before Gilboa, that David began his policy of sending gifts to the elders of Judah in an attempt to woo them away from a reigning King Saul.

1 Sam. 28: The Philistines prepare for war against Israel; David is ordered by Achish to march with the Philistines.

Samuel is lamented and buried in Ramah; Saul bans necromancy.

The mention of Saul's famous ban just prior to his seeking out Samuel's ghost is a Davidic ploy to sully his name. Samuel was alive at the meeting at En-dor, therefore Saul was innocent of the alleged sin.

The Philistines muster an army to invade Israel; they pitch their tents at Shunem; Israel encamps at Gilboa.

Deserted by God, Saul, visits the 'woman of En-dor' on the eve of battle; she raises the ghost of Samuel, who admonishes Saul; Saul returns to camp, very dispirited.

1 Sam. 29: The Philistines muster all their armies at Aphek; Israel musters at the fountain at Jezreel; during their march into Israel, the Philistines demand that Achish send David back to Ziklag.

The Philistine camp at Aphek, many miles southwest of Shunem their final encampment in the valley of Jezreel. This information should have come before the verse in the previous chapter that describes their pitching at Shunem.

1 Sam. 30: David returns to Ziklag, to discover it has been sacked by the Amalekites; all the women, including his wives, have been taken captive. Under a threat of death from his own men, David pursues the raiders; two hundred men stay behind at 'Besor';

David and his men were involved in covert operations against Saul at this time. The story of the Amalekite raid and David's reprisal belongs to the period prior to Saul's war against the Amalekites, which had resulted in their annihilation. Its misplacement here is an escaped Egyptian slave gives David the location of the raiding party; David is victorious over the raiders, rescuing his women, and taking much spoil; David resolves a dispute over the dividing of loot between combatants and non-combatants.

a Davidic attempt to build an alibi for David, who, in reality, was working covertly for the Philistines at Gilboa (see chapter 9).

David sends gifts from the booty to the elders of Judah.

This policy was begun a year earlier, and its success can be gauged by the tribe of Judah's absence at the battle of Gilboa.

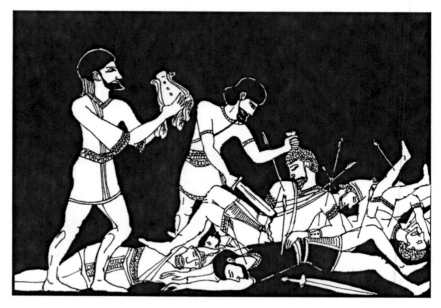

The Death of Saul

9

'How' The Mighty Fell
The Death of Saul

The Philistines mustered and they marched to Shunem and encamped; and Saul gathered all Israel, and they encamped at Gilboa. (1 Sam. 28:4)

As Saul stood on the northwest-facing slopes of Mount Gilboa, the first rays of dawn glinting on the countless iron spear tips of the Philistine host, drawn up in battle array against him, he must have known that he had no hope of victory. Thanks to the efforts of his son-in-law, practically the entire levy of Judah had stayed at home, and worse still, some of his elite Israelite warriors had been lured over to the Bethlehemite (1 Ch. 12: 20-21).[1]

Nevertheless, Saul and Abner had to deal with the situation as best they could, and with extreme urgency. Faced with such dire circumstances, their options were limited – either to fight to the last man, or tactically withdraw.

For Saul 'the Lord's anointed', this choice must have been especially painful. In spite of his apparent antagonism towards sections of the religious establishment, Saul was evidently a devout man who would have considered himself and his heirs ordained by God to rule in perpetuity. Therefore, that same burden of duty that had seemed so daunting to him at the time of his coronation would now harden his resolve to protect his crown and his fledgling dynasty at all costs. In the light of all this, we can see why it would have been unthinkable for Saul to consider surrender. He had devoted himself and his family to the service of the people in accordance with the will of God. Neither his kingship nor his kingdom were his to give up.

It would have been perilous to launch the army into the field, even *with* Judah's full participation. Their absence meant that such a tactic was out of the question. Even allowing for Abner's military reforms and recent successes against lesser enemies, Israel was unready to risk all in a pitched battle against a fully restored and rejuvenated Philistine army. To repeat the mistake of the previous generation at Aphek would have been unforgivable. Therefore, the only sensible option could have been a withdrawal.

Trans-Jordan Israel seems to have been effectively beyond the range of the Philistines, as there is only minimal evidence of their ever having ventured across the river.[2] Thus, Gilead would have offered a relatively secure base from where Israel could regroup and continue to prosecute a war of attrition. Saul would have reasoned that a diminished Israel was preferable to no Israel at all. Circumstances change – why not bide his time and await developments between the ambitious David and his Philistine sponsors? Once the son of Jesse had a free hand, he could prove to be an unpopular ruler of Judah. His ambition might get the better of his judgement and compromise his handling of the alliance. If so, his Philistine masters would undoubtedly prove less tolerant than Saul had been. In fact, given the volatility of the new status quo, it might not be too long before opportunities arose to reverse the situation.

In the context of this story, it is interesting to note that many years later, the then King David himself was forced to make a near-identical tactical withdrawal across the Jordan. When he was losing the civil war against his son – Absalom – David used Gilead as a place to re-group his forces until he was able to launch a counter-offensive that was ultimately successful. Moreover – in common with Abner and Ishbosheth – during his Trans-Jordan exile, he also based himself in Mahanaim (2 Sam. 17:24).[3]

Another crucial piece of information regarding the mindset of King Saul in the build up to the coming battle was the apparent absence of the Gileadites from the army of 'all Israel'.[4] As we will read presently, the men of Jabesh-Gilead did not learn of the death of Saul until after the battle (1 Sam. 31: 7). Bearing in mind how inconceivable it is that Saul's most devoted and loyal subjects – the men of Jabesh – ignored the call to arms, their absence points to the probability that the mustering at Gilboa was intentionally only partial. Saul probably never intended to risk the whole army of Israel in a single decisive engagement with the Philistines.[5]

Once having decided on a retreat of the remaining body of the army, Saul had to make certain it went smoothly.

We know that Israel mustered at the 'fountain of Jezreel' (probably the Spring of Harod – 1 Sam. 29:1). The absent ranks of Judah notwithstanding, a general Israelite withdrawal would have entailed the movement of a substantial body of men, who would be exposed to the danger of a rear assault from the Philistines, as well as possible harrying from opportunist Canaanites seeking revenge or wishing to ingratiate themselves with their masters-to-be. To avoid such hazards, Saul would have had to mount a rearguard that could buy time for his troops as they crossed the Jordan.

This being the probable case, it seems odd that Saul himself remained behind to command what could be nothing more than a dangerous holding action. Normally, a reliable officer would have been the choice to command such a force. However, there was nothing normal about this situation; hence Saul, no doubt concerned about securing his royal house, would have had other ideas.

Saul may have believed that, in the event of his own death, Jonathan would yield at least part of the kingdom to David. Paradoxically, the desperate plight that now confronted him might have presented an opportunity to ensure the future integrity of his realm.

The king remained at Jezreel to oversee the holding action, but as will become clear as the battle unfolds, with every intention of making good his own escape. Meanwhile, Saul sent Ishboshet, his most 'reliable' son, across the Jordan into Gad/Gilead, together with the bulk of the army under the command of Abner (2 Sam. 2:8).[6]

Much earlier in the narrative of 1 Samuel, we may discern an allusion to the idea that Saul was prepared to sacrifice Jonathan. The highly apocryphal story of Jonathan tasting of the forbidden honey and falling under his father's curse may be seen as a retrospective insertion alluding to sinful intimacies between Jonathan and David. The Bible is quite clear on what was to be done to such transgressors, and apparently so was Saul (1 Sam. 14:16-46).

Whatever the symbolism of the story, the honey episode offered later redactors an explanation for why the noble Jonathan had to die before he was able to fulfil his alleged chosen path of serving David (1 Sam. 20:12-16; 23:16-18). In reality, the entire honey and curse episode may originally have been derived from the fact that Jonathan's untimely death was engineered by Saul. The story of Jonathan's death may then in fact represent a genuine example of Saul's pragmatism, and almost David-like ruthlessness. While the desperate situation may have demanded the most awful measures of expediency, Saul's sacrifice of Jonathan and his two remaining brothers at Gilboa would seem to be his least forgivable and most morally questionable historical deed. If however, our hypothesis is correct, one can immediately see the benefits to Saul if things had gone according to plan and he himself had survived the battle.

At a stroke, the problem of what to do with his unreliable heir would have been solved, leaving Saul free to devote the rest of his life to consolidating his position in "free Israel" and grooming his new reliable heir, Ishboshet. Furthermore, the heroic death of Jonathan would have imbued the house of

Saul with additional glory. Such an outcome might even have rejuvenated his reputation and kingship to such a degree, especially in contrast to the treacherous Philistine mercenary David, that Saul might have been in a position to launch a counter-attack as early as the following spring.

As we are told absolutely nothing about Melchishua and Abinadab, we can only hazard a guess as to why they shared in their brother's fate. Possibly, like Michal and Jonathan, they had also been under David's spell. Perhaps they were regarded as equally unreliable heirs by their father. If they had escaped the notice of the Davidic author, it may simply have been because they were, as things turned out – by their deaths on Gilboa – merely peripheral characters.

> ## Conclusion 28
> Saul intended that Jonathan should die commanding a suicidal rearguard action against the Philistines.

Dividing of the Army

From the minimalist, near-identical descriptions in 1 Samuel and 1 Chronicles, it is impossible to draw a precise picture of the Battle of Gilboa. All we know is that the Philistines were drawn up at Shunem, on the north-eastern side of the Jezreel Plain, with the Israelites based opposite, at the hamlet of Jezreel itself (1 Sam. 29:1), at the south-eastern side of the valley. Between the protagonists lay about three miles of, for the most part, gently undulating countryside, bisected by the depression of the brook of Harod – bordered on its southern edge by the northern slope of Gilboa (then probably wooded), curving downwards in an easterly direction until it broadens into the open spaces of the Jordan valley itself.[7]

The geography offered Saul two routes for the retreat of his main army. The first followed hard on the curve of the Gilboa massif, taking the Israelites away from the Philistines and toward the river. From there, the army would have continued along the Jordan Valley, possibly all the way to the Jordan fords south of Zaphon, where, even allowing for the relatively swollen waters of the early spring, they could have effected a crossing. However, as previously stated, an army is rarely more vulnerable than when it is in retreat. Even under cover of darkness, the valley route would have been dangerously exposed to the attentions of both the Philistines themselves and any Canaanite inhabitants of the adjacent city of Bet-shean. Hence, it seems likely that Saul directed his troops along the slower mountain route, over the back of the Gilboa massif, concealed from enemy eyes.

Another aspect of the battle which does seem clear from the Bible description is that combat occurred on and around the mountain itself.[8]

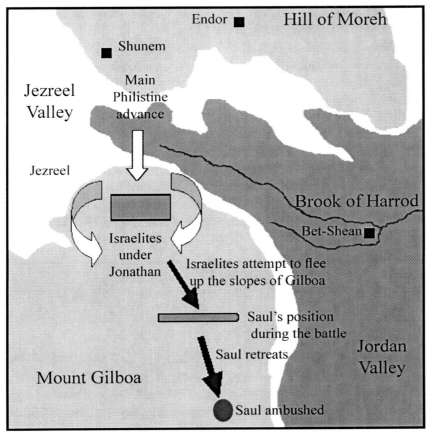

Gilboa with pre-battle lines

This would be consistent with the normal Israelite desire to engage their enemies on hilly terrain. With the possible exception of Mizpah, where the Philistines were a shadow of their normal selves, the Israelite victories were confined to areas where such topography gave Israel the advantage. The Philistine army favoured formal battles in level, open country, where their chariots (including battle carts drawn by teams of oxen) and heavy infantry were supreme – such as at Aphek, in the Plain of Sharon. The fact that the host of Israel failed to meet them in the valley itself would have been no surprise to Achish and his comrades.

Saul, for his part, would have held fast to Mount Gilboa, benefiting from the relative advantage of being above the approaching enemy. He might also have hoped that by exploiting any cover afforded by vegetation on the mountain slope, he could conceal the true size of his force until the last possible moment.

With the bulk of the Israelite army either making its arduous way to the Jordan fords or already safe across the river, we can now attempt to estimate the size of Saul's remaining force.

We know that Saul and Jonathan led a standing regiment numbering at least three thousand men (1 Sam. 13:2). However, at Gilboa, we can assume that a significant part of this force was attached to Abner and Ishboshet. Bearing in mind that each 'knight' would have been accompanied by at least one lightly armed attendant, we can surmise that Saul's army at the Battle of Gilboa might have comprised between two and three thousand men. The narrative gives us no information as to the size of the Philistine host, but considering the 'gathering of all the Philistine armies' in 1 Sam. 29:1, their army must have outnumbered the Israelites by a substantial factor. Nevertheless, the Israelite rearguard, comprising as it did many of Israel's elite warriors, was well placed and suited to delay the enemy long enough to permit the successful withdrawal of the main army.

Conclusion 29
The Israelite force at Gilboa was merely a rearguard designed to cover the withdrawal of the main army.

The Battle of Gilboa[9]
The descriptions of the battle in both 1 Samuel (31:1-3) and 1 Chronicles (10:1-3) are virtually identical in their detail and their brevity. Unfortunately for the modern historian, Bible authors, in common with most other recorders of national epics down the ages, developed selective amnesia when recounting their people's defeats. By contrast, their descriptions of Israelite victories, such as those of Deborah/Barak (Jg. 4: 11-24), Gideon (Jg. 7: 19-25) and especially Saul himself at Michmash (1 Sam. 14), contain sufficient detail as to constitute useable tactical aids to modern generals.

The accounts of the Battle of Gilboa do at least contain certain clues which permit us to reconstruct the crucial elements of what must have been a dramatic, if one-sided, encounter. The versions in both 1 Samuel and 1 Chronicles present an extremely condensed account of a battle which may in reality have lasted hours. The facts we can glean from them are as follows:

- The men of Israel were routed by the Philistine army (1 Sam. 31: 1; 1 Ch. 10:1);
- The Philistines pursued Saul and his sons (1 Sam. 31: 2; 1 Ch. 10: 2);
- Saul's sons were slain (ibid);
- Saul's retreat was cut off – he was surrounded and wounded by arrows (1 Sam. 31: 3; 1 Chron. 10: 3);

· Saul either falls on his own sword, or is killed by an Amalekite (1
  Sam. 31: 4; 2 Sam. 1: 10; 1 Ch.10: 4).

By combining this information and our graphic knowledge of the overall
site of the battle, and by examining these details in the context of our
general reassessment, we can – despite the sparseness of detail – arrive
at a plausible reconstruction of the Battle of Gilboa.

As we have already ascertained, it was essential for Saul to draw the
Philistines up the slope towards his own men. By so doing, he could at
least slow down their chariots and somewhat blunt the effect of their
archers, slingers, and spear throwers.

At some point, he gave the order for Jonathan and his men to charge
down the slope onto the approaching enemy. Several hundred heavily
armed soldiers, aided by gravity, crashing into the Philistine front ranks
made a dramatic impact, but once the initial shock had been absorbed, the
sheer weight of enemy numbers overcame the Israelites, until their thin
lines finally broke. At this point, Jonathan might have expected his father
to lead his remaining men down from their higher position in a second
wave to reinforce his crumbling front. If he did have that expectation, he
was to be sorely disappointed. Once the Israelite line broke, their fate was
sealed as the Philistine chariots and archers swept round in an outflanking
manoeuvre up the gentle western slopes. Meanwhile, thousands of heavy
infantrymen poured through, over, and around the small body of men.

Many of the chariots from the far wings of the Philistine force had
continued up the mountain slope towards the point where Saul's men had
earlier been spied. Despite the distance and elevation between the king and
his pursuers, he was aware that he could not delay. Once the chariot ponies
and oxen reached the ridge and delivered their cargo of archers, the terrain
on the uplands of the Gilboa massif would be to their advantage.

While Saul made good his escape, those Israelites still embroiled in
battle on the lower slopes, sought to flee back up the hill, but they were
doomed. Along with the royal princes, they were completely outflanked,
overrun and cut to pieces.

The Ambush

It is the contention of this hypothesis that Saul did not intend to die that
day on the slopes of Mount Gilboa and took every precaution to prevent
his retreat being cut off by the Philistines.

From his vantage point, high above the battle, he had more than
adequate warning of any potential outflanking manoeuvre on the part
of the enemy. The king and his companions were onlookers, who would
have shielded themselves from the obvious risks of being close to the

combat. However, there was one unobvious danger that even Saul, a veteran commander of exceptional ability, had not considered: ambush by a concealed force of Israelite guerrilla troops.

As Saul and his men rapidly traversed the broad, rounded ridge that forms the summit of Mount Gilboa, deep in collective mourning for their fallen comrades, they may have sensed a stirring from the pine trees and scrub that lined their path. Then, in a split second – barely enough time to tighten their grip on the shafts of their spears – they found themselves showered by a hail of arrows. Those who survived the first volley instinctively formed themselves into a shield around the person of their king. By now, however, the archers had found their range, and with each successive volley of missiles, the shield of men became ever thinner as the Mighty Ones and their servants were gradually cut down.

1 Sam.31: 4: *Eventually, Saul, terribly wounded by arrows, found himself isolated and cut off from retreat.*

Saul said to his armour bearer, "Draw your sword and run me through so that the uncircumcised may not run me through and make sport of me." But his armour bearer, overawed, refused; whereupon Saul grasped the sword and fell on it.'

A point of note is the richness of detail describing Saul's death, which in this respect stands in stark contrast to those of numerous other Israelite warriors, from Jonathan himself to Judas Maccabaeus (1 Mac. 9: 18). The brutal truth is that, following a total rout such as Gilboa, there would have been few, if any, among the defeated to give an eyewitness account of such a specific scene. The only purported witness to Saul's death – in the 1 Samuel and 1 Chronicles accounts – is the armour bearer; however, according to both versions, he too falls on his sword, emulating his master. Furthermore, it seems most improbable that the Philistines would have wanted to spread a story that detracted from their direct involvement in the slaying of their greatest enemy.

A fair, if cynical, conclusion would be that the description of Saul's death is merely apocryphal, a small piece of pro-Benjamin propaganda that with time became accepted lore – so much so that King David found it expedient to acknowledge the veracity of the story by the time he reburied Saul. However, the genuine source of the death scene is not so difficult to discover when a little detective work is brought to bear on the matter.

The Marks of Betrayal
The narrative now describes the terrible aftermath of the battle of Gilboa for Israel:

1 Sam. 31:7-10: On hearing the news of the disaster, the Israelites of Jezreel fled across the Jordan to Gilead, abandoning their land and their towns to the victors.

The next day, the Philistines discovered the bodies of Saul and his sons. After decapitating the dead king, they stripped him of his armour and . . . they placed his armour in the temple of Ashteroth:[10] and they impaled his body on the wall of Bet-shean.

It is important to note that, according to 1 Samuel, the Philistines did not discover the body of Saul until the next day.

Given the obvious implausibility of a scenario, whereby Philistine warriors approaching the King of Israel at his moment of death (as described in all three accounts), simply leave his body – their greatest trophy of victory – undisturbed until the following morning, we must consider the probability that in fact, the Philistines neither witnessed, nor contributed to the death of Saul. Moreover, the additional information that his corpse was laying in its armour upon discovery indicates that whoever in fact killed him, did not hang around to gloat. This seems to put the lie to some scholarly speculation – articulated most forcefully by David Rohl – that Saul was killed by Canaanite allies of the Philistines from the city of En Ganim (modern Jenin).[11] Surely, Canaanites of this persuasion would have been only too keen to present such a glorious trophy to their new, all powerful masters – the serans of the Philistines.

Whereas in reality, whoever killed the King of Israel had no need of credit points with the Philistines and, more crucially, no desire to be associated with the act.

Bet-shean was the closest major town to the battlefield of Gilboa. With its Canaanite population, it was also less likely to have been deserted in the aftermath of the Israelite defeat, thus providing the victors with a possibly enthusiastic audience for their gory trophy.[12] Additionally, Bet-shean's prominent position at the eastern opening of the Jezreel valley ensured that the torso of Saul would serve as an effective and chilling reminder of Philistine supremacy to all who passed by – especially those Israelites fleeing across the Jordan into Gilead.

However, if the inhabitants of Bet-shean were glad to see the end of King Saul, there were others among his possibly non-Israelite subjects who had contrary ideas on the subject. When the people of Jabesh-gilead learnt what had befallen King Saul, 'all the stalwart men set out and marched all night; they removed the bodies of Saul and his sons from the wall of Bet-shean and came to Jabesh where they cremated them. And they buried the bones, under a tree at Jabesh, and fasted seven days' (1 Sam. 31:12-13).[13]

The people of Jabesh-Gilead owed their liberty to King Saul, so, for them in particular, the thought of his body savaged and defiled, an object of derision and contempt, was intolerable. However, their poignantly heroic act tends to obscure a significant fact and an important piece of evidence relating to the exact nature of Saul's death.

That being the case, the condition of the bodies, as observed by the Gileadites, while they prepared them for cremation, must have influenced much of the subsequent description of the battle, including the deployment of Saul and his sons.

Sword wounds on the bodies of the three sons would indicate death while fighting the enemy at close quarters. By contrast, the king's torso might have revealed numerous arrow punctures,[14] suggesting that he had originally been at some distance from his assailants. This in itself would have informed his Gileadite embalmers that Saul had been apart from his sons when he met his end. The additional presence of a single catastrophic stab wound would have indicated that the king, immobilised by the arrows, was finally dispatched with a sword. It would explain, too, the consistent tradition that Saul died after his sons, when fleeing the scene.

Conclusion 30
The tradition that Saul died separately from his sons is based on evidence gathered during the ritual purification of his and his sons' battle-scarred remains prior to cremation.

Thus ends the narrative of the first book of Samuel.

Crowns, Bracelets and Amalekites

The second book of Samuel begins three days after David's return from slaughtering the Amalekites, with the arrival at Ziklag of a young runner from Gilboa.

2 Sam. 1:1-27: The runner's clothes were torn and there was dust on his head. After prostrating himself at the feet of David, he recounted the terrible news of Israel's defeat. The youth described how, during the battle, he had found Saul mortally wounded, attempting to fall on his sword, and how he had complied when asked by the stricken king to run him through. The youth, an Amalekite, then produced the crown and amulet of the late King of Israel and presented them to David as evidence of the truthfulness of his story.
". . . Then I took the crown from his head and the bracelet from his arm, and have brought them here, to my lord."

After seeing the proof of Saul's death, David commanded his men to mourn for their late king until the evening.

So furious was David with the Amalekite for having slain the Lord's anointed that he had him executed on the spot. The rest of the day was spent mourning and lamenting the lives of Saul, his sons, and the other fallen men of Israel.

This alternative account of Saul's tragic end, when set alongside the duplicate accounts already discussed, cannot but raise grave suspicions as to whether we have any reliable information about the episode at all.

The casting of an Amalekite as Saul's killer was surely a pro-David propagandist's mythological strike against Saul – by suggesting a direct punishment for Saul's 'crime' of sparing Agag. In other words, to pious eyes, the ethnicity of Saul's executioner in this version of his death had the ring of divinely ordained 'poetic justice'.[15] In the same way, placing David's slaughter of the Amalekite raiders and his righteous dispatch of the Amalekite youth on either side of the death of Saul was intended to highlight Saul's failure and disobedience in his battle with Amalek the previous year.

In reality, the fiction of the Amalekite youth was necessary to explain the presence at Ziklag of Saul's royal crown and bracelet immediately following the battle of Gilboa. Unlike armour, crowns and bracelets are easily and quickly removed. Thus, whoever the real killer of King Saul was, he found the temptation of possessing the two symbols of Israelite kingship impossible to resist. Just as the story of the Amalekite raid on Ziklag provided an alibi for David just prior to and during the battle at Gilboa, the story of Saul's final, desperate plea to the youth was intended to remove the genuine killer from the scene of the regicide.

Thus, we have two contradictory accounts of Saul's last moments, one possibly from the men of Jabesh and the other probably from the mouth of David. While the former paints a picture of a heroic death in which Saul takes on himself the full burden of a tragic destiny, the latter gives the king a relatively ignoble end as a supplicant to a passing teenager. In reality, both are myths; in the one case it is a confection that blends fact and rumour indiscriminately, and in the other, a screen behind which a criminal could conceal his guilt.

Conclusion 31
David created the alternative version of Saul's death to explain his possession of the royal crown and bracelet within days of the battle of Gilboa.[16]

'The Use of the Bow'

Even the most conscientious reader of biblical texts may miss vital clues, especially those embedded in seemingly superfluous stretches of narrative. How many, for example, have overlooked the apparently innocuous verse that precedes David's lament to Saul and Jonathan? 'And David intoned this lamentation over Saul and Jonathan – He commanded the Judahites be taught [the use of] the bow. It is recorded in the book of Jasher. . . .' (2 Sam. 1:17-18). This apparently gratuitous reference to archery lessons has puzzled scholars down the ages. The King James Bible turns the entire verse into an aside, placing it in parentheses. Creativity has more than one way to suppress something awkward.

Some commentators explain the verse by proposing that the lament itself was a battle hymn, sung perhaps during military training – presumably during archery practice.[17] A superficially more plausible theory suggests that the nature of Saul's death – as alleged in 1 Samuel and 1 Chronicles – taught David the tactical value of archers within an army, and thus the lament was as much a reminder to Judah and Israel of their former military limitations under Saul as a eulogy. Yet the implication that the army of Saul could have vanquished Amalek, Zobah, Moab, and Ammon, and held its own against the Philistines for over a decade without archers seems highly dubious.

Such theories presume a link between the "bow" (Heb: keshet) verse and the following lament; often, keshet is said to have some musical, historical, or folkloric relationship to the lament. But if, as is likely, the verse slipped into this location simply as a result of editorial inertia, attempts to bind it to the surrounding text are doomed to futility.

The later redactors and compilers of the narrative who inserted these scraps were as ignorant of their relevance as we are today. They included them because, despite their loss of apparent historical meaning, they were irrevocably woven into the core tradition. What may have begun life as a vivid parallel record, perhaps contained within the lost book of Jasher, probably faded with time into an obscure, anomalous addendum.

The forgotten history in this instance may be that the keshet and arrows which spelt Saul's doom, were perhaps those of an ambush set by David and/or his fellow 'sons of Judah'.[18]

King of Judah

With Saul's crown in his possession, David's next move was inexorable:

2 Sam. 2:1: Following the deaths of Saul and his three sons, David moved his base to Hebron where he was anointed King of Judah.

After the battle of Gilboa, the population of north-central Israel was again faced with the choice of flight or subjugation. The Philistines had exacted revenge for their defeats at Michmash, Mizpah and Elah. David, no doubt with the grateful cooperation of his victorious allies, had himself anointed as their vassal ruler of Judah and established Hebron as his capital.[19]

2 Sam. 2:5-7: *He then sent a message of congratulation to the brave men of Jabesh for their remarkable display of loyalty and heroism in rescuing the remains of King Saul. He also let them know that he now ruled in Judah.*

David sent messengers to the men of Jabesh-gilead, and said unto them, "May the Lord bless you for the kindness which you have displayed to your lord, Saul. . . . Now take courage and be brave men, for your lord Saul is dead and the House of Judah have already anointed me king over them."

In other words, David was saying to the men of Jabesh; 'your king is dead; if you don't accept me as your new master, be ready for a fight. . . .'[20]

Ultimately, he got a fight – a civil war lasting seven years, between his Judahite forces (with Philistine allies), and the army of Israel commanded by Abner and Ishboshet, son of Saul – second and forgotten King of Israel.

Orthodox Sequence	**Major Variants**
1 Sam. 31: The Battle of Gilboa; Israel flees before the Philistines; Saul's sons are killed; Saul is wounded by arrows; Saul and his armour bearer fall on their swords; the local Israelites flee across Jordan, abandoning their cities to the Philistines; the Philistines decapitate bodies of Saul and sons – and then nail the torsos to wall of Bet-shean; the men of Jabesh launch a daring raid, and recover the bodies of Saul and his sons; the bodies are cremated and then buried in Jabesh-Gilead.	The picture handed down to us of the death of Saul and his sons is based upon the conclusions of the Jabeshites who prepared their torsos for cremation.
2 Sam. 1: Three days later, David gets the news of Saul's defeat from an Amalekite runner; the youth, presents David with Saul's crown and amulet; David executes him for slaying the Lord's anointed; David laments for Saul and Jonathan.	David concocted the story of the Amalekite runner to explain the presence of the royal crown and amulet at Ziklag so soon after the battle of Gilboa.
2 Sam. 2: David is anointed king at Hebron.	

David Dictates to his Scribe

10
'To the Victor . . .'
King David

'Saul is said to have been more pious than David, gentle and generous, the real elect of God.' (An anonymous Haggadist)

With Saul and Jonathan out of the way, and their surviving troops across the Jordan in Gilead, the coast was now clear for David to take formal control over Judah.

2 Sam. 2:8-3:12: As David was assuming his kingly role in Judah, Abner made Ishboshet, Saul's one remaining legitimate son, king over the rest of Israel. A bloody civil war then commenced between Ishboshet's supporters and those of David. During one battle, Abner killed a brother of Joab, David's commander in chief.

Abner's influence in Israel grew greater than that of Ishboshet. Eventually, the two men fell out over Rizpah, one of Saul's concubines, and Abner declared his intention of defecting to David, together with the army.

David continued to have sons by all of his wives.

The Legacy of Saul[1]
On the face of it, Saul's legacy lay in tatters, the bulk of his kingdom divided between his mortal enemy, the Philistines, and his loathed pretender. His crown was on the head of his weak and ineffectual son,[2] and his once mighty army reduced to fighting a war of attrition against their brother tribe. Between two and seven and a half years after his death,[3] the disintegration of his kingdom culminated in the murders of both Abner and Ishboshet, the surrender of his army, and the coronation of David as king over All Israel.[4]

There were other aspects of Saul's legacy, however, which survived the destruction of his kingdom and that remain evident to this day, within the traditions of all the extant royal houses of Europe. The first beneficiaries of this abstract and enduring bequest were David and his successors.

Saul overcame the hitherto supreme authority of the clergy and demonstrated that, with a mix of astute military leadership, courage, compassion, understanding, and just a touch of expedient ruthlessness, Israel could flourish under secular rule. He did away with decisions based solely upon the ecstatic ramblings of priests and shamans. Moreover, Saul needed prodigious enthusiasm and energy to accomplish his revolution. By his success in thus shifting the balance of power and influence within Israel, he left for his successor David the blueprint for royal government, sanctioned by God. It would be hard to overstate the importance of this part of Saul's legacy, not merely to Israel but to western society in general.

Saul's rule over All Israel and Judah lasted about ten years, during which time he laid the foundations of the Israelite nation state. He graphically demonstrated that the union of Israel and Judah created a formidable and thus potentially durable entity. In consequence, the previous theocratic, tribal confederacy was superseded by a monarchist, pan-tribal nation. Saul had shown that All Israel had little to fear from her immediate neighbours, and in time could rise to great influence in the larger world.

The relatively complex and abstract Israelite notion of deity, together with Samuel's reluctance to anoint a king and Saul's innate humility, produced a revolutionary royal creation: the man-king, divinely chosen and sometimes 'divinely inspired', but in and of himself a mere mortal. By accepting Samuel as his guide and conscience, Saul initiated a governmental style that nearly all his successors followed, to the word if not to the letter. His novel example of an answerable monarch – albeit answerable to a single holy man – was courageous in a world separated by over two thousand years from Magna Carta. The formal clergy, meanwhile, found themselves reduced to the role of ceremonially rubber-stamping the authority of the man-king.[5]

Unfortunately for Israel, for Judah, and for history, the ambitious David was not content with this inheritance of a balanced and workable form of governance. By centralizing the Israelite cult and by emulating the customs of his imperial contemporaries, such as the maintenance of a large harem and the building of opulent palaces, he sought – as proclaimed on various occasions and most explicitly in Psalm 2:6-7 – to raise himself, and thereby his successors, to the level of son of God:[6] ' "But, I have installed My king on Zion, My holy mountain!" Let me tell of the decree: the Lord said to me, "You are My son. I have fathered you this day." ' In so doing, he mutated the seed bequeathed to him by Saul and began a process that led directly, sometimes gloriously but more often ignobly, to the eventual destruction of the entire Israelite nation.

While David was aided by aspects of Saul's legacy in his gradual and inexorable rise from Philistine vassal to Israel's best known king, the loyalty Saul continued to inspire in his people from beyond the grave became a thorn in David's side. In addition to the daring action of the men of Jabesh in rescuing Saul's remains, the memory of the late king in the hearts and souls of Benjamin and Israel provoked unrest and reprisal well into David's long reign and beyond. Despite David's attempt to endear himself to the Saulides by his protection of Jonathan's son, Mephiboshet (2 Sam. 9), the wounded sensibilities of his northern subjects were further lacerated by his purge of the house of Saul. The popular uprising, led by the Benjaminite rebel Sheba, late into his reign (2 Sam. 20) attests to the fact that David never succeeded in convincing Israel of his right to rule over them.[7]

The Lament

Of all King David's attempts to allay the resentment of many of his northern subjects, none is more affecting than his wonderful lament to the fallen Saul and Jonathan.

Placing the lament in the Samuel text immediately following the battle of Gilboa, at the very moment that David learnt of Israel's defeat, is an obvious exercise of 'narrative license' on the part of the author. Even allowing the possibility that David was the poetic genius implied by the ascription of numerous psalms to him, it stretches credulity to imagine that he was capable of breaking into sublime verse at a moment's notice. Moreover, such a passionate outburst against the 'uncircumcised' slayers of Saul and Jonathan would not have been well received by his Philistine masters.[8]

Whenever the lament was actually conceived, it was probably intended for a special occasion honouring the slain heroes. David's re-interment of the bones of Saul and Jonathan at the Kish family sepulchre at Zelah is likely to have been that occasion (2 Sam. 21:12-14).

Should this be so, the fact that David paid homage to his predecessor so soon after murdering Saul's two illegitimate sons and five grandsons graphically illustrates his conflicting priorities at the time (2 Sam. 21). On the one hand, he felt compelled to remove all male remnants of the house of Saul; on the other, he had to win the trust of his northern subjects by honouring the memory of their beloved king.

We can picture the scene at Zelah: The gathering is large, comprising all the princes and elders of Israel and Judah, and many more besides who have come to honour the memory of Saul and his noble house. The king is dressed in the sackcloth of mourning, his red Moabite hair dusted with ash in an ostentatious display of humility before the tomb of Saul.

Benaiah – the commander of the royal guard – and a large section of the Cherethite and Pelethite[9] troops stand posted a respectable distance away, but well within sight, as a warning and a precaution against anyone becoming emotionally overheated and disrupting the proceedings.

Following a ceremony of dedication, led by Zadok the priest, consisting of offerings and chanting, the bloodcurdling banshee wails of the women mourners rise upwards on a thick cloud of smoke and incense into the evening sky. Gradually, as the keening subsides, and against a sombre background of quiet humming by the attendant Levites,

David intoned this dirge over Saul and his son Jonathan . . .

"Your glory O Israel,
Lies slain on your heights;
How have the mighty fallen!
Tell it not in Gath,
Do not proclaim it in the streets of Askelon,
Lest the daughters of the Philistines rejoice,
Lest the daughters of the uncircumcised exult.

O hills of Gilboa –
Let there be no dew or rain on you,
Or bountiful fields,
For there the shield of warriors lay rejected,
The shield of Saul,
Anointed with oil no more.

From the blood of the slain,
From the fat of warriors –
The bow of Jonathan
Never turned back;
The sword of Saul
Never withdrew empty.

Saul and Jonathan,
Beloved and cherished,
Never parted
In life or in death!
They were swifter than eagles,
They were stronger than lions!

Daughters of Israel,
Weep over Saul,
Who clothed you in crimson and finery,
Who decked your robes with jewels of gold.

How are the mighty fallen
In the thick of battle –
Jonathan, slain on your heights!
I grieve for you,
My brother Jonathan,
You were most dear to me.
Your love was wonderful to me
More than the love of women.

How have the mighty fallen,
The weapons of war perished!" (2 Sam. 1:17-27)

There can be little doubt that David did an effective job. The respect displayed towards Saul, David's proclaimed love of Jonathan, and his curse upon Gilboa hit just the right note that evening at Zelah, as they have continued to do down the ages. However, the hypothesis presented here is that the unequivocal expressions of sorrow and outrage in David's lament were false.[10]

Conclusion 32
David's lament was first recited at the reburial of Saul and Jonathan, after the anti-Saul purges, and was intended to bring the curtain down on the House of Saul and his Benjaminite dynasty.

'The Blameless Hero'
David's insincerity in the great lament is confirmed in another piece of poetic prose constituting the whole of chapter 22 of 2 Samuel (and repeated almost verbatim in the eighteenth psalm).

The poem provides us with a vivid insight into the mind of David with regards to the tragic events at the battle of Gilboa.

At this point, we will do well to remember the alleged scene at Ziklag, as narrated in 2 Samuel 1, where David, grief-stricken and outraged by the news of the battle, breaks into an emotional lament. With this scene in mind, we should now consider the heading of the poem:[11] 'David addressed the words of this song to the Lord after the Lord had saved him . . . from the hand of Saul.' For the most part, the piece indulges in a eulogistic affirmation of God's defence of David, but intermingled with the expressions of praise are several oblique references to the overthrow of Saul. When they are extracted and then juxtaposed in their original order, they make illuminating reading: ' "All praise!" I called on the Lord, And I was delivered from my enemies' (2 Sam. 22: 4); 'He let loose arrows, and scattered them . . .' (2 Sam. 22:15).

For I have kept the ways of the Lord
And have not been guilty before my God;
I am mindful of all his rules
And have not departed from His laws.
I have been blameless before Him,
And have guarded myself against sinning –
And the Lord has requited my merit,
According to my purity in His sight.
With the loyal You deal loyally;
With the blameless hero, blamelessly.
With the pure You act in purity,
And with the perverse You are wily.
To humble folk You give victory,
And you look with scorn on the haughty. (2 Sam. 22: 22-28)

Who made my legs like a deer's,
And set me firm upon the heights;
Who trained my hands for battle,
So that my arms can bend a bow of bronze! (2 Sam. 22: 34/35)

I pursued my enemies and wiped them out,
I did not turn back till I destroyed them.
I destroyed them, I struck them down;
They rose no more, they lay at my feet.
You have girt me with strength for battle,
Brought low my foes before me,
My foes – and I wiped them out.
They cried, but there was none to deliver;
To the Lord, but he answered them not.
I pounded them like dust of the earth,
Stamped, crushed them like dirt of the streets. (2 Sam. 22: 38-43)

The God who vindicated me
And made peoples subject to me,
Rescued me from my enemies,
Raised me clear from my foes,
Saved me from lawless men! (2 Sam. 22. 48/49)

. . . Who deals graciously with His anointed,
With David and his offspring for evermore." (2 Sam. 22:51)

These verses offer a slightly compressed but graphic description of Saul
and his army's fate on Mount Gilboa, the 'heights' of the famous lament.
Hidden among the lyrical praise the poetry might be taken as generalised

allusions to David's divinely assisted victories over non-specific enemies, one of whom happened to be Saul. However, the heading confirms that the poem is David's glorification of his 'deliverance' from – i.e. overthrowing of Saul. In addition, he attempts to vindicate his own role in the affair by casting God as the de facto executioner and by a paradoxically hubristic reminder of his own purity and humbleness relative to Saul – the breaker of divine law. 2 Samuel 22 is David's – 'the blameless hero's' – personal antidote to the great lament.

The dichotomy that exists between the lament and the poem is quite consistent with the carrot-and-stick style of governance typical of a tyrant king ruling over a tribal people. In this case, the lament is David's conciliatory carrot to Benjamin and the northern tribes, while 2 Samuel 22 is the stick with which he reminds all his people of his supremacy, based on the direct favour of God.

Elhanan

Of all the warriors who risked their lives in the service of the 'greatest King of Israel', it is perhaps Elhanan who deserves most credit. Not simply for slaying Goliath, but – more importantly – for putting the lie to the most famous myth in the books of Samuel, and thereby, allowing us to catch a glimpse of the true history of the foundation of the Kingdom of All Israel: 'A champion of the Philistine forces stepped forward; his name was Goliath of Gath, and he was six cubits and a span tall.' (1 Sam. 17: 4); 'The shaft of his spear was like a weaver's beam . . .' (1 Sam. 17: 7); 'Again there was fighting with the Philistines at Gob; Elhanan the son of Jaare-Oregim the Bethlehemite killed Goliath the Gittite, whose spear had a shaft like a weaver's beam' (2 Sam. 21:19). The deed of Elhanan is placed long after the death of Saul, at the time his usurper was king over All Israel in his own right. It is depicted as a constituent of David's ultimately successful campaign against his former sponsors, the Philistines. While it is possible that Elhanan had acted on behalf of Saul, it is most likely that the chronological placement in 2 Samuel is correct.[12] Perversely, the clue lies in the earlier David and Goliath myth.

Within that narrative, there is a peculiar verse that makes no apparent sense at all. This insertion reads: 'And David took the head of the Philistine, and brought it to Jerusalem; and he put his weapons in his own tent . . .'[13] (1 Sam. 17:54). What at first seems to be a riddle now serves to illuminate the way.

David captured Jerusalem after he had reunited Saul's kingdom in the eighth year of his rule. Until that date, throughout the reign of Saul, including the time in which the David and Goliath myth is slotted into the narrative, Jerusalem was a Jebusite city. It would have been virtually impossible and certainly pointless for the slayer of Goliath to take his grizzly trophy to the city during this period. Three verses later, we are further confused by being informed that '. . . when David returned after killing the Philistine, Abner took him and brought him to Saul, with the head of the Philistine still in his hand' (1 Sam. 17:57).

At this point, the David and Goliath narrative has moved from the realms of mythology into farce. Are we now to believe that Saul was waiting for David in Jerusalem? If so, was the Israelite king a guest or some sort of ally of the Jebusites against the Philistines, or had he temporarily conquered the city and made it his HQ during the battle that took place at Elah? Or is the story suggesting, even more bizarrely, that David carried the head to Jerusalem and then back to Elah for some unspecified reason prior to presenting his trophy to King Saul?

In the face of such implausibility, we are forced to conclude that the author of 1 Samuel was a-none-too skilled practitioner of collage, pasting together elements of many scattered events – Saul's various battles with the Philistines, David's alleged actions as a possible participant in some of these military encounters – for the sake of a vivid tale. His deficiencies as a collagist become especially glaring, of course, when he tells us that Goliath was felled twice, once by David and once by Elhanan.[14]

However, it was almost certainly Elhanan who slew the giant of Gath, at 'Gob', not Elah. He would then have dutifully presented his trophies to King David, who in turn would have locked up the great sword in his royal tent before leading his troops back to his capital, Jerusalem, where he might have displayed the champion's head in triumph.

Over time, David's and Elhanan's parts in the matter naturally became confused until, consistent with the ever-growing mythological status of the legendary lion-fighting youth, the event was distilled into a Davidic fantasy. By contrast, the role of the factual hero survived only in the form of two remnants of genuine history.

Bethlehem of Zebulun

An interesting and potentially illuminating footnote to the Goliath debate derives from the description of Elhanan as a Bethlehemite. This has led to speculation that he was none other than David himself and that Jaare of Jaare-oregim is a version of Jesse.[15] Commentators of this persuasion consider "David" to be a throne name, either earned by Elhanan during his time as a Philistine dwd (commander) or after he became Dwd-in-chief, so to speak, of the Israelite nation.[16]

In spite of its undoubted attractiveness, the plausibility of this theory is nevertheless highly strained, both by the existence of two distinct records which are set in two distinct eras, and by the fact that Elhanan is explicitly portrayed as being in the service of David. Moreover, the Jesse-Jarre-oregim equation is dubious in the extreme, somewhat reminiscent of newspaper 'word-ladder' games, whereby over five stages one turns for example, coal into snow. By the same technique Moses could become Aaron and Ezekiel could be made into Jezebel.[17]

In any event, with the exception of the distinct identification of Elhanan in 2 Samuel, the name appears high on a list of heroes in the service of King David in the First Book of Chronicles (in 11:26): 'The valiant warriors: Asahel brother of Joab, Elhanan the son of Dodo from Bethlehem.'

The discrepancy in paternity – Jarre-Oregim vs. Dodo – notwithstanding,[18] it does seem that an Elhanan of Bethlehem was a distinct and distinguished soldier who served in King David's army.

It should also be noted that there were two Bethlehems (literally house of bread) in ancient Israel: the famous Judahite city and another Bethlehem in Zebulun, to the northwest of the Jezreel Valley. The tribe of Zebulun was noted for the courage of its warriors and their loyalty to David. This is also borne out in 1 Chronicles (in 12:34), where it states: '. . . of Zebulun, those ready for service, able to man battle line with all kinds of weapons . . . giving support wholeheartedly . . .' Thus, the chronicler informs us that the tribe from which Elhanan possibly hailed was known for its 'wholehearted' support for the king. Given the value David placed on cementing the loyalty of his northern subjects, the survival of the Elhanan verse within the pages of 2 Samuel may be seen as serving a strategic purpose.

It is easy to see how these facts could have contributed to the historical muddle. If Elhanan was indeed a Zebulunite and not a Judahite, the existence of two distinct, competing traditions becomes explicable.

Conclusion 33
Goliath was killed by Elhanan during King David's war against the Philistines.[19]

One Nation, Two Peoples

Following David's defeat of the Philistines, the early part of his reign was dogged by a series of rebellions and revolts. In particular, the civil war which resulted from the most serious of these, the revolt of his son Absalom (2 Sam. 13-19), nearly cost him the throne, and the rebellion of the Benjaminite Sheba son of Bichri (2 Sam. 20), which represents the last recognized attempt by Benjamin to regain its position of supremacy in Israel and Judah.

The domestic peace achieved by David towards the end of his reign, which continued so famously throughout the reign of Solomon, was established and sustained by the virtual enslavement of the entire Israelite population. The two kings' rule may have been wise, but if so, this was wisdom forged in iron and maintained by thuggish sidekicks, such as Joab, who willingly absorbed the resulting public resentment so that their patrons could continue to shine, untarnished, above the darkness.

However, there were those amongst David's subjects who refused to be silenced or have the wool pulled over their eyes. Perhaps the most vociferous of these was a descendant of Saul's, by the name of Shimei son of Gera. His often overlooked denouncement of David (in 2 Sam. 16:7-8) – when the latter was fleeing from Absalom – was recorded by the Judahite scribes secure in the knowledge that his words would be regarded as a despicable calumny against the Son of God. Yet, in the context of this revision, they represent shocking and frank testimony as to the relative authenticity of the Davidic versus the Saulide claim to the throne of All Israel:

> "Get out, get out, you criminal, you villain! You murderer! The Lord
> is paying you back for all your crimes against the family of Saul,
> whose throne you seized." [20]

David's long wars of expansion, the maintenance of his pocket empire, and the vast building projects undertaken by his successor depended on a dragooned and tethered populace. And as with all empires built on the sweat and blood of resentful subjects, its strength was illusory. At the very first opportunity, during the reign of David's grandson Rehoboam, Israel threw off the oppressive yoke of Judah, uttering the battle cry coined by Sheba a generation earlier:

> "We have no portion in David,
> No share in Jesse's son!
> Every man to his tent, O Israel!" (2 Sam. 20:1)

Jeroboam then became the first king of the northern tribes of Israel since Ishboshet son of Saul.

As for the fate of Benjamin, in what perhaps amounts to the most poignant of all the ironies contained within this history of Saul, the tribe found itself, on the division of the kingdom, likewise split in two, one part falling within Judah and the other absorbed into Israel. Though personalities arose from time to time who proudly claimed their descent from Rachel's second son,[21] the tribe of Saul gradually lost its distinct identity. As Benjamin, the original royal tribe of Israel disappeared, its true history, together with that of Saul, became hostage to the exigencies of Israelite and, more critically for us today, Judahite tradition.

After David himself, perhaps the proudest protector of Judahite tradition is 'the Deuteronomist',[22] the alleged and anonymous compiler of many biblical texts, including the book that bears his name in addition to Joshua, Judges, Samuel (1 and 2) and Kings (1 and 2). Writing some four hundred years after the death of Saul and some three centuries following the disappearance of Benjamin, he felt secure enough to place these complimentary – albeit reflective – words into the mouth of Moses, in the thirty-third chapter, verse twelve of his eponymous text:

Of Benjamin he said:

"Beloved of the Lord,

He rests securely by Him;

Ever does He protect him,

As he dwells between His shoulders."

This retrospective blessing given to an extinct tribe might reflect a belated sense of gratitude on the part of the Judahite scribe – gratitude to those who, during Israel and Judah's darkest days, lit the torch of freedom, took on the might of their foes, protected the Israelite people – 'the beloved of the Lord' – and led the way to regal nationhood.

List of Conclusions

1.   The stories of the 'wicked sons' in the book of Samuel confirm that hereditary rule was established in Israel before the end of the era of the judges. These stories represent an attempt by pro-David partisans to consign potentially competing dynasties to oblivion.

2.   Confused chronology permitted the personality of the single historical Samuel to be fragmented and pressed into service by a variety of agenda-driven authors, thus obscuring the historical Samuel.

3.   The first meeting between Saul and Samuel occurred long before the disaster of Aphek. Samuel had not yet achieved national standing, and Saul was still a youth. This meeting became confused with an occasion following the battle of Aphek when Saul received a low-key, military-related anointing as 'ruler' of Israel.

4.   'Hand of the Lord' was a metaphor for Saul – the genuine victor of the single battle of Mizpah. The description of 'General Samuel' was an invention of a later anti-monarchist author.

5.   Saul was simply Saul.

6.   The cultic practices of eleventh-century BCE Israelites and their new king were syncretistic.

7.   The triple anointing of Saul reflects his historical evolution from nagid (Prince) of Israel, to melech (King) of Israel, to melech (King) of All Israel.

8.   Saul was captain of Israel for one year, King of Israel for two years, and King of All Israel for ten years.

9.   Saul was well into middle age by the time he became king over All Israel.

10. The "ophlim" disaster which struck the Philistine homeland provided a window of opportunity for the start of the Israelite resistance.

11. Saul's first campaign was not against Ammon, but against the Philistines when he was still only a nagid,

12. The joint rule of Samuel and Saul engendered an ambiguity in their respective roles and tense relations between the two leaders.

13. Saul's anointing as King of Israel (without Judah) was a direct result of his successful war of liberation against the Philistines.

14. Saul was crowned King of All Israel following his victory over Ammon and his earlier successes against the Philistines.

15. The chronologically confused records of two reprimands of Saul by Samuel are the result of the anti-monarchist perspective superimposed on the earlier pro-David narrative.

16. What was in reality a common, everyday event was distorted by the propagandist into a royal anointing, when he entered court as an accomplished warrior and musician.

17. The true history of David's recruitment is reflected in the first version of his introduction to King Saul.

18. The three accounts of Saul's spear throwing are apocryphal, pro-David distortions of the actual tensions which existed between the king, his heir, and the would-be usurper.

19. David's taking of Keilah was part of a planned rebellion against Saul in which the House of Eli and the four hundred malcontents were co-conspirators.

20. The falling out between Saul and Jonathan at the new moon banquet occurred as a direct result of the meeting at Ziph between David and the heir to the throne, when Jonathan ceded his future kingship of Judah to David.

21. Behind the confused narrative of David's initial time on the run from Saul lies the history of a failed insurrection by an unpopular pretender against a popular king.

22. The two descriptions of the sparing of Saul's life are pro-David myths, created to mask a meeting that resulted in David's banishment from Israel.

23. David bribed the princes of Judah to win their loyalty at the expense of Saul.

24. David provoked Israel's war with Amalek during his time at Ziklag.

25. Samuel was alive at the time of the battle of Gilboa.

26. The En-dor narrative is a corrupt account of the last meeting between Saul and a living Samuel.

27. The sacking of Ziklag is chronologically misplaced; it occurred about a year prior to the battle of Gilboa.

28. Saul intended that Jonathan should die commanding a suicidal rearguard action against the Philistines.

29. The Hebrew force at Gilboa was merely a rearguard designed to cover the withdrawal of the main army.

30. The tradition that Saul died separately from his sons is based on evidence gathered during the ritual purification of his and his sons' battle-scarred remains prior to cremation.

31. David created the alternative version of Saul's death to explain his possession of the royal crown and bracelet within days of the battle of Gilboa.

32. David's lament was first recited at the reburial of Saul and Jonathan, after the anti-Saul purges, and was intended to bring the curtain down on the House of Saul and his Benjaminite dynasty.

33. Goliath was killed by Elhanan during King David's war against the Philistines.

Timelines:
Comparative Orthodox and Revised Chronology

1: ORTHODOX TIME LINE

1 Samuel Time Markers	Sequence of Events Bold refers to incidents thought to be purely fictitious
	(1) Eli, high priest and judge of Israel – based in Shiloh
	(2) Battle of Aphek – Israel defeated – Ark captured by Philistines – Eli dies
7 months after Aphek – Ark begins 20-year sojourn in Kiryath-Jearim	(3) Plague hits Philistia – Ark returned to Israel – Placed in care of Abinadab in Kiryath-jearim – remains there for 20 years
	(4) Battle of Mizpah – **Samuel leads Israel to victory** – Philistines quashed for the rest of Samuel's lifetime – Samuel judges Israel from Ramah
Samuel's allotted 7 days start	(5) Samuel anoints Saul "Captain of Israel" – **Samuel commands Saul to meet him at Gilgal in 7 days time**
	(6) Samuel gathers Israel at Mizpah – Saul anointed King of Israel
	(7) Battle of Jabesh-Gilead – Saul leads army of All-Israel to victory over Nahash of Ammon – Saul anointed King of All-Israel at Gilgal
	(8) Saul forms army of 600 men
	(9) Jonathan liberates Geba
Samuel's allotted 7 days end	(10) Saul musters army at Gilgal – Philistines launch raids from Michmash – Saul's army dwindles – Samuel fails to appear and Saul makes sacrifice – **Samuel turns up and rebukes Saul** – Philistines occupy Israel – Israelites forbidden to own weapons
	(11) Battle of Michmash – Saul and Jonathan lead Israel to victory and expel Philistines
	(12) Saul wins victories over Moab, (13) Edom, (14) Zobah

(15) Saul defeats Amalekites – **final rupture with Samuel**

Samuel anoints the boy David future king at Bethlehem

(16) Great warrior David employed by Saul as court musician and armour bearer

Boy David kills Goliath at (17) battle of Elah – David takes Goliath's head to Jerusalem – **David becomes national hero** – David at Court of Saul – **David weds Michal**

(18) David flees Gibeah and goes to Samuel, then Nob then Gath, and then Adullam and gathers his family and gang of malcontents – David leaves his family in care of the king of Moab – Saul massacres priests of Nob – David occupies town of Keilah – David flees Keilah when Saul approaches – David takes refuge in southern Judah

Samuel dies

(19) Nabal episode

David's
16 month
sojourn in
Philistia
begins

(20) David flees to Gath, becomes servant of Achish – receives Ziklag – raids non-Judahites

(21) Philistines invade Israel with David – **David sent back to Ziklag** – David battles Amalekites – David sends gifts of spoil to Judahite elders – Saul dies at Battle of Gilboa

3 days after
Gilboa

David receives news of Saul's death at Ziklag – (22) Composes great lament

2: REVISED TIME LINE

'Saul'
Year

Sequence of Events
Bracketed numbers refer to orthodox positioning of each event (see previous section)

-18   (1) Eli, high priest and judge of Israel – based in Shiloh – Samuel born

13   Saul anointed prince of Benjamin by Samuel

15   Saul weds Ahinoam

16   Jonathan born

18   Ishboshet born

30   Saul takes Rizpah as his concubine

43   (2)Battle of Aphek – Philistines capture the Ark – Eli dies – (5) Samuel appoints Saul "Captain of Israel" – (8) Saul gathers 600 men to his cause – (11) Saul raises the standard of resistance at Gilgal – (9) Jonathan liberates Geba – Philistines occupy Michmash and

	take control over central Israel – Israelites under philistine control banned from owning weapons
43+7 months	(3) Earthquake strikes Philistia and surrounds – plague follows – Ark returns to Israel – Ark in care of clan of Abinadab for 20 years
44	(10) Battle of Michmash – Saul leads army to victory – Saul clears Philistines out of central highlands – Saul's army swells to 3000
45	(4) Battle of Mizpah – Saul leads Israel to decisive victory over Philistines – (6) Saul crowned king of Israel at Mizpah by Samuel – Saul's victory results in unification of southern and northern Israelite tribes – Saul signs peace treaty with Canaanite tribes within his kingdom
46	(12) Saul campaigns against Moab – Samuel goes on successful diplomatic mission to elders and princes of Judah – (16) Amongst others, David and his brothers enrolled into Saul's elite guard
47	(17) Battle of Elah – Philistines, fearful of united Hebrew kingdom, invade Judah – Saul victorious – David fights bravely
48	(7) Nahash of Ammon invades Gilead and lays siege to Jabesh – Battle of Jabesh-Gilead – Saul leads army of all Israel to great victory – Samuel crowns Saul king of all Israel at Gilgal
49	(13) Saul campaigns against Edom
50	(14) Saul campaigns agaist Zobah
52-55	(18) David leads failed rebellion against Saul – Saul executes priests of Nob – (19) Nabal Episode
55-56	(20) David and small army flee Judah and join Achish of Gath – Achish gives David Ziklag as base – David stirs up trouble on Saul's southern border, by raiding Amalekites – David sends bribes from Amalekite spoil to Judah elders – Amalekites launch reprisal raids into southern Judah
57	(15) Saul leads successful campaign against Amalek – Samuel retires from public life
58	(21) Battle of Gilboa – Philistines, with David, defeat Saul on Mount Gilboa – Saul killed – David crowned king of Judah in Hebron – Ishboshet crowned king of Israel in Manahaim in Gilead – seven year war begins between David and Ishboshet
65	Ishboshet murdered and David made king of all Israel in Hebron – David takes Jerusalem – has Ark moved to new capital
66+	Elhanan kills Goliath at Gob – David re-inters remains of Saul and his sons at Zelah – (22) David reads great lament

The (Hypothetical)
'Book of Saul'

The following is presented in the form of a 'Book of Saul'. While it does not claim to be a one hundred percent accurate history of the rise and fall of Saul, it attempts to suggest a plausible alternative account to that presented in the muddled and biased pro-David First Book of Samuel. Moreover, it includes some assertions, which could only be hinted at in the necessarily circumspect main text. These assertions merely represent the conviction of this author, and are based upon informed reasoning as much as scholarship. The reader is free to accept or dismiss them as she/he sees fit The citations reveal the sources and/or clues for each episode or event.

I

High Priests, Judges and Princes
The Theocracy

Thirty years before the battle of Aphek, Israel was judged by the high priest Eli, from Shiloh (the resting place of the Ark of the Covenant) – in the heart of Ephraim (1: 3). Eli was assisted by his two sons, Hophni and Phinehas, and his grandson Ahitub (14: 3). Ahitub was the son of Phinehas, and his own son, Ahia, was in his infancy.

At that time, the respected Ephraimite/Levite shaman, Samuel was employed by the Benjaminite elder Kish to anoint his thirteen-year-old son Saul as a tribal prince (9; 10). Two years later Saul married Ahinoam who bore him four sons, Jonathan, Ishboshet, Abinadab and Melchishua, and two daughters, Merab and Michal (14: 49-50). When Ahinoam could give him no more children, Saul took a concubine, named Rizpah, who bore him two further sons – Armoni and Mephiboshet (2 Sam. 21: 1-14). Saul's closest companion was his cousin Abner, son of Ner (Kish's brother) (14: 51).

Over the ensuing thirty years, Samuel became ever more revered. Eventually he decided to share the burden of his work with his two sons – Joel and Abijah. While he based himself in his home town of Ramah, in Benjamin (7: 17) he sent his sons to judge in the south of the country – in Judah and Simeon – and set them up in Beersheba (8: 1-2).

II

The Battle of Aphek
The Fall of the House of Eli

By this time, the Philistines had established themselves in five city-states along the south-western shore of Canaan. They formed a military confederation that began to encroach into western Judah and southern Israel (Jg. 3: 31; 15: 9). The lands which held the greatest appeal for them were the great fertile valleys of the Jezreel and the Jordan River. The central and northern tribes, who had only recently secured these valuable possessions from the indigenous Canaanite population (Jg. 4), gathered an army at Ebenezer, intending to push the Philistines into the Sea. The army of the Philistine confederacy confronted and held Israel at Aphek (4: 1-2), slaying some four thousand men.

In desperation, the commanders of the Israelite army sent for the Ark of the Covenant from Shiloh. It duly arrived at the Israelite camp, escorted by Hophni and Phinehas. When the men of Israel beheld the Ark in their midst they let out a great battle cry which temporarily unsettled the Philistines (4: 4).

Nevertheless, in the ensuing battle, Israel was heavily defeated, the sons of Eli were slain, and the Ark was captured (4: 10-11).

Amongst the Israelite survivors was a contingent of Benjaminites, led by their prince, Saul (now forty-three years old) and which included Abner and Jonathan (in his late twenties). Realizing that most of his senior commanders were either dead or had fled in panic, Saul sent a fellow clansman to Shiloh to deliver the news of the Ark's capture to Eli (4: 12).

On hearing of the death of his sons and the loss of the Ark, the aged high priest collapsed, broke his neck and died – he was ninety years of age (4: 18).

The Philistines followed up their great victory by overrunning most of Israel (8: 14) and destroying Shiloh (Jem. 7: 12-14; 26: 6-9). The Israelites were condemned to a life of serfdom prohibited by their new masters both from owning weapons and the manufacture of metal tools, and having to get their farm implements sharpened by Philistine smithies (13: 19-21).

III

The Resistance
The Partnership of Samuel and Saul

Taking with them the sacred Ephod, the surviving members of the House of Eli fled to Nob in northern Judah (21: 1). Eli's great grandson Ahia was made the new high priest of Israel (14: 3).

The charismatic Samuel, meanwhile, found himself as the de-facto leader of 'free Israel'. He set up his base in an unconquered enclave in the eastern lowlands of Benjamin, at the cult centre of Gilgal. There, he was joined by – amongst others – Saul and his clan, and together they raised the banner of resistance (10: 8; 13: 4/15).

Requiring a military leader, Samuel soon decided that Saul was an ideal choice for his general and anointed him 'captain' of Israel. In an attempt to imbue the new 'nagid' with even more authority, Samuel initiated him in the sacred prophetic rites (10: 1/10/26).

The war of liberation began with a successful guerrilla attack led by Jonathan, on the Philistine garrison at Geba (13: 3-4).

The Philistines retaliated by launching reprisal raids deep into Benjamin and Ephraim (13: 17-18), taking hostages as they went (14: 21) and establishing a fortified position at Michmash (13: 16/23).

IV
The Wrath of God
A Window of Opportunity

Seven months after the battle of Aphek, the Philistine city-states, together with adjoining parts of Israel and Judah were struck by a massive earthquake which toppled the great statue of Dagon in the temple of Ashdod. As bodies lay rotting under rubble many survivors of the original catastrophe succumbed to a lethal plague. Amid the ruins of the temple in Ashdod, the Ark of the Israelite God miraculously escaped damage, leading the Philistines to the conclusion that the disaster was His punishment upon them (5).

In an attempt to appease the wrath of God, the Philistines returned the Ark to Israel, where it was deposited into the care of the Benjamin/Levite clan of Abinadab of Kiryath-jearim (6: 7-21; 7: 1).

Meanwhile, with their motherland decimated, the Philistine garrisons within Israel suddenly found themselves isolated and vulnerable. By then, Samuel and Saul's 'army' had grown to six-hundred men (14: 2).

Seeing a window of opportunity, the captain of Israel mustered the troops at Gilgal, from where he planned to make a lightning strike against Gibeah (13: 15). Impatient to attack, Saul performed the pre-battle rites himself rather than wait for Samuel (13: 8-14).

The judge's ire notwithstanding, Saul duly liberated Gibeah and declared it his HQ (13: 16). He and Samuel had the Ark transferred to Gibeah from Kiryath-jearim (14: 18), at which point Ahia arrived from Nob (14: 3).

V
The Battle of Michmash
The Rise of Saul

Saul immediately prepared for an assault on the Philistine garrison at Michmash. Making the most of his limited numbers, Saul planned a pincer movement, whereby Jonathan would lead a diversionary attack on the enemy's rear, followed by a frontal assault against the Philistines – led by himself (14: 4-15/20-23).

Just prior to the battle Saul summoned Ahia with the Ark so that his men would be emboldened by the knowledge that God was once more in their midst (14: 18). However, Ahia, eager to re-establish his family's prestige, made it clear that he wanted to lead the Ark into combat. Saul, fearing a repeat of Aphek, and intent on cementing his own authority – with the backing of Samuel – refused the wishes of the high priest (14: 19).

The battle itself was a significant victory for Israel. The two-pronged attack caused the Philistines to panic and culminated in their total rout (14: 23). As chaos spread through the garrison, the Israelite hostages therein turned on their captors (14: 21). News of the slaughter travelled across the countryside of Benjamin and Ephraim like wildfire (13: 4) and thousands of Israelites emerged from their hiding places in the hills to join in the slaughter (14: 22). By the evening, the army of Saul, exhausted by its exertions, had succeeded in clearing the Philistines out from the central highlands of Israel (14: 23/31/46).

Following the battle, the elders and princes of Israel approached Samuel and asked him to anoint Saul as their king. Both the judge and his general opposed the request – the former, because of the threat posed to his own supremacy – and the succession of his sons – (8: 1-6), and the latter out of a sense of humility (10: 22).

During the following year, Saul formed an elite standing regiment comprising three thousand warriors – two thousand under his command, at Michmash, and one thousand under Jonathan based at Gibeah (13: 2). The organization and training of the levy of Israel was placed in the hands of Abner (14: 50).

Ahia, who had felt slighted by Saul before the battle, returned to Nob in a state of resentment and bitterness.

In the meantime, Samuel returned to Ramah, from where he continued to judge Israel (7: 17).

VI

The Battle of Mizpah
The Supremacy of Saul

The following spring, Saul was ready to finish the task he had started at Michmash.

The Philistines retained control over the Sharon and Jezreel plains, thus depriving the Israelites of good arable land and compromising communications between Saul and the northernmost tribes.

Saul and Abner believed that the army of Israel was now sufficiently armed, trained and confident to take on the still much weakened Philistine confederacy in open battle. So Samuel mustered the entire levy at Mizpah, to ritually prepare the army for combat (7: 5).

As soon as the serans of the Philistines heard that the Israelites were gathered for war they quickly amassed as large a force as they could, and putting their hopes in a pre-emptive strike, marched rapidly on Mizpah (7: 7). As the Philistine army approached, in full battle array, a freak storm erupted, transforming the terrain into a quagmire, totally incapacitating their chariots, and severely hampering their heavy infantry (7: 10).

Taking full advantage of the situation, Saul unleashed his more mobile, lightly armed Israelite troops upon the stricken Philistines. The ensuing battle was a consummate victory for Israel, with the main part of the enemy force being slaughtered where they stood. Those who could flee were chased all the way to Beth-car (7: 11).

The success at Mizpah reversed all the gains the Philistines had made nineteen months before. The Israelites were again masters of their heartland. In a graphic gesture of celebration, Samuel and his sons set up a victory stele at Ebenezer, the site of the Israelites previous defeat (7: 12-14).

However, on Samuel's return to the high place at Mizpah to conduct the victory rites, he and Saul were confronted by the elders and princes of Israel, repeating their demand that Saul be crowned their king (8: 19). This time Samuel and Saul reluctantly agreed (8: 21/22).

To confirm the primacy of God in the matter, Samuel conducted a symbolic ceremony of lots whereby Saul was revealed as being the chosen of the Lord (10: 20-21).

Thus it was, just a year after his anointing as captain, Saul was crowned at Mizpah, before the Ark of the Covenant, as Israel's first king – he was forty five years old (10: 24-25).

In spite of his overwhelming popularity, there remained amongst the powerful families of Ephraim and Manasseh, the priesthood, and indigenous Canaanites, those who resented Saul's coronation, and refused him tribute. Wishing to avoid internal strife so early in his reign, Saul decided to overlook these insults (10: 27).

VII
The Battle of Elah
The Army of All Israel

After his coronation, Saul made Gibeah his capital and designated the clan of Abinadab official guardians of the Ark (2 Sam. 6: 3-4). Ahia remained the nominal high priest and retained the sacred Ephod at Nob (14: 3).

During the following two years Saul conducted successful campaigns against the Moabites (14: 47) and made a peace treaty with the Canaanites who lived within the kingdom (7: 14).

Saul and Samuel both believed that unification of Israel and Judah was vital to the future security of the Israelites. Saul requested that Samuel and his sons should use their considerable influence within Judah and Simeon (16: 4) to convince the tribal elders and princes to join the new kingdom.

One of the first places Samuel visited during his diplomatic mission was Bethlehem where the highest ranking elder was Jesse, of the clan of Boaz. The venerable Judahite prince greeted the judge of Israel enthusiastically, and pledged his sons to the service of Saul. In return, Samuel anointed all eight of Jesse's sons as princes of Judah (16: 5-13).

Samuel completed a successful mission, establishing a military alliance between Judah and Israel. In spite of their battered condition, the Philistines reacted to this threatening development by occupying the Shephela – the corridor between the confederacy and Judah. Saul in turn, honoured his treaty obligations by blocking the Philistines at the valley of Elah (17: 1-2). Amongst his army were four of Jesse's sons, including David (17: 13/22). The ensuing battle was yet another resounding victory for the men of Israel, who together with their Judahite allies pushed the enemy all the way back to the coastal plain (17: 52).

The impressive performance of David in battle caught Saul's eye, who made the son of Jesse his royal armour-bearer (16: 19-21).

Although the Philistines continued a war of attrition (14: 52), their defeats at Mizpah and then Elah were so decisive, that it was a further decade before they were sufficiently recovered to launch another invasion into Israelite territory (7: 13).

VIII
The Battle of Jabesh
The United Kingdom

In the spring of the third year of Saul's reign over Israel, King Nahash of Ammon, in a challenge to the new Israelite alliance, launched a surprise incursion into Gilead (in northern Transjordan) and laid siege to the city of Jabesh (11: 1).

Nahash felt threatened by the burgeoning kingdom on his western frontier, and decided to call Saul's bluff by staking out his claim on Gilead. He gambled that Judah would fail to repay their debt to Israel, and that the Israelite king would regard a campaign across the Jordan as too risky an undertaking. It was in this spirit that he allowed the people of Jabesh to send to Saul for assistance (11: 3).

However, the King of Ammon had made a fatal misjudgement. The answer to Saul's call to arms was rapid and total. For the first time in Israelite history the entire levy of Israel and Judah mustered in one place – at Bezek – on the western shore of the River Jordan (11: 8). At first light, the following morning, Saul launched a three-pronged attack against Nahash with devastating results. Before the day was out, the army of All Israel had succeeded in repulsing the entire Ammonite force and liberating the people of Jabesh and the whole of Gilead (11: 11).

By popular demand, Saul – now in his forty-eigth year – was anointed by Samuel as King of All Israel at the subsequent victory celebrations held at Gilgal. In an act of clemency, Saul officially pardoned all those who had hitherto refused him tribute (11: 12-15).

The following spring, Saul led a successful campaign against Edom on Judah/Simeon's southern border (14: 47).

During the fifth year of Saul's reign over Israel and Judah, he undertook another victorious expedition – this time against Zobah – to secure the exposed north eastern fringe of the kingdom (14: 47).

IX
David at Gibeah
Seducer and Pretender

After David was promoted to the position of king's armour bearer, he revealed himself as an accomplished bard and musician (16: 19-21). Before long, Jonathan and Michal were seduced by David's charms (18: 1/20) and both came to adore him. However, for all the force of his personality, the son of Jesse possessed a weak character (17: 28) overly susceptible to their adulation.

Gradually, a desire grew in David's heart to become a member of the royal family. In time he came to believe that a future marriage to one of Saul's two daughters was his by right. When Saul married off Merab – the eldest of his two daughters – to the Manassehite prince Adriel (18: 19), David felt himself to have been slighted.

The resentment David felt at the loss of Merab caused him to undermine the loyalty of Jonathan towards his father (18: 3). Unaware of these developments, Saul remained impressed with David, coming to regard him as an ideal political match for his younger daughter, Michal (18: 20-21). However, David's subsequent betrothal to the princess merely increased his ambition. He spread the rumour of his kingly anointing at the hands of Samuel (16: 18) and gathered support among fellow Judahite hotheads within the royal guard (22: 6).

After a time Saul became aware of David's pretensions and seditious behaviour (18: 9), but was constrained from acting punitively out of fear of offending Judahite sensibilities. Moreover, he was also restrained by Jonathan's pleas on his friend's behalf (18: 13). The one course of action open to him was the breaking off of the betrothal between David and Michal (22: 54) and sending the Bethlehemite away from Gibeah (18: 13).

With the door to the royal family now firmly shut, an indignant David began to plan an outright Judahite rebellion against Saul. Putting his time away from Gibeah to good use, he established secret contacts with several enemies of Israel, including the Philistine seran of Gath, Achish (21: 10), the King of Moab (22: 3) and Nahash, King of Ammon (2 Sam. 10: 2). Furthermore, he conspired with the high priest, Ahia and set up an arms and supplies dump at Nob (21: 1-9).

About the time of the Nob conspiracy, Jonathan persuaded his father to allow David to return to Gibeah (19: 4-7). However, relations between Saul and David had deteriorated too far. Following a particularly violent altercation, David decided to slip away from Gibeah and put his plans for Judahite revolt in to effect (19: 11-12).

David made off for the cave of Adullam in Judah where he met with his clan. Using his considerable family wealth, the Bethlehemite prince soon amassed a mercenary band of some four hundred men, including the brothers Joab and Abishai, the sons of Zeruiah (22: 1-2).

Fearing for his family's safety, David then left Judah for Moab where the king – both out of filial considerations (Ruth. 18-22) and a shared loathing of Saul – granted him and his family asylum (22: 3-4). It was the fifth year of Saul's reign over All Israel.

X

The Failed Rebellion
The Fall of the House of Eli

During his time in Moab, David maintained constant communications with Achish of Gath and Ahia at Nob. After about a year in exile he felt the time had come for an attempt to prize Judah away from the grasp of Saul.

Following a discreet re-entry into Judah, he and his band made straight for Nob, where they received arms and supplies. Unbeknown to David and Ahia, their meeting was witnessed and overheard by Saul's chief herdsman Doeg, the Edomite – delivering cattle for sacrifice (21: 7).

Following a pre-arranged plan with Achish, David then marched on the Judahite town of Keilah, where he staged an apparent liberation from a Philistine raiding party. After chasing off the complicit 'enemy', David entered the town in triumph bearing gifts including cattle, 'captured' from the Philistines (23: 1-5).

Meanwhile, Doeg informed Saul about Ahia's meeting with David. Saul summoned the high priest and his family to Gibeah, and summarily executed eighty-five of them, including Ahia himself (22: 9-20).

Abiathar, the son of Ahia, escaped the massacre and, carrying the sacred Ephod, made straight for Keilah where he joined David (23: 6).

Nevertheless, the Keilahites remained loyal to King Saul and appealed to him for help. Saul responded immediately by marching to their rescue, leaving David no alternative but to abandon the town. To punish the Keilahites for their 'disloyalty' to himself, David liberated two hundred of their male slaves, whom he incorporated into his mini army (23: 7-13).

Having failed to spark off a Judahite rebellion, David retreated into the wilderness of Ziph to regroup (23: 14). When the Ziphites emulated the Keilahites and informed Saul of David's presence, the king set out in hot pursuit, and this time succeeded in encircling the renegade and his men. However, David managed to get a message to Achish, who then launched a raid into the Shephela, forcing Saul to withdraw. David retired deeper into the wilderness of southern Judah (23: 19-29) where he spent the next three years as an outlaw.

Saul married Michal to prince Phalti of Gallim, a rival Judahite prince to David (25: 44).

XI
Nabal and Abigail (cf. 1 Sam. 25)
Protection, Wife Stealing and Murder

Nabal was a wealthy livestock farmer based in Maon, in the Carmel region of southern Judah. Moreover, he was an important tribal prince of the house of Caleb, and therefore superior to David – a Boazite, and half Moabite – in the Judahite tribal pantheon.

In his efforts to win over Judah to his cause it was crucial for David to convince the likes of Nabal to turn away from Saul. Unfortunately for the Bethlehemite, Nabal, like many others, was staunchly loyal to the king. Thus, when David's brotherly overtures failed to impress the Calebite, he turned to coercion by offering to 'protect' Nabal's flocks, for the small price of meat and wool. Nabal rejected this in the strongest terms, reminding David of his treachery to his master, King Saul.

This was more than the self-proclaimed anointed of the Lord could tolerate. Leaving two hundred men behind to guard camp, he and the remaining four hundred armed themselves, and set out to take revenge on Nabal and his household.

However, on their march to Maon, they were intercepted by Nabal's beautiful wife Abigail, who pleaded for mercy on behalf of herself and her household. Smitten by Abigail's beauty, David struck a deal whereby he would refrain from harming her if she agreed to do away with her husband. Abigail agreed to David's terms and returned to her husband with the 'good news' that she had convinced the son of Jesse to leave them alone.

A relieved Nabal then held a celebratory feast during which Abigail poisoned him. When her husband eventually died, Abigail surrendered herself, her household and all her late husband's cattle to David.

When David and his men returned to camp with Abigail, her household and the livestock in tow, friction broke out between the two groups of men over the division of the booty (30: 21-25).

The removal of Nabal represented a significant victory for David in his struggle against Saul. At a stroke he had rid himself of one of the few Judahites whose influence was more than equal to his own, and by the possession of Abigail, her entourage and the livestock had gained stature, power and wealth.

However, the fact that David had achieved this by coercion still troubled him. He knew that ultimate control of his tribe could only come through gentler forms of persuasion.

XII

The Intermediary
Jonathan's Disgrace

Unable to tolerate the continued presence of an ever more powerful pretender within the borders of his kingdom – but wary of a potentially damaging civil war – Saul decided to broach a treaty with David. It was the eighth year of his reign over All Israel.

Saul sent Jonathan to Ziph to speak with David, to prepare the ground for a meeting between himself and the pretender. However, Jonathan went beyond his brief: in addition to arranging the future meeting he agreed to cede Judah to David upon the death of Saul (1 23: 16-18).

Jonathan returned to Gibeah in time for the new-moon banquet, where he related the details of his compact with David. Saul was enraged and hurled a spear into the wall behind David's empty place, next to that of Jonathan. The crown prince left the scene in disgrace (20: 30-34).

A few days later, as arranged, Saul met David in southern Judah under the flag of truce (24; 26). In return for an oath of non-belligerence on the part of Saul, David made obeisance to his king. Moreover, David in turn swore to refrain from attacking Saul's subjects and agreed to leave the kingdom (26: 19-20; 27: 8-12).

Thus, in the eighth year of Saul's reign over All Israel, David and all his people crossed the border of Judah into the territory of his friend and ally, Achish seran of Gath (27: 2).

XIII
Ziklag
David and – his ally – Goliath

The settlement of Ziklag, situated at the southern periphery of the land of the Philistines, and bordering the south-west of Judah/Simeon, was presented to David and his people by Achish seran of Gath (27: 6). In return, David provided his new master with copious amounts of booty extracted from savage raids deep into the northern Negev (27: 8-12). Moreover, he sent generous gifts of loot to all the princes of Judah to woo them away from Saul (30: 26-31), and likewise, lured many elite Israelite warriors to Ziklag with promises of riches (1 Chron. 12: 1-14).

After a short time, David's activities in the Negev began to threaten Amalekite control over the strategically vital region between Israel and Egypt. The Amalekites responded by launching reprisals against cities and towns in southern Judah/Simeon, including the plundering of an unguarded Ziklag (30: 1). Saul's hand was forced and, in the spring of his ninth year as king over All Israel, he mustered the army at Telaim in the northern Negev. However, because of David's success in seducing much of his tribe, only those Judahites directly affected by the Amalekite raids answered the call to arms, about a third of their total levy. Nevertheless, after a long and gruelling campaign, the Israelites were victorious, and at the subsequent victory celebration at Gilgal, Saul granted Samuel the honour of executing Agag, the captured King of Amalek (15: 1-33).

In spite of Saul's great victory, by the end of the following year most of Judah, lured by David's bribes, had seceded from the kingdom.

As David's influence grew, the rumour of his royal anointing at the hand of Samuel began to take hold in the minds of the men of Judah. Samuel realized that as he was the only witness to the falsity of that lie, his life was in serious danger. Thus, with Saul's co-operation he quietly slipped away from Ramah and surreptitiously travelled to the northernmost part of the kingdom, well beyond the reach of David and his agents. After a short time, a second rumour took hold in Judah and Israel that the old judge had passed away. His 'death' was deeply mourned by all the people (28: 3).

XIV

Ishboshet
The Second Royal anointed by Samuel

In the spring of Saul's tenth year as King of All Israel, the Philistine confederacy – now fully recovered from the earthquake and plague and taking full advantage of Israel's reduced military circumstances – mustered their combined armies – including David and his troops – at Aphek, as they had done thirteen years earlier (28: 1-2; 29: 10). They then marched into the Jezreel valley, where David and his men – now over a thousand in number – branched off into the hills to operate covertly against Israelite targets (29: 10).

Unwilling to confront the enemy advance on open ground, Saul gathered the levy of Israel (minus the men of Gilead [31: 11]) at the Harod spring near the town of Jezreel (29: 1). The Philistines camped at Shunem, on the opposite side of the valley. As soon as Saul spied the might of the Philistine army he realized that with his depleted forces he could not win a pitched battle (28: 4-5).

At nightfall on the eve of the hostilities, Saul, together with Abner and Ishboshet, disguised themselves, so as to hide their identities from Jonathan and his men. After making a covert exit from the camp of Israel, they rode around the Philistine position to En-dor. There, at the home of a local pagan priestess, they met with Samuel, who anointed Saul's youngest son as heir to the throne of Israel (28: 7-25).

On his return to camp, under cover of night, Saul sent the bulk of the army away under the command of Abner and Ishboshet, to regroup on the east bank of the Jordan (31: 7; 2 Sam. 2: 8). By daybreak, Saul had deployed two thousand men under Jonathan, Abinadab and Melchishua's command, to protect the rear of his retreating army. He positioned them half way up the north-west facing slope of Gilboa, while he and his three hundred strong force, waited on the uppermost ridge of the great hill.

XV

Gilboa
Saul's Death – David's Triumph

At first light the Philistines, in full battle array, advanced across the eastern end of the valley of Jezreel and up the slopes of Mount Gilboa towards Jonathan's position. The climb over the rocky and scrubby terrain hampered the advance of the heavily armed infantry. At fifty meters they met with a volley of Israelite arrows and stones, and at twenty meters Jonathan shouted the command to charge.

In tight formation, the Israelites hurtled themselves against the sluggish Philistine front lines. Despite their numerical inferiority, the Israelites – veterans of thirteen years of campaign and victory – briefly checked the progress of the Philistines, sending a shockwave throughout the column. However, the impact was short lived, and within minutes the overwhelming disparity in numbers began to count. Like a leaking dam, the Israelite line crumbled, gradually at first and then with a rush, as the Philistines poured through, over and around them. As Jonathan and his brothers attempted to retreat up the slope, they were overrun and outflanked by enemy soldiers and slain (31: 1-2; 1 Chron.10: 2).

Having learnt some time earlier from his scouts that Saul had mustered the Israelites at the Harod Brook, David decided to make his way to the rear of Saul's position. His original plan was to aid the Philistines by cutting off the retreat of the remnants of the main Israelite army after their inevitable routing. He had not foreseen however, the actions of Saul in withdrawing the main levy across the Jordan. But, once he had witnessed the deployment of the rearguard, David suddenly realized that a far greater 'prize' than defeated remnants were about to fall into his lap. Seeing that Saul and his bodyguards would undoubtedly follow hard on the heals of Abner's army, it was not difficult for David to guess the route the king would take and where best to set up a deadly ambush (2 Sam. 22:34; Pss. 18: 32-33).

Satisfied that the withdrawal of the main army had been accomplished, and unwilling to come to Jonathan's aid, Saul and his three hundred remaining troops beat a hasty retreat away from the tragic scene across the broad, wooded plateau of the Gilboa summit.

They had travelled only a short distance when they noticed movement in the pine trees and thickets that lined their path. An instant later they found themselves under a withering hail of arrows. The effect was devastating, leaving most of the men either dead or wounded. Those left standing had little time to react before a second and then a third wave of missiles laid them low. Those closest to Saul sought desperately and instinctively to shield him from harm, but he too was grievously wounded (31: 3; 2 Sam 1: 18; 1 Chron. 10: 3; Pss. 18: 14/38).

Working with urgency, David and his men finished off those who had survived the arrows. When they discovered Saul – terribly wounded – Abishai suggested that he should dispatch the king and David, granted him his wish (26: 8).

As soon as Saul was dead, David snatched the crown from Saul's head and pulled the royal bracelet from the dead king's arm (2 Sam. 1: 2-10).

Wary of being connected with Saul's death, David and his men then headed straight back for Ziklag (2 Sam. 1: 1).

The next morning the Philistines discovered the body of Saul and his sons. Although the royal crown had been looted, the king's corpse was still in full armour. They then stripped all the bodies and decapitated that of Saul, before nailing all four to the walls of the city of Bet-shean. The following day, in a daring raid, the men of Jabesh-Gilead recovered the royal remains and gave them an honourable funeral (31: 8-13).

Many years later, following his purge of the house of Saul, David re-interred the remains of Saul and Jonathan in the Kish family sepulchre at Zelah (2 Sam. 21). The ceremony culminated with the first rendition of the great lament (2 Sam. 1: 17-24).

Afterword

The accepted characterization of Saul is one of the great human portraits in all literature – factual or fictitious. Perhaps this is the reason that few have ever dared to challenge it. Whether seduced by the power of Saul's biblical portrayal, or from fear of damaging something precious, most of those scholars who have sensed problems with 1 Samuel's description of Israel's first king, continue to do little more than hint at their own misgivings.

Nevertheless, the author of this work – at the risk of being labelled a literary vandal – has dared to offer the world a more historical Saul: a Saul, no less, human; no less flawed; and certainly no less vulnerable than the biblical king. The main distinction between the man of 1 Samuel and the man of history lies – not so much in deeds and words, but in the interpretation we place upon those deeds and upon those words. This hypothesis has treated the biblical narrative in the same way a photographer handles a negative film. By taking the negative text, and dipping it in the solution of truth, we have seen a far more positive image of King Saul develop before our eyes. By stark contrast, we have also become aware of a far more negative historical David than we could ever have imagined.

However, this hypothesis notwithstanding, the strongest testament to the greatness of King Saul is that, despite all the damaging propaganda of 1 Samuel, he remains a much loved and pitied individual.

Pious Jews, Christians and secularists alike, instinctively sympathise with the son of Kish. It is as if we all know, deep down – that whatever his failings – Saul was dealt a bad hand. His treatment at the hands of Samuel, David and even God, as described in the Bible was grossly unfair and undeserved. And, it is this innate understanding that strikes against the very essence of our cultural and intellectual conditioning. Everything that is decent in the contemporary reader is instinctively drawn to the character of Saul. Whether he is grasping desperately at the cloak of Samuel at Gilgal, or standing alone – wounded, betrayed and surrounded by death – on the top of Mount Gilboa, we see a premonition of our own destiny – at the hands of both man 'and God'. Thus, we discover an empathy with Saul which is both painful and tangible, and it is perhaps there the real problem lies – for above all else, Saul was as vulnerable as any normal man.

It is possible that the attraction of David in contrast to Saul – to Jews in particular, faced with an almost daily struggle for survival – is his apparent invulnerability. While Saul seemed to represent a historical dead-end, the 'eternal House of David' offers the promise of hope. However, the shadow of the very human Saul remains, both attractive and troubling.

Thus it is hardly surprising that in the modern State of Israel, it is David and not Saul who is revered above all other biblical heroes. The concept of Zionism is inextricably linked with the fabulous personality who selected the Jebusite pagan high place to be the capital of his kingdom. Each and every city has a major road or square dedicated to his memory. Famous hotels and institutions bear the name of the son of Jesse. Patriotic songs, poems, and books sing his praises and extol his virtues. For pious men and women, he is a role model and an ideal whose deeds of courage and honour act as a guiding light and an eternal inspiration, and whose admitted barbarities are indulgently swept aside as understandable human frailties. Since the thirteenth century, the very emblem of Judaism itself, the six-pointed star, has borne David's name. Indeed, the fact that today I am a 'Jew,' and not a 'Benji' or an 'Ephra,' bears witness to a tribal self-belief and sense of destiny that are rooted in the myth of a pious shepherd who rose to become a lion-hearted king in spite of his persecutors.

Few greater challenges have ever been made to this received portrait of King David than that laid down in Baruch Halpern's book, *David's Secret Demons* – sub-titled: Messiah, Murderer, Traitor, King – (2001).

David's Secret Demons comprises 480-pages of masterful academic scrutiny, of (primarily) the second book of Samuel, in which the King David of history is extracted from the King David of myth as cleanly and as convincingly as a pea being squeezed from a pod. No objective reader could fail to be impressed by the cogency and persuasiveness of his gruesomely stark portrait of Israel's greatest king. Indeed he shows how, far from being the merely flawed, but intrinsically noble J.F.K. of his day, King David was closer to Genghis Khan – but with excellent PR.

Yet, where messiahs and iconic heroes are concerned, few of us are truly objective and thus, a book that should logically have shaken the Judeo-Christian world to its foundations merely succeeded in ruffling one or two pious feathers and raising a few scholastic eyebrows. Halpern's attempt to re-educate the world about King David was like parents trying to convince their children of the non-existence of Santa Claus. But, whereas a parent can rest assured that her/his child will eventually grow out of the need for Santa, Halpern could entertain no such certainty of eventual intellectual maturity with respect to the vast majority of pious Jews and Christians.

The lesson in all this is a depressing one, especially for the likes of me. For, if an illustrious, internationally respected scholar such as Baruch Halpern could barely cause a ripple upon the steely surface of received certitude how much less likely that a work by an obscure 'outsider' will make the slightest impression.

Perhaps my one hope lies in the fact that unlike David, Father Christmas or the Turin Shroud for that matter, Saul is not an iconographic image – he is merely a misunderstood and maligned character from history. Although, this book challenges the received picture of the young David in a way similar to Halpern's treatment of the older King David, its fundamental task – to restore King Saul to his rightful place in history – is advantaged by him being a sympathetic and accessible personality. Most readers, pious and secular alike, will have few reservations when it comes to granting Saul a 'fairer hearing' than he has thus far enjoyed.

It is probably a foolish and hubristic dream, but I dare to hope, that a fairer hearing for Saul may plant a seed in the universal consciousness of the Judeo-Christian world, whereby eventually, Israel's first king will take his rightful pre-eminent place in the pantheon of biblical heroes. And, in the process, pious and secular people alike will learn to see the historical David for who he really was. Where Baruch Halpern's 'front door' approach failed to shake pious resolve, perhaps this 'back door' attempt to put the record straight will succeed.

My second dream is that one day, when my first dream has come to pass and the planted seed has germinated, the Israelites and Judahites of today will put right a grievous three thousand year old wrong and give due honour to the memory of Saul. I believe that the day when modern Jews learn to revere the memory of Saul with equal reverence to that which we presently accord to David, is when finally, after two millennia of persecution and horror, we finally grow out of our belief in a Davidic Santa-Claus. It will mark the time when the Jewish people have truly grown up, when we understand that our old icons have served their purpose and reached their sell-by date.

So far as the Jews are concerned, the mythical David and all his symbols belong to an era when survival, within a mostly hostile Diaspora, was an ever-present concern. For previous generations, until very recently, faith, hope and aspiration, represented by iconic symbols and emblems were integral and therapeutic. For Jews, struggling to maintain their identity within an alien environment, the iconography of David and his golden city was the guiding light through the murk of dispersion – it was the super magnet that ensured that the millions of scattered filings would one day re-coalesce.

With the foundation of the modern State of Israel, the magnet had done its job, and suddenly everything had changed.

Although there was and is still daily death and horror, uncertainty and insecurity, Jews are at last in a position to defend themselves and forge their own destiny.

As the situation has changed, so should our icons and our aspirations.

The historical David was by any standards, an awful man, a "murderer, a tyrant, and a traitor". As for the demographic and geographical aspirations expressed by the mythical David, only the most intransigent and fanatical of his modern day followers believes or actually desires that they should or could be fulfilled. In other words, an ideal which acted as a guiding light to the Jews of the dispersion manifests as a blueprint for conquest and repression within the context of the modern State.

The historical Saul, by stark contrast, presents a picture of courageous pragmatism, which, for the most part, and to its eternal credit, modern Israel successfully demonstrates – even as I write these words – in its dealings with its troublesome and hostile neighbours.

My third and final dream reflects this aspiration and imagines a time in the future when the people of Israel sing songs, name magnificent hotels, main streets and town squares, and build monuments to the memory of Saul. It imagines the Shield of David replaced with a symbol of Saul (perhaps the double crown of Israel and Judah) between the two blue bands – symbols of the Mediterranean Sea and the River Jordan – upon the flag of Israel.

The seemingly inevitable loathing, intransigence and unreasonableness of her neighbours notwithstanding, the people of modern Israel could do worse in their search for inner national harmony than revoke their age old allegiance to the ideals of David and re-unite under the banner of Saul, founder, redeemer and first and only true King of All-Israel.

Appendix A
Who wrote Samuel?

The identity or identities of the original author(s) of the books of Samuel have long been the subject of scholarly speculation. Scribes mentioned within the text itself are obvious candidates, as are the possible later scribes who may have worked in the courts of all the Judahite kings (2 Sam. 8:17). David and Solomon themselves are often mooted as at least partial authors, as is one of their successors, the 'restorationalist' King Josiah.[1] There is a substantial body of opinion that sees in the antimonarchist words of Samuel at Mizpah a direct echo of sentiments expressed by several of the later prophets, especially Hosea.[2] This perceived influence upon the text is commonly referred to as the "Prophetic Source". Another candidate is the famous post-exile Judahite scribe, Ezra.[3] The only two points that all academics agree upon is that Samuel himself was not the author (he dies/disappears halfway through the narrative), and that, whatever the exact number of original writers, the final version is the work of more than one hand.

Many scholars observe two distinct prose styles woven throughout and talk of an early and a late 'tradition' and or 'strand', the former reflecting a finer literary standard than the latter.[4] The early tradition, they tell us, is sympathetic to Saul and may be derived in part from the lost Book of Jasher, itself a probable constituent of the original 'Deuteronomistic' group of writings that includes Joshua and Judges[5] – The Deuteronomist being the eponymous author of the fifth book of Moses, and, in the view of most modern scholarship, the "scroll of the law" [which may or may not be the same thing], which was "discovered" during the cleanup of the Temple ordered by King Josiah during his seventh century reformation (2 Kings. 22: 8), and whom it is further believed at least recorded and edited a host of hitherto oral sagas and remembrances. The late tradition, on the other hand, is antimonarchist and probably first emerged during the Elijah-to-Jeremiah era, 8-700 BCE. The books as a whole would have been edited long afterwards, either by Ezra or, later still, perhaps when the Hebrew Bible was translated into Greek as the Septuagint.[6] The final 'tinkering' can be dated to perhaps some eight hundred to a thousand years later (to the ninth century CE), when the Tanakh took its final Hebrew form, in the shape of the Massoretic text (from the Hebrew massorah – or 'tradition').[7]

This core theory and many others are all of great interest; however, the only thing of which we can be absolutely certain is that Judahite/ Judean/Jewish scribes put down the final form, either while living in their native land or in exile, looking back on past glories. Awareness of a philo-Davidic bias is a fundamental key to an objective reading of the 1 Samuel narrative.

Closely related to this Judahite bias, and with an equal influence on the finished text, is the common perspective of all the contributors to the Samuel books, that being pious fatalism. In other words, whatever happened was to serve the ultimate divine agenda. If the Kingdom of Judah went through a difficult time, it was a punishment from God; if things went well, it was a divine reward. This formula was used throughout the Bible, and resulted in some fine storytelling, especially for the pre-monarchy era. Any enemy of Israel who prevailed was an instrument of God. On the other hand, an enemy who suffered military defeat was revealed as an obstacle to the fulfilment of the will of God. Up until the time of Saul, for the most part (with the exception of some instances of intertribal strife), the agenda was clear: Israel versus the rest, and God over all.

Such pious presupposition is especially marked in the stories of certain exalted individuals such as Moses and Aaron. To explain their failure to enter the Promised Land following the desert wanderings, the biblical narrative ascribes to them single specific 'sins' that are remarkably similar to the 'sin' of Saul (2 Ex. 32: 1-35). In contrast, the story of David's youth and rise to pre-eminence was mythologized in order to vindicate his usurpation of the throne.

However, pious presupposition was not necessarily either righteous or consistent. For example, genuinely criminal, wanton, and heretical behaviour on the part of David and Solomon went seemingly unpunished, as they lived out their old age in indolent splendour.

The shaping of the narrative in accordance with pious presupposition did at least have one laudable result: it gave rise to some of the most indelible mythmaking in the Bible. The images of Moses looking longingly at Israel from the peak of Mount Pisgah, of Saul's confrontation with Samuel at Gilgal, and of David's admonishment by Nathan represent mythological literature at its most powerful and poignant.

Another confusing factor for scholars and readers of today is the style of biblical prose. It is important to remember that stories such as those related in Samuel were originally transmitted through the spoken word. To ensure that the listener remembered the plot and the all-important message, this 'oral tradition' made use of a clear and simple episodic structure. Long, factually accurate accounts of complex relationships could not have been assimilated. Furthermore, the average storyteller of ancient times lacked the literary tools with which to relate concurrent events. The expedient solution was to repackage history as a rigidly episodic tale.

Narrative 'Moods'
Any reasonably seasoned reader of the Tanakh can sense several distinct moods in the narrative of 1 Samuel. Whereas there seems little reason to argue with the accepted academic view that the book is the result of a grafting of at least two distinct traditions, I have dared to suggest the influence of two further authors. Thus, I propose a total of four moods detectable within the pages of the first book of Samuel. For the moment, let us call them A, B, C, and D.

Mood A is that of the glorious, miracle-working judge and prophet Samuel – general, kingmaker, rainmaker, and national saviour. It begins the entire story and weaves its way throughout the plot. This mood is aggressively antimonarchist, loaded with impassioned warnings against the concept of kingship. The roots of A are to be found in the era of the prophet Hosea (circa 740 BCE), when a series of 'corrupt' (in pious opinion at least) Judahite and Israelite kings and clerics provoked the rise of a pious fundamentalism.

However, it seems unlikely that these alleged sentiments of Samuel, in written form, would have got past contemporaneous royal censors. For A's first formal appearance on tablet or parchment, we must look for an interregnum when there was no king to be riled by such inflammatory sentiment. The first such era in post-Davidic Judahite history followed soon after the Babylonian exile, during the days of the Persian Empire, when the man in charge of Hebrew sentiment was Ezra the Scribe. Taking on the role of a latter-day Moses, Ezra's main task was to guide the physical and spiritual resettlement of his brethren within Judah and to raise the morale of a once proud people deprived of their king. A good method could have been to remind them through the words of past prophets how much better off the people were when they lived without a king. In addition, as Samuel was the very prophet who formally instituted the monarchy, who better to cast in the role of antiroyalist mouthpiece? Ezra may have drawn Samuel in both Hosea's and his own image, but with added value. To impart extra authority to the words of Samuel, special attention was drawn to his mythical reputation as a Moses-like miracle worker on intimate terms with God. Ezra would have been drawing on accepted tradition but giving that tradition a completely new purpose. His Samuel was not speaking to the elders and warriors of Israel assembled at Mizpah and Gilgal but to the people of Judah five hundred years later.

Thus, let us rename mood A 'Ezra/Prophetic'.

B is Saul's – monarchist – mood. It presents the new king as tall, handsome, and valiant; as the monarch who, with his knightly son Jonathan, began the liberation of Israel. It is the pre-David mood, in which Saul's achievements are fully recognized. The portrait it draws is of a modest, dutiful son who becomes a reluctant and merciful king. B reveals Saul as the Lord's anointed and Israel's messiah (meshiach). The Samuel of this mood is first and foremost a kingmaker. He appears as a local holy man unknown to Saul who willingly anoints the young Benjaminite when required by God to do so. There is affection between the two men, and even friendship. Mood B depicts a man who turned a defeated rabble into an organised and formidable army with the explicit encouragement and cooperation of the prophet Samuel. The Saul of these passages is a rational man whose devotion to God is tempered by the exigencies of the moment. The tensions between king and judge, while no doubt based on a modicum of historicity, are in truth more a result of the uneasy fusion of two contrasting moods. The end product, however, is a Samuel apparently split down the middle.

C is the David – monarchist – mood, attributable to him and/or his successors. It can be divided into two parts. The first presents us with a mighty man of valour and beauty who is also a talented musician. The second brings forth the boy hero – slayer of giants, bears, and lions – and the new anointed of the Lord. Both are universally adored, beloved of Samuel and of God. Once David appears on the scene, Saul is metamorphosed into a doomed, depressed paranoiac. Although the influence of mood C can be detected in the pre-David narrative, it is with the very introduction of David into the drama that Saul, too, becomes an awkward amalgam of two disparate personalities. The fact that three underlying traditions inhabit the text is evidenced by the bizarre permutations of identity undergone by Saul, David, and Samuel. A worthy Saul becomes unworthy in order to justify David's pretension to the throne. David is the dutiful servant of the Lord's anointed while at the same time regarding that title as his own. Samuel is more confusing and confused than anyone. He apparently risks his life by going behind the back of the king he created and loved, to anoint someone else to be king instead, while all the time abhorring the very idea of monarchy. Even God comes across as muddled, petulant, and fickle. One moment He commands Samuel to make Saul king. The next moment He expresses His feelings of rejection with displays of thunder and lightning. Finally, He admits that He was mistaken in His initial choice and opts for somebody else. What we have learned to revere as a mythic religious drama is, in truth, barely distinguishable from farce.

As if all this were not enough, there is the final mood, D – the colouration of the final editing. Exactly when that took place is difficult to say.[8] The window is a large one, somewhere between the fifth and second centuries BCE. D is the output of a person or persons working at a great distance in time from the events recorded. It is an attempt to harmonise all three of the aforementioned traditions into a cohesive whole. Whether or not these editors had access to texts long lost to us, their basic agenda was strongly influenced by the conflicting national moods of their post-Davidic era. Babylonian, Persian, Ptolemaic (Macedonian-Egyptian) and Seleucid (Macedonian-Syrian) rule had caused many Judahites to yearn for the past glories of David and Solomon. However, their subsequent experiences under the restored monarchy in both its Maccabean and Herodian incarnations had left the bulk of the population sceptical about the institution. This ambivalence is strongly felt in the extremely equivocal final edit. We are nonetheless indebted to this final, error-prone text, for without its assiduous inclusion of even the most suspect apocryphal material, we would not have before us the many awkward narrative juxtapositions that ultimately give the game away.

1 Samuel therefore emerges as a selective blend of four distinct strands formulated over the greater part of the first millennium BCE. Up to this point, the four moods have been described in the order in which they appear – A, Ezra/Prophetic; B, Saul/Monarchist; C, David/Monarchist; D, Final/Pious-Nostalgic. However, their chronological order must necessarily read: B, Saul; C, David; A, Ezra/Prophetic; and D, Final/Pious-Nostalgic. This sequence is another fundamental key to arriving at a more believable historical picture of the reign of King Saul.

Appendix B
Psalms of David?[9]

Whereas much of modern scholarship considers the linkage untrustworthy, pious people rarely question whether David actually composed the Psalms attributed to him. The truth probably lies somewhere in-between. While it is likely that a great deal of the poetry and prose was adapted or even copied from earlier traditional songs and praises,[10] and that much of the material has suffered from biblical re-editing, the partial authorship of David and/or his scribes remains plausible. After all, we are not dealing here with writings named for a person who could not possibly have been their author or sponsor, as could be argued, for example, of two-thirds of the books named after Samuel.

The word psalm derives from the Septuagint's ancient Greek psalmoi, meaning instrumental (probably string) music and its verbal accompaniment. The Hebrew word is Tehillim, or praises. The ascriptions, such as 'Psalm of David', and 'Psalm of Asaph', may date from the construction of the Septuagint and, presumably, are based on sources and references long lost to scholarship and thus impossible to challenge or verify. The existence in the Tanakh of far older songs, such as those of Miriam and Deborah, prove that David did not initiate the tradition of Hebrew song, and it is impossible to determine from what point in Israelite history music and song became associated with cultic ritual. Both Eli's rebuke to Hannah (1.Sam. 1:13-14) and her song (1 Sam. 2: 1-10) could be understood to imply that oral prayer, at least, was an extremely ancient Israelite practice.[11] From Solomon's time onward, the reciting and chanting of the psalms by choruses of Levites was an established Temple ritual.

Appendix C
Heterodoxy versus Orthodoxy

Pious opinion is generally suspicious of all critical analysis of sacred texts, especially when the reputation of a universal hero and icon such as David is at stake. For Jews, David is the greatest King of Israel and the founder of Zion. For Christians, he is, in an admittedly enigmatic way, the ancestor and spiritual harbinger of Jesus Christ. Both faiths look toward the seed of Jesse for messianic redemption. It is apostasy to find catastrophic fault with the Lion of Judah, the Lord's anointed, and the progenitor of all our messiahs past and yet to come.

Scholarship within this pious milieu can be broadly divided into two sub-groupings. The first are primarily 'theologians' for whom the theological message is paramount and the historicity merely incidental.[12] The second are primarily 'pious historians' for whom the theological content is a crucial element in 'understanding' the history. It is the unenviable task of these scholars to balance historic plausibility against the exigencies of faith, and to 'explain' the many textual, factual, chronological and ethical 'inconveniences' thrown up in the "sacred text".[13]

Although the secular academic establishment has no such problems, it tends to distrust anything that smacks of amateur sleuthing into its closely held preserve. Academic intolerance, while understandable, is just as stultifying, scholastically speaking, as the pious variety.

The average biblical historian and/or archaeologist views any major challenge to conventional theories – especially those pertaining to chronology – as pointless troublemaking, even when the challenge originates from within the academic circle itself. Brave indeed is the historian or archaeologist who dares stray profoundly from the straight path of academic convention.

Aside from academic orthodoxy concerning the text itself, there exists a 'permitted range' of theories on the actuality of the people and events described.

On one side are those whose vocation in life is to minimize as far as possible the historicity of the narrative. While acknowledging the beauty of the Tanakh and its cultural value, they regard most of the content as a quaint mythological aggrandizement of small local events that took place under – for the most part – indifferent eyes of far greater and more important neighbouring powers. Many within this group are united in the conviction that Samuel is of late editorship, thus diminishing its historicity in relation to their own, more recent, Christian texts.[14]

Opposed to them on the other side of this 'permitted range' are those theorists who, while agreeing with the broad drift of the argument, express some minor differences of opinion over detail. For example, in the context of this study, they place a tad more weight on David's regional importance and make great play of the few and minuscule contemporary non-biblical references to his reign. Whereas the former group tends to cite these tiny cross-references as proof of Israel's relative insignificance, the latter group argues that any such mention does at least prove Israel's importance, albeit minor. It is a typical glass-half-full/half-empty debate.[15]

So far as this study is concerned, the other distinct difference is that most academic opinion within the second school leans towards an earlier editorship for Samuel. In scholarly circles, the first group is sometimes referred to as 'minimalist' or 'rejectionist', while the opposition is dubbed 'maximalist'. The main preoccupation of the two groups may be more political than scholarly, the former seeking to minimize modern Jewry's claims on the Holy Land, the latter attempting to validate them.

However, on the main points, the two schools of thought are almost indistinguishable, insofar as they both believe that the Samuel books are a beautiful description of a quasi-historical sequence of events related to the founding of Hebrew nationhood and of incidental importance to the larger contemporaneous world. The narrative is probably the result of a blending of traditions, and would have been edited into its existing form during the mid to late first millennium BCE. The two schools would also more or less concur that Samuel himself was a parochial shaman, while Saul was a local warlord succeeded by David, Israel's first genuine king. Samuel's importance lay only in his being representative of the old theocracy and, as such, having authority to anoint captains and kings and ensure the important support of his religious community. Saul was a noble but essentially brutish man whose courageous attempt to forge a kingdom was doomed by his own ineptitude, while David was a charismatic, ruthless, and brave opportunist with an eye for the main chance.

The Chronology Heresy

For hundreds of years, Jewish historians working within the European Diaspora have produced many large and impressive tomes about the Tanakh. Whether out of expedient deference to their Christian host nations or because of the overwhelming dominance of Christian and/or secular academic convention, or merely from their own innate scholarly conservatism, their writings tended to be Jewish-flavoured restatements of the prevailing view. While inferences and conclusions may have been distinct, the fundamental reading was the same. Nobody made waves.

The veritable revolution that accompanied the great archaeological discoveries of the last two centuries was met by Jewish academics in a similar manner. The few works that dared to utter any trace of dissent were cloaked in apologetic obsequiousness. In effect, the study of Bible history from a Hebrew perspective remained tied to the general scholastic consensus.

Nevertheless, with the inception of the State of Israel, Jewish academics shook off their previous deferential attitude, and replaced it with a spirit of surging self-confidence. A new generation of Israeli archaeologists arose with unfettered access to the countless ancient sites that dotted their reborn nation. The world of ancient historical scholarship began to buzz with the names of Yigal Yadin, Ofer Bar-Yoseph, Ephraim Stern, and Ehud Netzer as they set about their maximalist quest within the soil of the Holy Land itself. Yet, despite their obvious Jewish predilections, these were scholars with their feet planted firmly on the ground that their gentile (and equally maximalist, though primarily *Christian*) forerunners, such as Flinders Petrie and Kathleen Kenyon, had opened up. Their energy and their bias notwithstanding, they were and remain creatures of the established convention.

Nevertheless, the new-found confidence meant that other, more radical voices also began to be heard. One of the most famous (or infamous, depending on one's viewpoint) challengers of conventionality was Immanuel Velikovsky.

The name of Immanuel Velikovsky, a Russian-born doctor of psychiatry, became synonymous with 'improper speculation' after he published *Worlds in Collision* (1950),[16] which presented a radical hypothesis linking many of the Bible's apparently supernatural events to an interplanetary catastrophe.

Braving a torrent of prejudice, hate and abuse from the scientific and historical establishment, he bravely (some might say stubbornly) stood his ground and eventually managed to get his work published.[17] His books inspired the first serious modern challenge to a number of academic holy cows, especially with regard to the synchronization of the chronologies of ancient Israel and Egypt. Velikovsky perceived that the conventional dating systems for the ancient Near East, based almost entirely on the anchorage of Egyptian chronology, were fundamentally flawed. He described how, by re-examining and realigning the time lines of all the Middle Eastern cultures of antiquity, one could bring them into harmony. For example, the Exodus, normally placed at the height of the all-powerful Nineteenth (Ramessid) Dynasty in Egypt, and thus condemned to the status of a minor event, is found at the end of the Middle Kingdom, when Egypt was in a state of collapse. Likewise, Solomon, who conventionally suffers the indignity of communicating with obscure kings of a declining Egypt, now instead finds himself entertaining the magnificent queen-pharaoh Hatshepsut of the Eighteenth Dynasty – and she in turn is revealed as none other than Sheba.

Most present day revisionists disagree with Velikovsky's most radical theories – such as the one quoted above – but nevertheless, emboldened by their master, they continue to make constructive and often inspired contributions to the debate of biblical chronology. In Britain, John Bimson, Peter James and David Rohl, to name but a few, have done much to challenge the conventions of our own age.[18]

Appendix D
Methodology

Unlike most historical research, including that into ancient Greece and Rome, the study of the books of Samuel cannot draw corroboration or refutation from a range of contemporary sources. The book of Chronicles, with an even more pro-Judah bias, skips over the details of 1 Samuel and does little more than copy 2 Samuel. Not until a thousand years later did the Jewish historian, Flavius Josephus (38-100 CE), concern himself with the events recounted in these books (Ant. V: 9 & 6; VI; VII). If there were ever any alternative contemporary traditions about Samuel, Saul, and David, they are long gone. The mysterious book of Jasher, mentioned at 2 Sam. 1: 18, had disappeared well before the time of Josephus.[19]

No doubt several factors put paid to the possibility of the survival of an authentic supportive or critical document. These may have included:

- A literary purge of perceived unfriendly material by the kings of Judah;
- The destruction and dispersion of the kingdom of Israel;
- The many lootings of Jerusalem, as well as other conflagrations such as the one that destroyed the great library of Alexandria in 640 CE.

In any case, attempting to establish ancient historical truths is a frustrating enterprise. It is difficult to move beyond a contest of versions – typically, one conventional and one revisionist. Because the science is so inexact and so often flawed by subjectivity, the received conventional certainties, for all their infectious confidence, are often nothing better than castles built on sand. Similarly, the methodologies of the revisionists are often contaminated with the lethal Axe-Grinder Virus.

Depending upon bias, the contemporary secular biblical commentator will state that Saul:

- (a) never existed;
- (b) was a small-time chieftain;
- (c) was an important warlord;

(d) was a minor king.

Only a few heretics dare to suggest that he:

(e) was a significant king who established Israel as a regional power. The mere fact that *King Saul* was written at all indicates this author's attitude with regard to the historicity and relative importance of King Saul.

Let us now return to the problem of the unsupported – *and* un-contradicted – source material.

While much is made of the differences (usually grammatical) between the earliest Hebrew, Aramaic and Greek bibles, it is their striking similarity that attests to the scarcity of any original source material other than what was actually included. As far as content and structure are concerned, they are all but identical. What is even more remarkable is that the Tanakh passages found in the Dead Sea Scrolls are equally faithful to the established biblical texts.[20] As for Josephus, with the tiny exception of one or two additional details, he merely retells the Bible story in a style palatable to his mostly Roman audience. The few other pre-Christian scriptural references are so scarce, and so brief, as to be almost useless to us. While the handful of biblical references to foreign rulers, and the scattered references to biblical characters on contemporary inscriptions, are of some value, their very rarity has made them more teasing than enlightening.[21]

The advent of carbon-14 testing and dendrochronological calibration (judging the age of wooden artefacts by the use of tree-ring analysis) means that the modern archaeologist can date most finds with extraordinary accuracy. However, if the revisionists are correct in their assertion that comparative chronologies of Israel and Egypt are out of synchrony, many of the lessons that have been drawn from archaeological discoveries may be seriously in error.

A good illustration of this hazard is Kathleen Kenyon's conclusion drawn from her renowned excavations of Jericho during the 1950s.[22]

The 'destruction layer' she discovered at Jericho failed to correspond to the date conventionally assigned to Joshua's entry into Canaan, thus she concluded that the story as recounted in the Bible was incorrect. She apparently failed to consider that the accepted dating could be erroneous, and that her 'destruction layer' could in fact be proof that the walls did indeed 'come a-tumbling down' at the hands of Joshua, albeit centuries earlier than is customarily thought.

In sharp contrast to Kenyon's Jericho excavations, which seemed to cast doubt on biblical events, there are a few discoveries that appear, at first glance, to do the opposite.[23]

Few objects in the field of biblical archaeology are given more credence than the famous Victory Stele of Merneptah, a large stone tablet on which a pharaoh boasts of the defeat of Israel (now housed in the Cairo Museum). Yet, nothing so clearly reveals the fragility of the standard methodology.

The excitement provoked by the discovery of the name of Israel on an Egyptian document from the thirteenth century BCE is understandable. It was the earliest extra-biblical reference to the People of the Book ever found. It seemed to prove that a community going by the name of Israel really did exist in Canaan as early as 1250 BCE (conventional dating). But wait a minute! According to most scholars, Merneptah was the pharaoh of the Exodus. What were Israelites doing settled in Canaan, when they were supposed to be tramping around the Sinai desert?

Naturally, theories were advanced to explain away the anomaly.

Some scholars proposed a series of settlements, suggesting that the Israelites had entered Canaan in waves of migration. Others recommended that the Exodus be re-dated to the time of an earlier pharaoh, which would imply that Israel had settled in the Promised Land by the time of Merneptah. There were (and are still are) commentators who proposed that the inscription was referring to a place – the Jezreel valley – and not a people – Israel – at all. A minority even theorized that the stele proved the entire Exodus tradition to be a mere fantasy.[24]

Eventually, those radical historians who dared to suggest that the reason for the anomaly was a misalignment in the chronologies of Egypt and the Bible showed that by making certain adjustments, particularly to the Egyptian records – for example, placing Merneptah three centuries later than hitherto believed – the two histories became corroborative. The only problem with their ideas was that they were *no more than* ideas; incontrovertible evidence that could justify a realignment of chronologies was not presented. In the final analysis, we are unlikely ever to know who, if anyone is correct, since the debate is between competing subjectivities. Aside from Merneptah's apparent brush with Israel, the stele tells us absolutely nothing about the history we would so like to understand.

For the period covered by this study, there is virtually no relevant extra-biblical material at all. In such cases, scholars shy away from detailed analysis of single episodes, preferring to stand back for an overview—rather as a cartographer designing a globe might concern himself primarily with oceans, continents, and countries. The end product omits all but the most prominent details.

An ironic and common consequence of this overview is that many of the most critical of biblical historians, when rearranging the grand picture of

Hebrew history, unquestioningly accept patent nonsense within individual episodes. While this might not matter in the case of a Samson, when such lack of discrimination is brought to Saul's story, the entire project may be fatally compromised.

Unless one accepts the 'new chronology' proposed by the likes of David Rohl there is virtually no extra-biblical evidence – either scriptural or archaeological – for the period covered by this study. While it would be tempting to 'use' Rohl's highly persuasive (not to mention corroborative) 'Amarna/Labaya' hypothesis to back up this study, this author felt that its introduction would be as much a distraction as a support of the 'core study'.

Fortunately, the hypothesis developed in these pages is not dependent on comparative chronology or archaeology. Whether King Saul was the first king of Israel; whether his reign lasted at least two and no more than forty years; whether his greatest foe was the Philistines; and whether he fell at Gilboa, to be eventually succeeded by David remain for the time being impossible to prove. Who the pharaohs of the day were is not an issue. The exact locations of the sites mentioned in the text are of academic interest only. Therefore, from the outset, the shackles of the standard methodology have been no impediment to our project.

Notes

Introduction

1. V.M. Berginer, 2000, *Neurological aspects of the David-Goliath battle: restriction in the giant's visual field, Israel Medical Association Journal.*
2. The site is unidentified, though it may be identical with Nob (cf. ch.7) according to O. Eissfeldt. 1943. 120-22 *Israelitisch-philistäische Grenzverschienbungen von David bis auf die Assyrerzeit. Zeitschrift des deutschen Palästina-Vereins 66:* 115-128. Reprinted. *Kleine Schriften* 2: 453-63.
3. According to S.G. Dempster (1992 in *ABD*, II, p.455), Jarre-oregim is the result of a "copying error" within the passage and it should read Jair – the 'oregim' ending pertaining in 2 Sam. 21:19 to "the shaft of his spear was like a *weaver's* beam".
4. See Baruch Halpern, 2001, *DSD*, pp.136, 137, 149, 275-76, and Simcha Brookes, 2005. *SATM.*
5. Arab: *Tell el-Husn*: mod Heb: *Tel Bet She'an.*
6. Anointing was employed for medicinal purposes, as part of the burial rites, for crowning kings and appointing priests – see M.D. Coogan and B.M. Metzger (co eds), 1993 *TOCB*. pp. 30-31
7. See Ex. 30:23-38 for the official recipe.
8. J.M. Allegro. *The Sacred Mushroom and the Cross.* 1970. p.56.
9. Herodotus. *Histories*: 6. 203-208.
10. The idea of a Josephic messiah became current following the failed 'Davidic' messiahship of Bar-Kochba during the first part of the second century (see A. Cohen, 1932, *Everyman's Talmud*, pp. 348-9 & n. 2) but had been conceived many generations earlier – see note 11 below.
11. Originally deduced from Gen. 49:10 – sometimes translated as, '*until Shiloh come*', i.e. when the sceptre passes from Judah back to Ephraim (i.e. Joseph). For further discussion see W. Ewing, 1909, In *Dictionary of the Bible, Shiloh,* 2 p.848.
12. See 1 QS. 9:1; cf. R. Feather, 1999. *The Copper Scroll Decoded.*
13. Ibid. pp. 217 / 237-238, and G. Vermez, 1962, *The Dead Sea Scrolls in English,* ch. 22, for a detailed description of the Essene Messianic tradition.

Chapter One

1. Conventional theory places the era of Israelite Exodus from Egypt until the judgeship of Samuel circa 1250-1050 BCE. However, the chronological information contained within 1.Kings.2:1, pushes the flight from Egypt back by another two centuries to around 1440. Similarly, most opinion maintains that the invasion of Canaan under Joshua – and the following period of settlement – occurred during the mid/late Nineteenth to mid/late Twentieth (Egyptian, Ramessid) Dynasties. However, different revisionists suggest various dates, ranging from an Exodus that coincided with the establishment of Hyksos rule in Egypt [see I. Velikovsky. 1952. *Ages in Chaos*, cf: ch. 2] (sixteenth century BCE) to a Samuel contemporary with the mid/late Eighteenth (Thutmossid/Amenhotep) Dynasty [D.M. Rohl. 1995. *ATOT*, cf: ch. 9].

   See K.A. Kitchen, 1992, In *ABD* II. pp. 700-708 – for a comprehensive overview of the Exodus.

2. See O. Eissfeldt, 1975, In *CAH* II, 2B, p. 568 – "From the beginning of the thirteenth century the Egyptian supremacy over Syria and Palestine that had been exercised continuously from the middle of the sixteenth century grew rapidly weaker and then finally ceased." Also see M. Noth. 1958. *THOI*, p.30 – "[E]vidence of Egyptian rule in Palestine . . . disappeared to all intents and purposes. Henceforward the country was left to its own fate".

3. Ibid: pp.17-24 & pp.101-104; also see T.L.J. Mafico.1992. In *ABD* III. pp.1104-06 – '*Judges and Judging*'; R.G. Boling. In Ibid. pp.1107-17 – '*The Book of Judges*' – for a thorough analysis of the subject.

4. A confederation of communities linked by a common cult usually worshiped at a central shrine – Shiloh, in the case of Israel (cf. note 23).

5. *A Sea People*: See *Amos*. 9:7; *Jem.* 47:4, which state that the original home of the Philistines was the island of 'Caphtor' – i.e. Crete. However, recent archaeological evidence seems to point towards Cyprus. In any event, it is generally accepted that the migration of the Philistines and various other 'sea peoples' was connected with the termination of the Cretan based Minoan civilization, possibly due to some natural cataclysmic event. See R.A.S. Macalister. 1965, *The Philistines, Their History and Civilization*, and T. Dothan and S. Gitin, 1990, *Ekron of the Philistines. BAR* 16/1: 20-25.

6. The peoples of ancient Israel – including the Philistines – were divided roughly into two demographic categories. The first were urban/agrarian, living in mostly lowland, walled towns and cities, such as Ekron and Bet-shean. Typically, the town would dominate the local agriculture and would offer security in times of war. The urban populations comprised traders, craftsmen and farmers. The second category was pastoral, based in small hill communities and homesteads, living mostly from herding. Within both sections of society, there existed the full gamut of classes, from wealthy land-owning freemen to bonded slaves. In the time of Saul, the vast majority of the Israelite population was made up of the pastoral category. Hence, many of the Israelite 'cities' alluded to in 1 Samuel were in fact merely villages and hamlets – sometimes tented – and have remained all but invisible to the archaeologists' trowel – see I. Finkelstein & N.A. Silberman, 2001 *TBU*. Ch. 4, for the latest archaeological thinking on the above.

7. Josh. 19:47-48 says merely that the southern coastal inheritance of Dan: "became

too little for them". However, Jg. 1: 34 states that Dan never succeeded in settling its maritime inheritance because of the hostility of the native "Amorites" (Canaanites), whereas the story of Samson (Jg. 13-16) has the Danites settled in the south, but in constant conflict with the Philistines.

8. 1 Sam. 4 can be read either as an Israelite attempt at expansion or a Philistine attempt at conquest.

9. According to Gen. 49: 5-7 the fate of the tribe of Simeon was to be dispersed throughout Israel. Certainly, most of the cities cited as Simeon's in Josh. 19: 1-9 are located in what effectively comprised southern Judah.

10. Arab: *Khirbet Seilun.*

11. The probable demographic composition of Gilead is discussed in chapter 3.

12. The name *Asher* is possibly the masculine equivalent of the Canaanite *Ashera* and/or *Ashteroth* and could represent evidence – together with the fact of the tribe's relative geographic remoteness from the national heartland – of Asher's non-Israelite origins [Noth. 1958. *THOI*, p.65 / footnote 2]. Moreover, both their patriarchal birth traditions (Gen 29/30) – making *Asher, Gad, Dan,* and *Naphtali* all sons of Leah and Rachel's handmaidens, Bilhah and Zilpah – and their peripheral geographical locations – to the extreme north and east of the Israelite heartland – all adds weight to the possibility of non-Israelite origins for these four tribes.

For the very latest in modern thinking on the development and evolution of the ancient Israelite nation see: I. Finkelstein and N.A. Silberman, 2001, *TBU*, Chapter 4. Finkelstein and Silberman present an Israel that evolved almost solely from within the indigenous Canaanite populations, as a series of urban/pastoral upheavals. According to this theory there was no bondage in Egypt, no Exodus and no violent invasion. Rather, the entire 'mythology' was a result of the puritanical revolution and retrospective piety of King Josiah and his scribes and was set down in writing during the seventh century BCE. This construction profoundly compromises all the biblical 'history' up to that time and reduces Saul, David and even Solomon to the roles of local highland chieftains. Moreover, it reveals Josiah, and not David to be the source personality for the Judeo-Christian messianic concept.

13. The *Philistines* constituted a distinct national entity until the Babylonian conquest in 612 BCE.

14. See I. Singer. 1992. In *ABD* V. pp.1059-61.

15. Modern scholarship contends that much of this supposed eleventh century demography belongs more properly to the eighth century BCE – especially in relation to Edom. Cf. I. Finkelstein & A. Silberman. 2001 *TBU*, p. 40.

16. See n. 12 above.

17. Many commentators regard the 'Joshua epic' as exclusively Josephic in character, representing a later Israelite migration into what had previously been Judahite territory, especially *vis-à-vis* Benjamin.

18. See M.D. Rehm and J.R. Spencer, 1992. In *ABD* IV pp. 297-311 for a full discussion of *Levites* and *Levitical cities.*

19. See C.L. Seow, 1992. In *ABD* I pp. 389: C.

20. It is interesting to note in this regard that within the patriarchal birth narrative, only Benjamin is born in the land of Canaan (Israel: Gen. 35: 16-19). Simcha Brooke's suggestion that "it is possible that the relative size of Benjamin has

been deliberately minimised in order to diminish its [regal] status" (2001, *SATM*, *p.91*), seems highly plausible.

21. In this context *Ephrathite* would seem to be describing Elkanah's tribal allegiance – i.e. to Ephraim.

22. See Num. 6:2 for a description of the vows of the Nazarite.

23. *Shrine* or more literally *sanctuary* (Heb. *hechal*), and possibly referring to the tabernacle – "tent of meeting" although according to O. Eissfeldt (1975. In *CAH*, II: 2B pp. 562/3) and others, the Shiloh *hechal* was probably a stone structure of relative grandeur.

24. R. Press doubts the reliability of the tradition linking Samuel with the Levitical priesthood at Shiloh, having more faith in the "earlier" narrative describing him as purely an [presumably] Ephraimite "seer" or prophet (1938. *ZFDAW*, Berlin).

25. Gk: *Antipatris* – Arab: *Ras el-'Ain* – mod Heb: *Tel Afeq*.

26. For example, S. Brookes states that "in the first of these references, Saul's tearing away of the hem of Samuel's robe represents the tearing away of Saul's kingdom. On the other hand, in the second reference it is David who tears away the kingship from Saul." 2005. *SATM*, p.74.

27. Ex. 25: 10-16: gives a detailed description of the Ark. Some scholars suggest that 'Ark of God' [*Yahweh*] is the oldest *style* and that 'Ark of the covenant' belongs to 'the Deuteronomist' (see Appendix A, p. 191 and n. 5) and thus, is more *recent*.

28. Also: *Ain Shems* and/or Ir-shemesh – Arab: *Tell er-Rumeileh* – mod Heb: *Tel Bet Shemesh*.

29. *Tell el-*Achar – close to the site of modern *Abu-Gosh*

30. *Amorites* is regarded as another general name for *Canaanites.*

31. *Beer-sheba* (mod Heb: *Beersheva*) – technically fell within the territory of Simeon.

32. It is implied in Jg. 9:2 that the concept of hereditary rule had taken seed well before the era of Samuel.

33. In both 2 Sam. 8:17 and 1 Chron. 6: Zadok's lineage is purported to be from Aaron, however, many scholars believe that he was actually connected to the pre-David Jerusalem of the Jebusites. They see a linkage with *Melchi-zedek* King of Shalem ' . . . priest of the most high God' mentioned in Gen. 14:18 and more crucially with the *definitely* Jebusite king of Jerusalem mentioned in Josh. 10: 1-3, *Adoni-zedek. Zadok* and zedek are identical in their meaning – i.e. 'righteousness'. Bearing in mind the scarcity of information regarding David's single-most important military conquest, it seems plausible to speculate that his acquiring of the "stronghold of Zion" (*2 Sam.* 5: 7) may have taken the form of some kind of pragmatic annexation, whereby the Jebusite elite – who anyway seem to have been more priests than kings – retained religious control over the holy shrine in the service of the Hebrew David – who was content remaining more king than priest. See D.G. Schiley. 1992. In *ABD* I. p.75.

34. This probability appears to be confirmed during the reign of David's successor, Solomon, who exiles Abiathar – the last of the Eli clan high priests – from Jerusalem, leaving [the Jerusalemite] Zadok as the sole high priest (*1 K.* 2: 26).

35. Many modern commentators resolve the apparent anomaly of this 'local holy

man' (i.e. 'seer') by suggesting that he was only associated with Samuel – the judge of Israel – by later redactors. See A.D.H. Mayes 1978. *The Rise of the Israelite Monarchy. ZFDAW*, Berlin pp.13-14, 17-18 (also see note 36 below).

36. This passage represents 'Samuel-as-seer' rather than the epic 'Samuel-as-prophet' of other passages (e.g. *1 Sam* 7: 7-15 and *1 Sam* 10) and has thus done much to convince the majority of modern commentators of a dichotomy in the narrative sources. See F. James 1939 *POT*, pp. 77-81 for a rational assessment of the problem.

37. See P. R. Ackroyd. 1993. In *TOCB*, pp. 674-677 – *The Books of Samuel* – for a thorough discussion of this argument.

38. Ibid.

Chapter Two

1. Arab: *Er-Ram.*

2. Several commentators doubt the reliability of Benjamin's purported diminutiveness at this time in Israel's history. S. Brooke's suggests that "the relative size of Benjamin has been deliberately minimised in order to diminish its status" by the pro-David redactor/s (2005. *Saul and the Monarchy*, p.91). Moreover, M. Gichon points out the likelihood that Benjamin was the de-facto front-line tribe "that suffered more directly than all the others [i.e. tribes], as it was plagued by the constant presence of a Philistine occupation force on its territory, Saul had the strongest motivation to raise the banner of freedom." (1997. *BOTB*, p.83).

3. *High place* – Heb: *bamah* or *bimah* – probably a stone platform topped off with an alter and/or a standing stone/s – perhaps in the form of a dolmen. These sites and other forms of 'sacred groves' were often holy to Israelite and indigenous Canaanite alike and were to become the targets of reactionary royal and prophetic displeasure following the centralisation of the Israelite cult upon that most famous 'high place' of all – Jerusalem. Paradoxically, modern Jews, bereft of their temple have been compelled to re-institute the plurality of the *bimah* in each and every synagogue throughout the world.

4. C.F. Kent suggests that these words "indicate that others in Israel were beginning to regard the young Benjaminite as a possible deliverer." (1910. *AHOTHP*, pp.117-8, vol. 1).

5. This is presumably referring to 'Ner' (1 Sam. 14:51).

6. 1 Sam. 9: 1, says that Kish was a *gibbôr hayil* (Heb) – a man 'of substance' (sometimes translated 'a mighty and valiant man'). Similarly, Ruth. 2:1 informs us that 'Boaz', a wealthy land owner from a high cast Judahite family, was the 'grandfather of Jesse' – and thus the great grandfather of David.

7. See C. Meyers. 1999. *TOHBW* (ed: M.D. Coogan), pp. 261-262.

8. See J.M. Allegro.1970. *The Sacred Mushroom and the Cross*, chapter 7.

9. See Chapter 6, p. 58-60 and note 24 for an alternative theory regarding the tradition of a 'staged' elevation from king-elect to full-blown monarch.

10. See W.R. Kotter and P.M. Arnold. 1992. In *ABD*, II, pp. 1022-24; IV, pp. 879-881; *Gilgal* and *Mizpah* articles respectively.

11. See ch. 4 p. 62 and endnote 7 for a discussion on the origins of the word *Hebrew*.

12. According to M. Noth "[t]he Deuteronomist Historian (see Appendix A p. 191: n. 1) supplemented the old tradition of Saul . . . by making Samuel win the decisive victory over the Philistines, thereby fundamentally misrepresenting the real historical background to the emergence of the monarchy." (1958. *THOI* p. 172, footnote 2). Furthermore, S. Brookes states that "[t]he story [of Samuel's military exploits] is highly generalised and probably a production of later prophetic revision" (2005. *SATM*, p. 84).Chapter two

Chapter Three

1. *Divine lots* – possibly the '*Urim* and/or *Thummim*', see 1 Sam. 28:6 (See ch. 7, note 14).
2. M. Noth states that in this form of election the man designated to be future king [i.e. *nagid*] had been proclaimed by a prophet in the name of [God]; when a man had thus been designated he could expect to ascend the throne at the next opportunity (1958. *THOI*, pp. 167-73).
3. See D.V. Edelman, 1992. In *ABD*, V, p. 990 for a concise discussion of the name *Saul*.
4. D.M. Rohl. 1995. *ATOT*, pp. 205-207.
5. In fact, some commentators do allude to the Mari texts to suggest that *David* was not originally his personal name but related in some way to the Akkadian word *dawidkm*, meaning commander or leader of soldiers (see M. Noth. 1958. *THOI*, note 2 p. 179). Furthermore B. Halpern postulates that not only is *David* not an Israelite name but that the *dwd* form is linked in some way to a Moabite ancestral cult (2001. *DSD*, pp. 266-270) – which would corroborate the information concerning David's ancestry contained in 4: 18-22 of the book of Ruth.
6. C. Meyers proposes that "the narrative of Saul's birth has apparently been appropriated for Samuel" (1999. *TOHBW*, p. 228)
7. Literally, before or within the Ark.
8. Probably modern *Tel el-Ful* ('Hill of Beans'). For a full discussion on the entire problem vis-à-vis the location and significance of "Gibeah of Saul" see S. Brookes. 2005. *SATM*, ch. 6. and F.W. Albright. 1924. *Excavations and Results at Tell el-Ful (Gibeah of Saul)*, Annual of the American Schools of Oriental Research; F.W. Albright., 1933. *A New Campaign of Excavation at Gibeah of Saul*, Bulletin of the American Schools of Oriental research.
9. This probably refers to those warriors who were fellow initiates of Saul into the sacred rites of 'prophesy'.
10. *Zelah* remains unidentified – the fact that Zelah was the site of Saul's family sepulchre implies that it was also his original hometown. Saul became associated with Gibeah after he had made it his royal capital, and would no doubt have been buried there too, but for his defeat at Gilboa. Similarly, Jerusalem became both 'the city (and burial site) of' the Bethlehemite, David. For hypotheses regarding the identity of Zelah see C.R. Conder. 1877. *Saul's Journey to Zuph. Palestine Exploration society – Quarterly Statement*, pp.37-40 and G. Dalman. 1930 *Jerusalem und sein Gelände. Schriften des Deautschen Palästina-Instituts 4. Gütersloh.*
11. Arab: *Tell el-Maqlub*.
12. Martin Noth asserts that this act was 'customary of the time' (1958. *THOI*, pp.

169) in stark contrast to F. James who describes the act as a spontaneous "form of liberating rage" (1939. *POT*, p. 98).

13. Modern '*Khirbet Ibziq*' (just west of the Jordan fords) – M. Gichon, suggests that the numbers presented in 1 Samuel are an accurate approximation of the military levy of All Israel – reflective of a total Israelite population of '750,000' people. He adds that 10% would have been a maximum 'substantial turnout' for a major war, i.e. twenty one thousand men. Moreover, Gichon proceeds to halve this number, out of 'conservatism', no doubt based upon his own appreciation of the situation vis-à-vis modern Israel (1997. *BOTB*, pp. 83-85). However, we might do better to compare the 30-50% figures from Samuel with those of other ancient peoples involved in total, national life-or-death war. Two examples come to mind:

1. At the Battle of Platea, [479 BCE] Sparta put its entire army – i.e. every Spartan man between the age of twenty and sixty – comprising around 5,000 men into the field, a figure well in excess of 10% of the total Spartan population, possibly somewhere between 20 and 30% (See Herodotus. IX: 30 and P. Connolly. 1977. *The Greek Armies*, pp. 28-9)

2. At the battle of Cannae [216 BCE], according to Livy, Rome confronted Hannibal's Carthaginians with an army numbering at least 50,000 (Polybius has 86,000) men. Bearing in mind that the census taken in 204 BCE (twelve years later) counted a total of 214,000 Roman citizens, this again indicates a turnout of somewhere between 20 and 30% of the Latin population (See Livy. XXIX: 37.).

Desperate times often call for extreme measures and thus, perhaps the two hundred thousand plus recorded for the armies of Saul, while being a gross exaggeration of the actual numbers, may at least reflect a disproportionate turnout vis-à-vis the general population. On the other hand, if the population assessments for mid – eleventh – century Israel as postulated by Finkelstein and Silberman in their 2001 book, *TBU* (pp. 130-45), are anywhere near correct, then Saul would have been pushed to raise a levy in excess of a thousand troops, let alone tens or hundreds of thousands.

14. The phrase *Belial* in the books of Samuel is commonly rendered "scoundrels" or simply reproduced in English form as I have done here. For a discussion on the various theories regarding the meaning of the word see D.W. Thomas, 1963. *bliyya'al in the Old Testament*, pp. 11-19 in *Biblical and Patristic Studies in Memory of R.P. Casey*.

15. See D.V. Edelman. 1984. *Saul's Rescue of Jabesh Gilead* (1 Sam. 11: 1-11) *Sorting Story from History*. *ZFDAW*, Berlin, 86: 195-209. Also see ch. 5, pp. 69-71 and n. 2 for further discussion of this problem.

16. Jg. 21: 8/9 suggests a long standing bond between the people of Benjamin and Gilead, which may go some way to explaining the strong empathy between Saul and the men of Jabesh.

17. Except for the fact that it was definitely a non-Israelite town, the archaeology at Bet-shean is inconclusive regarding who occupied the city during this period. The consensus – such as exists – points towards an indigenous Canaanite presence under a waning form of Egyptian governance. See P.E. McGovern. 1993. In *ABD*, I, p.695, & 2001. *AEHL*, pp. 84-5, and F. James. 1966 *The Iron Age at Beth Shan*, pp. 150-53.

18. *Baal* can also be translated as 'master' or 'lord'. However, it is most strongly associated with various Canaanite deities.

19. Commentators see 1 Chron. 8: 29-40 & 9: 33-44 as evidence of Saul's 'Gibeonite heritage, lending further weight to the probability of his syncretistic beliefs', Cf S. Brookes. 2005. *SATM*, p.174.

20. See M. Grant. 1996. *The History of Ancient Israel*, p76). According to I. Finkelstein and N.A. Silberman, the 'Israelites' of this period would have been virtually indistinguishable from their Canaanite neighbours, from whom they were still in the process of emerging, thus not only would Saul's religion have been to a large extent 'Canaanite', but so would his own ancestry (2001. *TBU*, pp. 97-122).

21. Possibly modern *Khirbet el-Metjer*.

22. See discussion and notes in Appendix A.

23. D.V. Edelman refers to this 'sequence' as a 'three-part kingship ritual, consisting of the designation of the candidate as *ngîd*, "king-elect", through anointing; his testing by performance of a military deed; and his subsequent conformation as king by coronation upon successful completion of the test.' (1992. In *ABD*, V, p. 990) – this of course presumes that Samuel intended or knew that Saul was to become king at the time of the first anointing.

24. Ibid.

25. While most commentators believe the formula to be merely corrupt, S. Brookes sees the verse as "expressing a joke on Saul's background." (2005. *SATM*, p. 51)

26. Those interested in this subject should read E. Thiele. 1965. *The Mysterious Numbers of the Hebrew Kings.*

27. E.g. *The New English Bible OT*, pp.376 and footnote.

28. E. Robertson. 1944. *Samuel and Saul, Bulletin of the John Rylands Library 28/1*, pp. 175.

29. See ch. 7 note. 6.

30. D.V. Edelman gives Saul a twenty-five year reign (1992. In *ABD*, V, pp. 992-3), basing her assertion around the 'corrupted' two in the regnal formula being a 'misprint' of twenty-two. She then goes on to arrive at a final figure "upwards of 25 years".

31. Some commentators regard 'forty' as being far too high. See D.V. Edelman 1992. *ABD*, II, p. 615.

32. See F. James. 1939. *POT*, p. 97.

Chapter Four

1. Josephus (*Ant.* 6.1:1) gives a particularly graphic description of an awful disease.

2. The description of the Philistine idol of Dagon falling prostrate before the Ark is probably an apocryphal echo of a catastrophic event, indicative perhaps of an earthquake – which would typically be followed by a highly contagious epidemic ('plague') of cholera or worse.

3. The general failure of modern biblical commentators to make this link between the 'ophlim disaster' and the Israelite resurgence under Saul is a puzzling one. It may stem from the obviously misplaced military campaign of Samuel – which

most commentators regard as either fanciful or to have been appropriated by the redactor from the career of Saul (see pp. 86-88) – or being wedged between the disaster and the rise of Saul, and/or an academic reluctance to give credence to a passage which on the surface seems so fantastical.

4. Also: *Michmas* or *Machmas* – Arab: *Mukhmas*.

5. Possibly *Gibeah / Gibeath-elohim* – Arab: *Jeba*.

6. LXX reads *ephod* here – not Ark: see ch. 7, p. 156 and note. 7.

7. Those interested in investigating the subject further should refer to N.P. Lemche. 1992. In *ABD*, III, p. 95 and his accompanying bibliography and S. Brookes. 2005 *Saul and the Monarchy*, pp118-20. For an interesting revisionist perspective see P. van der Veen. 1989. *The el-Amarna Habiru and the Early Monarchy in Israel, Journal of the Ancient Chronology Forum* 3, pp 72-78.

8. Akkadian: *Ayaluna* – Arab: *Yalo*.

9. *Altar* – Heb: *mizbeach*. Possibly a sacred victory stone or stele (1 Sam: 14.35).

10. See 1989. *TAOTB*, p. 74, and J.M. Miller. 1974. *Saul's Rise to Power: Some Observations Concerning 1 Sam 9: 1-10: 16; 10: 26-11: 15 and 13: 2-14: 46. Catholic Biblical Quarterly*, 36: 157-74.

11. Baruch Halpern maintains that the Ark remained in Kiryath-jearim for the entire length of Saul's reign. Moreover, he suggests that K.J. was a Gibeonite town and that the Ark was a non-Israelite artefact, in which Saul had little, if any interest (2001. *DSD*, p.153). This hypothesis would seem to be consistent with Saul's ostentatious rejection of the Ark before the battle of Michmash.

12. See D.M. Gunn. 1993. In *TOCB*, p. 680 and G. W. Wade. 1928. *OTH*, pp. 221-22. By contrast H. Tadmor asserts that the conflict between Saul and Samuel was due to a culture clash between the new royal 'tyranny' and the old 'traditional leadership' (1976. *AHOTJP*, p. 92), whereas S. Brookes suggests that "Samuel and Saul were not involved with each other". Their 'relationship' was created in "later prophetic circles whose main objective was to support prophetic authority over the king". (2005. *SATM*, p. 173)

13. See M. Noth. 1981. *The Deutenronomistic History*, p. 55 (and see Appendix A p. 324 n. 5).

14. The iron weaponry of the *Philistines* was harder and thus deadlier than the bronze of the *Hebrews* – see M. Gichon. 1978. *BOTB*, pp. 81; 82.

15. Unidentified – though possibly *'Ain Karim'* or *Beth-Horon*.

16. The choice of *Eben-ezer* for the site of the victory stele was highly symbolic, and confirmed the new Israelite supremacy over the Philistines within the central hill country. Eben-ezer literally means 'the stone of the helper', and is possibly identical with Aphek on the southern Plain of Sharon. The possibility that the stone was erected in or very close to Aphek, and became the new name of that place in the minds of the victorious Israelites, may have resulted in the confusion over the identifying of ostensibly *two distinct* places. However, recent archaeology seems to underpin the theory that we are in fact dealing with one place with two names. See M. Kochavi and A. Demsky. 1978. *An Israelite Village from the Days of the Judges, Biblical Archaeologist Review*, 4/3: 19-21. However, another school of thought sees the two *Aphek/Ebenezer* battles as a sort of theological symbolic 'good and evil' mirror image rather than historic events.

17. Saul's 'humility' became a motif in pious Jewish thought – e.g. see the *Haggadic* quotation heading chapter 10.
18. It is one of the few consistent textual features of 1 Samuel, that Judah's presence or absence at any particular gathering is always clearly stated.
19. See J.M. Miller. 1974. *Saul's Rise to Power: Some Observations Concerning 1 Sam* 9: 1-10: 16; 10: 26-11: 15 and 13: 2-14: 46. *CBQ*, 36: 157-74.

Chapter Five

1. Probably identical with Nahash: 2 Sam.10: 2 & 1 Chron.19.1 – making him the father of Shobi.
2. Although there are a minority of scholars who support this position (see n. 6 below), the vast majority never even consider it, and of those who do, most go on to reject it out of hand. Even a more radical commentator such as Simcha Brooks asserts "that the Ammon war is correctly placed" and also that "the Philistines were not the principle enemy at this point" and "only became hostile because of Saul's emergence as a rising threat". (2005. *SATM*, pp. 100-4). A seemingly rational position which however, opens up an entirely original can of chronological worms. For example, where does the Philistine prohibition on Israelite iron production fit into this scenario – before or after the Ammonite war? If before, how did Saul emerge victorious as a weaponless and 'army-less' chieftain? If afterwards, Saul would have had to suffer some unmentioned catastrophic defeat at the hands of the Philistines between the Ammonite war, and his presumed re-emergence at Michmash – a possibility for which there is absolutely no textual evidence!
3. E.g. see C.F. Kent.1910. *AHOTHP*, p.118: G.W. Wade.1928. *OTH*, p.215: G.G. Yates. 1965 *A Guide to the Old Testament*, p.110: O. Eissfeldt. 1975. *CAH*, II 2: B, p. 570 and M. Gichon. 1997. *BOTB*, pp. 83/84.
4. See J. Baldwin 1988. *TOTC 1 and 2 Samuel*, p. 81. In this context, it is possible that the Saul was bound by treaty to go to the relief of Jabesh – assuming that the town was not part of his kingdom (see D.V. Edelman. 1984. *Saul's Rescue of Jabesh-Gilead* (1 Sam. 11: 1-11) *Sorting Story from History. ZFDAW*, Berlin).
5. See H. Tadmor. 1997. *AHOTJP*, pp. 92-94 for a description of the Israelite military structure at the time of Saul.
6. J.M. Miller suggests that it was the victory at Michmash – his "first battle" – which led to Saul being made king over the central hill country (1974. *Saul's Rise to Power: Some Observations Concerning 1 Sam. 9: 1-10:16; 10:26-11 and 13:2-14:46. CBQ 36: 157-74*) D.V. Edelman, on the other hand, claims that the battle of Jabesh "almost certainly would have had to take place after Saul had become an established king. . . . " (1992. *ABD*, V, p. 993).
7. For a plausible maximalist view of the military achievements of Saul and the scope of his influence see M. Gichon. 1997. *BOTB*, p.92; and O. Eissfeldt, who sees "no reason to consider" the victories of Saul as "paltry" (1975. *CAH*, II: 2B, p574). In contrast, according to the minimalist hypothesis – gaining favour rapidly today – typified by such scholars as Israel I. Finkelstein and N.A. Silberman, even David and Solomon – let alone Saul – were minor hill-top tribal chieftains, in command of a few hundred men, at best (2001 *TBU*, p. 190).
8. Jos, *Ant.* 6:7.3 states that Saul's conquest of Amalek extended south-west as far

as *Pelusium of Egypt* at the *NW* tip of the Sinai peninsular on the Mediterranean coast.

9. Akkadian; *Supite*: Arab; *Suba*? Mod; *Tel Zova*.

10. K.D. Schunk states "that clans forming the tribe of Benjamin may have originated outside the land of Canaan" (1992. In *ABD*, I p. 671 B: 1). See also J.B. Pritchard. 1955. *Ancient Near Eastern Texts Relating to the OT*.

11. Ex.18:13-15 and Jg.4:5 give vivid descriptions of the 'laid back' style of Israelite government under the regime of the Judges, from Moses onwards. F. James, in his affectionate biography of Israel's first king imagines Saul living "in Gibeah, apparently in real simplicity" (1939. *POT*, p.101) and H. Tadmor states that "Saul emerged as a military leader, on the pattern of the leaders in the period of the Judges" (1976. In A*HOTJP*, p.92). In contrast J. Miller regards the rule of Saul as a "challenge to the permanent-judge model" (1974. In *A History of Ancient Israel and Judah*. pp.124-49).

12. Ibid – J. Miller, who sees Saul as a "self-proclaimed protector/ruler. However, according to F. James "As the people gave their loyalty to Saul, so he gave himself to them." (1939 *POT*, p.115).

13. See B.S.J. Isserlin. 1998. *TI*, p. 68; and M. Grant. 1996. *THOAI*, p. 75.

14. Some commentators regard the marriages of his two daughters (1 Sam. 18:19; 2 Sam. 21:8) as possible additional evidence that Saul 'sealed political alliances' with strategically important neighbours (D.V. Edelman. 1992. In *ABD*, V, p. 998).

15. E.g. M. Noth. 1958. *THOI*, pp. 78-79.

16. See B. Halpern. 2001 *DSD*, p. 156.

17. David Rohl casts Saul as the Habiru leader and Amarna correspondent with mid Eighteenth-Dynasty Pharaoh – Amenhotep III, known as *Labayu* or *Labaya* (1995. *ATOT*, ch. 9). Immanuel Velikovsky on the other hand, places Saul as the un-named ally ('*the one*') of the Egyptian general Ahmose, servant and general to Eighteenth Dynasty Pharaoh Kamose, in their war against the Amu-Hyksos, or Amalekites (1952. *AIC*, ch. 2).

18. Some commentators suggest that the marriage of Saul's eldest daughter Merab to *Adriel ben Barzillai the Meholathite* (1 Sam. 18: 19; 2 Sam. 21: 8) was by way of forming diplomatic relations with Jezreel based Canaanites, rather than fellow high ranking Josephites (see D.V. Edelman, 1992. In *ABD*, V, D: 5, p. 998 and also ch. 6 pp. 88-89 and n. 14).

19. 1958. *THOI*, pp. 175-6.

20. 1939. *POT*, p. 102.

21. Modern: *Telalim* (in the north-central Negev).

22. E.g. the famous image of Ramesses II (1279-1212 BCE) in the Cairo museum, grasping the hair of three prisoners (one African and two Asiatic) just prior to despatching them with his battleaxe, is a commonly repeated motif in ancient Egyptian 'battle art'.

23. While many commentators agree, that two rejections are duplications or doublets of a single "event" and that they indicate 'parallel traditions' few theories are postulated as to *why* this apparent editorial error occurred, except to suggest – bearing in mind the numerous other examples of repetition in the Samuel texts – that it might be a sort of literary form intended to stress crucial ideas and events. In this case it might simply represent a double affirmation of David's

right to take over the kingdom from Saul (W. Brueggemann. 1992. In *ABD*, V,
D: 4, p. 972).

24. Archaeological finds throughout modern Israel confirm that animal sacrifice was
widely practised in ancient Israel and Judah at the time of Samuel and well into
the following millennium; e.g. the Israelite temple in Arad (northern Negev – i.e.
southern Judah) complete with alter, dating from tenth-century BCE and similar
finds dating from the period of the United Monarchy, at Megiddo (Building 338;
Shrine 2081), Lachish, Taanach (Stratum IIB), Bet-Shean, Tell Qasile (Temple
118) and Tel Amal (Stratum III). (2001. *AEHL*, pp. 43, 498).

25. R. Press agrees with this conclusion and believes that the two stories as related
in 1 Samuel are [pro-David] revisions intended to mask traditions which were
originally pro-Saul attempts at explaining his failure to establish a dynasty and
reworked to justify David's usurpation (1938. *Der Prophet Samuel, ZAW*, 56, p.
209/10). Meanwhile, opposing this hypothesis are those who see these verses as
betraying the hand of a 'prophetic redactor' attempting to stress the authority of
God [i.e. the prophet] over that of the king (e.g. B.C. Birch. 1976. *The Rise of the
Israelite Monarchy: The Growth and Development of 1 Samuel 7-15*, Society of
Biblical Literature Dissertation Series, p.74-85 and A.D.H. Mayes. 1978. *The Rise
of the Israelite Monarchy. ZFDAW*, 90, p. 330).

Chapter Six

1. *'Oil'* – Heb: *shemen* (from which the English word 'semen' is derived)
– alternative meanings include: 'fertile', 'fecund', 'rich-oil', 'rich-liquid' and
'rich-oil-of-fertility'.

2. O. Eissfeldt. 1975. In *CAH*, II 2: B, p. 573.

3. With regard to Saul's tensions with the clergy, even a philo-Davidic historian
such as H. Tadmor felt compelled to state that "young David shrewdly exploited
these differences and derived maximum benefit from them." (1976. In *AHOTJP*,
p. 93). Also see note 22 below.

4. 1 Sam. 16:18

5. It is interesting to note here that some pro-Saul commentators see Samuel in
an unflattering light – out to preserve his own power at all costs, by playing
Saul against David and visa versa. This is a seductive theory and in many ways
seemingly consistent with the biblical narrative (See L. Eslinger. 1985. *Kingship
of God in Crisis: A Close Reading of 1 Samuel 1-12*. Bible and Literature.10;
D.M. Gunn. 1980. *The Fate of King Saul. JSOT,* Supplement 14.and R. Polzin.
1989. *Samuel and the Deuteronomist*).

6. B. Halpern sees the anointing story of David by Samuel as a "supersession of
Saul's dynastic claim on the throne of Israel" and regards Samuel (amongst
others) as a crucial figure for "confirm[ing] David's authority against the House
of Saul." (2001. *David and Saul – DSD*: 16, pp. 368).

7. The valley of Elah lies about ten miles west of Jerusalem, and its capture by Saul
would have secured the south-easterly borders of his kingdom. He would have
achieved control over the important road from the north Judahite hill country,
across the valleys of Sorek and Elah itself, down into the Philistine plain (See
H.J. Stoebe. 1956. *Die Goliathperikope 1 Sam 27-28: 5 und die Textform der
Septuaginta. VTS*, 6 pp. 397-413).

8. In a display of particularly imaginative – not to say admirable – pious intellectual athleticism – J. Baldwin explains David's visit to Jerusalem as a sort of precocious stratagem, whereby he is reminding the Jebusites of Israel's dominance. However, even she is forced to admit to finding the episode "surprising" (1988. *TOTC 1&2 Sam*, p. 128).

9. B. Halpern makes some interesting – if slightly tongue-in-cheek – observations regarding David's victory over Goliath, illustrating the huge advantage in mobility a light infantryman – i.e. David – would have had over a sluggish heavy infantryman – i.e. Goliath – in single combat (2001. *The Surprising David – DSD*, pp. 8-13).

10. In common with most commentators, F. James regards the first account of David's recruitment into Saul's army (1 Sam. 16:14-23) as stemming from an earlier tradition and as the more historically reliable and says that, because of its contradictions and inconsistencies, "the Goliath story is by far the more improbable" (1939. *POT*, p. 121).

11. M. Grant says that Saul "had to be belittled as a prelude and contrast to the glory of David" (1996. *THOAI*, p. 75).

12. *Wickedness* (1 Sam. 17:28) is normally mistranslated as *naughtiness*! The Hebrew *rah always* means *wicked* or *evil* in a biblical context.

13. See J. Baldwin. 1988. *TOTC* 1&2 Sam, p. 127.

14. B. Halpern suggests that the entire story of David's time at the court of Saul is a fabrication intended to prove his affiliation with the king and his royal family, and thus further legitimise his usurpation of the throne. In addition, he believes that the David's betrothal to Michal is the only genuine linkage to the court of Saul, and even that only dates from after Saul's death during the reign of Ishboshet (2001. *In Saul's Court – DSD*, pp. 284).

15. *Meholath* – possibly *Mehola* in Manasseh. *Gallim* – thought to be south of Jerusalem, and thus within Judah. This scenario is consistent with the concept of Saul attempting to bond the kingdom by marrying his Benjaminite offspring into the princely clans of Joseph and of Judah, although other commentators see these marriages in much broader strategic terms. See chapter 5, note 14.

16. E.g. H. Tadmor – see note 3 above.

17. *Naioth* – unidentified, though possibly some form of sacred site or building within or near Ramah (J.M. Hamilton. 1992. In *ABD*, IV, p. 1001).

18. F. James believes that this passage "can hardly be depended on for facts." (1939. *POT*, p. 92), as does G.W. Wade who is struck by the apparent counterintuitivness of David's fleeing northwards, away from his homeland of Judah and deeper into Saul's territory (1928.) *OTH* p. 228).

19. See for example J. Levenson. 1978. *1 Samuel as Literature and History. CBQ*, 40, pp. 11-28; However, most commentators disagree with this hypothesis because, they say, in this era, possession of the royal harem was regarded as proof of royal legitimacy in and of itself (e.g. D.V. Edelman. 1992. In *ABD*, I, p. 118). This line of thought fails to consider both the implausibility of such a close textual juxtapositioning of two Ahinoams and, the obvious possibility that David may have actually kidnapped Ahinoam and made her a hostage – another common tactic in eleventh-century diplomacy. Such a scenario would further explain Saul's apparent tentativeness in his pursuit of David. Nathan's remarks in 2 Sam. 12: 8 may then suggest that David only added Ahinoam to his harem

following Saul's death, when he felt safe from Saul's vengeance.

20. Ibid.

21. B. Halpern does not consider Nathan's remark corroborates the hypothesis presented here, but sees it merely as part of a late attempt at a Davidic apologia intended to highlight David's propriety with regard to Saul's possessions. Moreover, he says that the David only acquired Saul's wives after the death of Ishboshet.

22. Whatever one's opinions regarding the historicity of the account of David's time as a courtier of Saul it is crucial always to bear in mind that the structuring of the plot is a device intended to explain the inexplicable – i.e. the legitimisation of David's "anointing" vis-à-vis the indisputable anointing of Saul. Thus the odd and erratic behaviour of all the key players can be seen as merely a hostage to the structural imperative (see D. Jobling. 1978. *Jonathan: A Structural Study in 1 Samuel*. pp. 4-25 in *The Sense of Biblical Narrative. JSOT*. Supplement. 7).

23. S. Brookes for one, thinks that "Saul's attitude towards David, as recorded in 1 Samuel, was a reasonable response to David's manipulative and devious behaviour." (2005. *SATM*, p. 72).

24. Mark Twain did, in effect write such a book, in allegorical form at least, with his 1889 novel, *A Yankee in King Arthur's Court*.

25. See note 21 above.

26. Ibid.

27. D.V. Edelman doubts that Jonathan played any significant military role in Saul's early campaigns against the Philistines, believing him to have been too young – i.e. under the legal fighting age of twenty (according to Num. 26: 2, 4) – at this stage (1992. In *ABD*, V. 4, p. 994). However, bearing in mind the exigencies of the period, that Jonathan was a crown prince from a military family possibly in his late teens as early as the battle of Aphek, and the probability that the military draft regulations set out in Numbers is almost certainly a pre-supposition from a much later age, there is no reason to doubt the fact that he was a fine – albeit very young – soldier.

28. B. Halpern. 1981. *The Constitution of the Monarchy in Israel*. 25, pp. 125-48 and D.V. Edelman. 1984. *Saul's Rescue of Jabesh-Gilead* (1 Sam. 11: 1-11): *Sorting Story from History. ZFDAW*, 96: pp. 197-99).

Chapter Seven

1. *Nob* – remains unidentified, although *Râs el-Mešârif* on Mount Scopus, overlooking Jerusalem, has been proposed (W.F. Albright. 1295. *The Assyrian March on Jerusalem. Annual of the American Schools of Oriental Research*, 4:139).

2. *Achish* – which is not considered to be a Semitic word – might be the same name or title as the seemingly long-lived *Ikausu* Philistine king of Ekron mentioned in Assyrian annals dating to around 681 – 629 BCE (1969. *Ancient Near Eastern Texts relating to the OT*, 2nd edition with supplements [ed. J.B. Pritchard, Princeton], p. 291) and has also been linked with *Agchioses*, a king from Asia Minor mentioned by Homer in the Iliad (2: 819).

3. Mod: *Horbat 'Adullam*; Arab: *Esh-Sheikh Madhkur*.

4. Unidentified, though, because of its close proximity to subsequent action at

Keilah (mod: *Khirbet Qîl*) some commentators have proposed modern *Kharas* (1962. *Interpreters Dictionary of the Bible*, [ed. G.A. Buttrick] p. 583 and P.K. McCarter Jr. 1980. *1 Samuel, AB*, p. 357).

5. If B. Halpern's highly plausible hypothesis, that David never spent time at the court of Saul is correct, then, in a sense, his genuine history starts here, with his emergence as a leader of a band of desperados – debtors, escaped bondsmen, disaffected Judahites and foreign freebooters. A contrast with the traditional image, of the harp playing, lion-slaying shepherd boy, and slayer of giants!

6. Commentators are split over this issue. Whether one believes that *Ahimelech* and *Ahia* (or *Ahijah*) are brothers (see P.K. McCarter Jr. 1980. *1 Samuel, AB*, p. 239 and K.W. Whitelam. 1992. In *ABD*, I, 1 p. 111), or the same man with different names (see J. Taylor. 1909. In *DOTB*, p. 18), often depends on how one interprets the information that they had the same father (1 Sam. 14: 3; 22: 9), and that there is no explanation given for the disappearance of the former. However, the most compelling evidence for them/him being one and the same individual lies in the timing of the name change. From the moment the priest (Ahia) meets David – and in effect becomes his ally – his name acquires the kingly appellation. Surely the hand of the grateful, pro-David redactor is at work bestowing a posthumous honour upon a loyal subject.

7. F. James sees a more prosaic explanation for Saul's behaviour, suggesting that the ritual was simply interrupted by the goings on in the Michmash pass following Jonathan's surprise sortie (1939. *POT*, p. 103).

8. Ibid.

9. In contrast, S. Brookes, amongst others, feels that "David deliberately tricked the priest [Ahimelech] into helping him" by concealing "the fact that he is a fugitive" and, "he lies by saying that Saul had him sent on a mission." (2005. *SATM*, pp. 64-65). Also see G.W. Wade. 1928. *OTH*, p. 229, n. 2.

10. See O. Eissfeldt. 1975. In *CAH*. II: 2B, p. 575.

11. According to S. Brookes, the Nob episode was "possibly the work of a later redactor. Since the incident is not recorded anywhere else in the Bible, not even in Chronicles. . . . " (2005. *SATM*, p.174).

12. Ibid: "It is unlikely that Saul evicted or killed them [the Gibeonites], not only because such an atrocity would have contradicted the image of Saul in 1 Sam. 15: 9 . . . but also because of his own genealogical links with the Gibeonites . . . " (pp. 50-51). Alternatively, as Baruch Halpern suggests, the Gibeonites, like all of David's allies during his rebellion against Saul were, in some way connected to the Philistines and Ammonites, and thus, a legitimate military target of the Israelite king (2001. *DSD*, p. 391).

13. See note 4 above.

14. *Ephod*: possibly derived from the Akkadian 'Epattu' (See P. Stern. In *TOCB*, p. 189). The Ephod is usually taken to be an elaborate priestly vestment. In the case of the high priest, and thus presumably Abiathar, it included the breastplate containing the 'urim and thummim' – the lots of divination (Ex.28: 30). However, in the story of Gideon, (Jg.8: 27) we read of an Ephod that took the form of a 'graven image', that is, some form of idol.

15. *Show kindness to* – alternatively translated as "have faith with . . . "

16. B. Halpern attests that "David allied with Nahash . . . [and] linked hands with just the non-Israelite elements whom Saul attacked." (2001. *DSD*, p. 325)

17. Modern *Tel-Ziph*, south-east *of* Hebron.

18. R. Kittel believes the accounts of Jonathan's pledges to David to be based on the possibility of his having been so disturbed by his father's decline, that he planned for a "regency with David as his right-hand man"; or some form of power-sharing agreement, whereby he and David became kings of their respective territories (1929, *Great Men and Movements in Israel*, pp. 125-6). In stark contrast, B. Halpern regards the entire story as "invented or inferred, not recollected", to legitimise David's usurpation of Saul and Jonathan (2001 *DSD*, p. 283). D. Edelman takes the scholarly middle ground, preferring not to dispute the friendship itself while doubting the reliability of the pledges (1992. In *ABD*, III, p. 946).

19. The Hebrew states *hichlimo* – meaning literally 'he [i.e. Saul] shamed him [i.e. Jonanthan]'; and /or 'he reproached him'.

20. See note 18 above.

21. S. Brookes states that "[t]he extent of the loyalty of the Judahites [to Saul] is clearly expressed by the people of Maon, Carmel and Zyph." (2005, *SATM*, p. 109). Other commentators have also made similar assessments include F. James. 1939. *POT*, p. 101; *H.* Tadmor. 1977. In *AHOTJP*, p. 95 and 1989, *TAOTB*, p. 75.

22. Even a philo-Davidic commentator like F. James seems to be aware of David's gangster traits – on a subconscious level at least – when accusing the wealthy Judahite landowner Nabal of "churlishness" for "insolently refusing David's request for protection money" (1939, *POT*, p. 123) – a particularly graphic example of the way piety can blind even the most erudite of scholars and contaminate objectivity.

23. See L.F. DeVries. 1992. In *ABD*, IV, p. 14. In contrast, G.W. Wade suggests the possibility that the people of Keilah were simply wary of suffering the same fate as the community of Nob (1928. *OTH*, p. 230). However, he also chooses to ignore the 'inconvenient' intervening piece of narrative regarding David's journeys to Gath and Moab – thus creating a graphic – but false – close juxtapositioning of the two events.

24. O. Eissfeldt (1975. In *CAH*. II: 2B, p. 578) hints at this probability, suggesting that David's ambition dates from his time at the court of Saul. Also see J.W. Flanagan. 1992. In *ABD*, V, 3: B, p. 963, who refers to David at this point as the "losing contender for succession" who then "withdraws to a remote and marginal region . . ."

25. Arab: *Khirbet el-Kirmil*.

26. E.g. see note 22 above. Amongst those scholars with a more critical view, Baruch Halpern is especially unequivocal regarding David's "protection racket" and regards Nabal's death of "natural causes" to be particularly "convenient" (2001. *DSD*, pp. 284 & 77).

27. S. Brookes – amongst others – agrees that the doublet represents "versions of the same story". She then goes on to suggest a highly original possibility, that "[t]hey could also represent events that took place near Gilboa before the battle . . . the main concern of the narrative [being] again to demonstrate David's innocence with regard to Saul's death". In other words, Brookes places the events at Gilboa, where Saul, with his dying breath, pleads with David to spare his family (2005. *SATM*, pp. 76-8).

28. In this context it is interesting to compare the language of 1 Sam.24: 14 & 26:20 with that of the Amarna correspondence contained within EA: 252.
29. See G.W. Wade (1928. *OTH*, p. 232), who also believes that on contextual grounds, the second version to be a record of the actual event.

Chapter Eight

1. See B. Halpern – 2001, *DSD*, pp. 302-6 "David's Philistine Pedigree" – for a compelling thesis which more than corroborates this position.
2. Possibly modern *Tell el-Khuweilfeh* near ancient Lachish. The huge strategic significance of Ziklag's position – controlling as it would one of the main caravan routes between Egypt and Asia – indicates the value Achish set by his Judahite protégé.
3. F. James, together with most other commentators, accepts the biblical account at face value and ponders for "[h]ow long David could have continued to throw dust in the eyes of Achish" (1939. *POT*, p.124), while never considering for a moment that the Seran of Gath knew and approved of the policy himself, and that the 1 Samuel redactor is merely covering up this uncomfortable truth. Indeed, Ziklag's remote southern position (see note 2 above) was perfectly chosen for just such a policy.
4. See F. James. 1939, *POT*, p.124; M. Noth. 1958. *THOI*, pp. 181-3.
5. E.g. see, *TAOTB*, pp.72 & 73; also see ch. 1, note. 21.
6. Ibid.
7. The conventional take is that Saul was attempting to strengthen his economic ties in the region, i.e. south Negev (see e.g. D. V. Edelman. 1992, in *ABD*, V, D: 4, p. 994).
8. Some commentators believe that the Amalekites whom Saul fought were located in an enclave adjacent to central Ephraim, well north of their traditional Negev haunts. They base this assertion primarily on the apparent remoteness of the southern Amalekites from Saul's main sphere of influence – i.e. the Benjamin and Ephraim central hill country – and certain biblical references regarding the southern Jezreel Valley (Ex. 17; Jg. 5: 14; 6: 3-7: 20; 12:15; 2 and 2 Sam. 1: 2-2: 26). This construction also fits in well with the idea that the Philistines mustering in Jezreel was immediately subsequent and reactive to an incursion by Saul, but inconsistent with the picture of a king who ruled All Israel, at least from Beersheba to Gilboa. See P.G. Van der Veen and U. Zerbst. 2002, *Biblische Archaologie am Scheideweg*.
9. Armies in the ancient world generally began campaigns in the spring or early summer when the climate and the terrain were most suitable for warfare, and the agricultural burden at its least demanding – see M. Noth. 1958. *THOI*, p. 177; D.V. Edelman, who employs the 'one campaign per year' rule as a guide to the minimum length of Saul's reign (1992, In *ABD*, V, D: 2, p. 993) and M. Gichon. 1997, *BOTB*, p. 111)
10. Jos. 6:7 states " . . . *from Shur to Havila* . . . " – Literally, Northern Sinai to SW Arabia! I. Velikovsky suggests that Havila be identified with the Egyptian-Hyksos headquarters of Avaris on the north-eastern Nile delta (*AIC, pp*. 95-99).
11. Also Ex.2 & 3 has Jethro as a 'Midianite'.
12. See note 9 above.

13   Some commentators believe that Saul was the aggressor here, eager to capture
     the strategically important town of Bet-Shean, win control of the Jezreel Valley,
     and secure stronger links with the northernmost Galilean Israelite tribes (cf:
     T. Koizumi. 1976. *On the Battle of Gilboa. Annual of the Japanese Biblical
     Institute*, 2:61-78). However, in light of the information contained within 2 Sam.
     2: 9 and the apparent range of Saul's previous military campaigns, their seems
     little reason to challenge the inference of the narrative (1 Sam. 28: 1-7; 29: 1;
     31: 1) that it was a massed Philistine incursion which started things off (cf: M.
     Gichon. 1997. *BOTB*, p. 93). While the recent discovery of Philistine style bio-
     chrome pottery in Bet-shean merely suggests a Philistine influence, or presence
     amongst the populace, it in no way negates the possibility that the town was at
     this time, and throughout the previous decade, under Saul's control. The pottery
     might just as easily represent evidence of plunder from Saul's victories over the
     Philistines, then given to the Bet-shean Canaanites to secure their loyalty – much
     in the same way that David divvied out spoil from his adventures to the people
     of Judah (see ch. 3, note 17).
14. Even a pious commentator such as F. James senses that something is not quite
     right here, when he suggests that the record of Samuel's death "is late" (and
     thus presumably unreliable) and that it "may idealise the respect paid to him."
     (1939, *POT*, p. 92).
15. H. Tadmor regards the linkage between Samuel and David to be historically
     questionable, especially in the light of the exclusion of Saul's family (1977. In
     AHOTJP, p. 92).
16. See B. Halpern. 2001, *DSD*, ch. 4 – *King David, Serial Killer*, to get a sense
     of why a powerful rival, such as Samuel may well have been, would have had
     good reason to avoid the attention of David at all costs.
17. Arab: *Solem*.
18. Possibly Arab: *Khirbet Safafeh* – mod: *Horbat Zazafot* (see note 21 below).
19. See ch. 3, note 20.
20. The subject of En-dor is perhaps the most polarising, scholastically speaking,
     contained within the story of King Saul. While the episode's strong spiritual and
     supernatural significance is irresistible for commentators of a pious persuasion
     it is barely mentioned, and often entirely ignored by critical commentators, who
     probably regard it as a complete invention of a late prophetic and/or pro-David
     redactor. Those amongst the latter grouping who do devote considerable time
     and effort to identifying and contextualising the material elements of the story
     (see notes 23 and 24 below) – e.g. the location of En-dor, her cultic background,
     Saul's journey to and from the camp of Israel etc. – presumably believe that
     Saul did in fact attempt to receive the word of the dead Samuel in the same way
     we know how the commanders of ancient Greeks and Roman armies generally
     consulted oracles and soothsayers before embarking upon campaign. How far
     any scholar believes Saul and the lady medium succeeded in this endeavour,
     depends entirely upon that scholar's view of spiritualism and the like. However,
     if the assertion of this study is correct, that Samuel was alive and kicking at
     the time of Gilboa, then there is no requirement for supernatural occurrences,
     successful or otherwise.
21. According to D.V. Edelman, it is equally possible that the location of En-dor
     could have been on Saul's side of the valley (1992. In *ABD*, II, p. 500).

22. Ibid and also e.g. see C.F. Kent. 1910. *AHOTHP*, pp. 131-2; G.W. Wade. 1928. *OTH*, p. 235.

23. Numerous other commentators have used the exact same adjective to describe the 1 Sam. 30 account of David's whereabouts during the Battle of Gilboa. Foremost amongst these are D. V. Edelman who writes "David's Amalekite battle provides him with an alibi" (1992. In *ABD*, V, D: 4 p. 995), while B. Halpern refers to the episode as "David's alibi for Saul's death" (2001. *DSD*, p. 79) and S. Brookes, states that the Ziklag episode "was fabricated to create an alibi for David at the time of the battle (2005. *SATM*, p.73).

24. E.g. see J. Baldwin. 1988. *TOTC, 1 and 2 Samuel*, p. 164: "David's Providential Rejection from the Philistine Army".

25. E.g. see M. Noth. 1958. *THOI*, pp. 180-1.

26. For further discussion on the whole issue of David's role at Gilboa see B. Halpern. 2001. *DSD*: cf pp. 78-81: "Saul and His Sons at Gilboa".

27. Ibid – Halpern suggests that these "defections" actually occurred before the battle when David was at Aphek.

Chapter Nine

1   See the previous chapter, note 13 for alternative suggestions for the background of the conflict and note 5 below.

2. Trans-Jordan Philistine "type" finds have been made only at *Tell Deir' Alla* – biblical *Succoth of Manasseh* (see A. Malamat, 1977. In *AHOTJP*, p. 86: "The Struggle Against the Philistines").

3. Arab: *Tell es-Sa'idiyeh*.

4. Cf M. Noth. 1958, *THOI*, p. 177.

5. M. Gichon points out that a section of Saul's army might have been consigned to shadow and observe the movements of Philistines along the coastal plain, from Aphek and then through the Carmel defiles into the Jezreel Valley (1997. *BOTB*, pp. 93-4). With this in mind, it is probable that Saul, wary of an incursion into the western approaches of the central hill country, would have felt compelled to detach a sizeable number of troops for the purpose of guarding against such an eventuality. This would have perhaps resulted in an even more depleted army at Gilboa.

6. There exist almost as many 'takes' on the entire battle of Gilboa episode, its cause and its course, and Saul's motivations and actions before and during the combat as there are commentators. M. Noth for example – in an uncharacteristic moment of biblical literalism – (1958, *THOI*, pp. 177-8) takes the view that the battle occurred in the second of Saul's 'two-year' reign, and was a direct Philistine "counter-attack" to their defeats at his hands the previous year. Saul's resistance at Gilboa, moreover, was knowingly suicidal and forced upon him by his failure to consolidate his power during the interim. D.V. Edelman, however, takes the opposite view (1992, in *ABD*, V, D:4, pp. 995-6), believing Saul to have gone on the offensive – against a Philistine/Canaanite alliance – in an attempt to secure the Bet-shean trade corridor to the Jezreel Valley. M. Gichon meanwhile (1997. *BOTB*, pp. 93-4), agrees with Edelman regarding the nature of Saul's enemy, but concurs with Noth, in regarding the Philistines and their allies as the initiators of the conflict. Ultimately, the way in which any given scholar assess

the Gilboa episode, depends upon their perception of the battle's context. The context of this hypothesis is a militarily weakened and overstretched King Saul, a rejuvenated and territorially ambitious Philistine confederacy, a dormant Judah (at best) and a power hungry and tenacious David. Which all points towards a Philistine aggression against a desperate King Saul.

7. For a graphic visual overview of the theatre of action at Gilboa, see the *TAOTB*, pp. 74-75.

8. Some commentators, presumably because of the mention of Philistine chariotry (often ox-drawn carts), prefer to place the battle on the plain itself, at the foot of the Gilboa range – see e.g. D.V. Edelman, 1992, in *ABD*, V, D: 4, pp. 995. However, as some expert military scholars have pointed out, the gentle western slope of the mountain would have been "easily traversable" for the Philistine forces (cf M. Gichon, 1997, *BOTB*. Pp. 93-4).

9. For two contrasting yet conventional readings of the battle see M. Gichon for an authoritative technical description – 1997, *BOTB*, pp. 93-4 and F. James, for an emotive literary version – 1958. *POT*, pp. 111-13.

10. *Ashteroth*: The plural/adjective form of *Astarte* or *Ashterah* – the Canaanite/ Sidonian (Phoenician) Goddess of fertility and war and consort of *Baal*. She is identical with the Babylonian, *Ishtar*. Hebrew etymological links with this near-eastern version of *Venus* are legion, and possibly include the name of the tribe of *Asher* (a pious alternative is offered in Gen. 30:13 and elsewhere) and that of Queen *Esther* – the Persian form of deity's name. See J. Day. In *ABD*, I, A. p. 492.

11. *ATOT*, pp. 216-19.

12. See note 17, ch. 3.

13. This information, regarding their burial rites would seem to prove the non-Israelite ethnicity of the Jabeshites and the possibility they may have been of Anatolian or perhaps Aegean stock (see D. Kurtz and J. Boardman. 1971. *Greek Burial Customs*).

14. B. Mazar postulates that engraved arrowheads and spear tips discovered at el-Kahdr near Bethlehem in 1953 belonged to archers in the service of King Saul (1986. *The Early Biblical Period*, pp. 87-8.). If David's archers had carelessly left their tell-tale inscriptions upon their arrowheads, and these had been discovered in the body of Saul, David's urgency, in attempting to pacify the men of Jabesh (2 Sam. 2: 4-7 and see n. 20 below) becomes even more understandable.

15. See B. Halpern. 2001. *Saul and His Sons at Gilboa – DSD*, pp. 78-81 for a definitive critical assessment of David's reconstruction of Saul's death and in particular, how it attempts to explain his being in possession of Saul's royal regalia.

16. Ibid and see note 23, ch. 8.

17. Cf M. Gichon. *BOTB*, p. 94.

18. S. Brookes agrees with this hypothesis, stating that "these archers were probably David and his men, who secretly made their way to Gilboa . . . " (*SATM*, p.175).

19. B. Halpern suggests the possibility that David had moved to Hebron before the battle of Gilboa (*DSD*, p. 296). This seems unlikely however, bearing in mind Ziklag's strong association with the alibi, and the fact that his vassal-ship in Hebron would have been big news from the moment of its commencement.

20. B. Halpern regards the Jabeshites apparent silence in reply to David's overtures as evidence of the hostility between the two parties. Moreover, he goes on to suggest that Abner setting Ishboshet up in Mahanaim was a direct response to the threat to Israel's "periphery" represented by a 'David-Ammonite' alliance in Transjordan (*DSD*, pp. 301-2 and see n.14 above).

Chapter Ten

1. For an eloquent, moving and conventionally sympathetic assessment of Saul and his reign read F. James' *An Estimate of Saul – POT*, pp. 113-16.
2. B. Halpern, amongst others, believes that the overall picture presented in the text at this point maybe hiding the fact – hinted at in 2 Sam. 2: 8&9 – that Gilboa may possibly have been a victory for Saul, albeit at the cost of his life, and that Ishboshet consolidated these northern gains of his father (*DSD*, p. 156). In stark contrast, the scholastic consensus argues against Halpern, in accepting the text's claim that Israel was routed at Gilboa, and moreover, despite the information in 2 Sam. 2: 9 (that Ishboshet was forty at the time of succession) asserting that Ishboshet was at most, only a callow youth when Abner made him king. However, it must be said that the latter hypothesis is underpinned by extremely tenuous reasoning with huge reliance on selected pieces of text. The argument goes something like this. At the time of the battle of Gilboa:
   - Jonathan only had one infant child – making him a man in his early to mid-twenties when he died;
   - Ishboshet was Jonathan's youngest sibling;
   - Their mother, Ahinoam, gave birth to six recorded children;
   - Allowing for failed births, infant mortality etc, the oldest Ishboshet could have been was a young teenager, and most probably an infant;
   - This probability is supported by the lack of any record of Ishboshet having children of his own;
   - Ishboshet was apparently not at Gilboa, indicating that he was under twenty years of age – the legal age for military service (Num 26: 2, 4).

   All very plausible, but also very dependent upon a selectively literalistic reading of the texts (see e.g. S. Brookes. *SATM*, p. 108 and D.V. Edelman. In *ABD*, II, pp. 615-17).

   For example, the entire construction rests upon the "fact" that Jonathan had only one infant child at the time in question. However, even if we accept this information as being accurate, is it not possible that either Jonathan and/or his main – perhaps only – wife, had fertility problems. Perhaps Mephiboshet's lameness was really an indication of just such a problem. Maybe he represented the one successful birth of many attempts. If this perfectly rational explanation was true, we can easily bump Jonathan up another ten years in age, and thus Ishboshet too, perhaps putting him in early to mid twenties. By the same token, perhaps Ishboshet himself had fertility issues; issues reflected in the story of Abner and Rizpah (2 Sam. 3: 6-11), whereby Ishboshet's uncle, in desperation, was attempting to create Saulide heirs through his own seed. Or perhaps Ishboshet did have children – unmentioned by the Davidic scribes – who were murdered together with their father in Mahanaim.

   Ishboshet's apparent absence from the battle of Gilboa is perhaps the weakest part of the hypothesis, bearing in mind that Abner too was apparently not a combatant. Certainly, they were not killed at Gilboa, but this neither proves they were *never* at the site, nor explains how they came to be at Mahanaim after the battle. The counter-hypothesis proposed in this book – that Abner and Ishboshet were sent away by Saul, together with the levy of Israel to regroup in Transjordan – is both plausible, and supported by the record of their long and stiff resistance to David over most of the subsequent decade.

Perhaps much of the debate originates from the regnal formula, giving Ishboshet an age of forty at his accession. For most critical commentators, 'forty' in biblical records immediately sparks off warning signals. It is nearly always a symbolic approximation – sometimes more approximate than others, as in this case, where it seems reasonable to assume that Ishboshet was in fact in his early twenties when he was crowned in Mahanaim.

3. The Bible's assertion that Ishboshet ruled Israel for only two years (2 Sam. 2: 10), sits at odds with the fact in 2 Sam. 5: 5 that he ruled over only Judah for between seven and eight years.

4. B. Halpern views Israel as being David's first conquest – *DSD*, p. 316.

5. O. Eissfeldt regards the Divine choice of Saul as "an act of grace" which constituted "the peculiar [i.e. unique] characteristic of Saul's kingship" and distinguished it from all the other kingdoms of the region. In other words, Saul's coronation was a reaction to a national emergency and the style of his kingship was coloured by this fact. Whereas a Pharaoh was a god, and the kings of Assyria and Babylon comprised a crucial element in the "cosmic order", Saul was merely a servant of his people and God, whose "factual power" lay in his supreme control of the tribal levy (In *CAH*, II 2: B, p. 571).

6. M. Noth believes that David's style of kingship was equally distinct as that of Saul. But whereas, Saul ruled by the grace of God, David's rule was a Divine expression of God's grace, whereby the king himself was proof of God's preferment of Israel, and exclusively through his (i.e. David's) seed, an active guarantor of a blessed and powerful future for the nation (*THOI*, p. 224).

7. See B.S.J. Isserlin (1998, *TI*, p. 69) who claims that the Saulide movement was still active in the reign of Solomon and B. Halpern (*DSD*, pp. 84-7; 479) who states that David did not gain full control over the kingdom until after the Absalom revolt – whom incidentally, he considers to have taken up the Saulide banner (*DSD*, pp. 94-103; 377-79).

8. Pious scholarship is pleased to take a contrary view, believing absolutely in the sincerity of the lament, and presumably the recorded time of composition; e.g. F. James, who does at least recognise that it represented "good policy" on David's part, but then ingenuously ascribes his impulsion to "his generosity"! (*POT*, pp. 125-7).

9. The *Cherethites* were (according to Ezk. 25:16) Sea Peoples of some description. Their constant companions in arms, the *Pelethites* were, according to most theories, also Philistines, the word being derived from *pl+sti* "Philistine". All of which must make particularly inconvenient and uncomfortable reading for the many fans of the "Lion of Judah". (See M. Delcor, 1978, *Les Kéréthim et les Crétois, VTS*, Leiden, 28: pp. 409-22 and H. Schult, 1965, *Ein inschriflicher Beleg für "Plethi"? Zeitschrift der deutschen Palästina-Vereins Zebahim*, 81: pp. 74-9). It is possible that the use of *Cherethite* and *Pelethite* by the Davidic

scribe was an attempt – albeit a poor one – to disguise the fact that David's elite regiment was Philistine.

10. B. Halpern regards the elegy as a component part of David's alibi for his whereabouts at the time of Gilboa, *DSD*, pp. 78; 295-6.

11. Cf J. Baldwin corroborates the above, but appears blind to the paradox created by the apparent juxtaposition of the psalm with the lament and its implication vis-à-vis David's role at the battle of Gilboa. *TOTC*, p. 287.

12. S. Brookes places the story in the Saulide Elah battle, while "putting aside the traditional story" (*SATM*, p. 108). However, as the only concrete clues to the chronology of the historical Elhanan episode are the textual errors contained within the "traditional story", this would seem to be an unfounded move.

13. Some translators (e.g. 1985, *Tanakh. The Jewish Publication Society*, *p.* 447 n: 'm'[ed: H.M. Orlinsky]) feel the need to explain this verse by stating that this incident occurred "after David's capture of Jerusalem" (2 Sam. 5). However, this fails to explain why the redactor felt the need to insert this information here. Why not place it in its correct chronological position in 2 Sam? The translator has correctly sensed that the verse is misplaced, but then failed to link it to the story of Elhanan – piously preserving the "David & Goliath" myth.

14. F. James' dubiousness over the "David and Goliath" episode attests to the fact that even pious scholarship senses a 'problem' here (See ch. 6, n. 8). For a reasoned argument for the validity of David's having at least killed Goliath at some time and at some place – not necessarily Elah – see G.W. Wade. *OTH*, p. 225. He does admit though, that "[o]f the acts and exploits which first won distinction for David, no fully trustworthy record remains." (ibid: p. 224).

15. E.g. J. Baldwin. *TOTC*, p. 286 & n. 1

16. Cf L.M. von Pákozdy, 1956, *Elhanan-der frühe Name Davids? Zietschrift für die alttestamentliche Wissenschaft*, Berlin, 68: pp. 257-59.

17. See. A. R. Honeyman. 1948. *The Evidence for Regnal Names Among the Hebrews. Journal of Biblical Literature*, 67; pp. 13-25.

18. Most commentators believe the two Elhanan's to be two distinct personalities (see B. Mazar, 1963, *The Military Elite of King David. VTS*, Leiden, 13: pp. 310-20).

19. E.g. H.J. Stoebe. 1956. *Die Goliathperikope* 1 Sam. 17 & 18: 5 *und die Textform der Septuaginta. VTS*, Lieden, 6: pp. 397-413 and H. I. Avalos. In *TOCTTB*, p. 258.

20. An alternative translation of this verse makes David responsible for the murder of the entire clan of Saul and not merely Saul himself (B. Halpern. 2001. *DSD*, p. 367): "Leave, leave, Man of blood, and wantonness. Yahweh has turned against you all the blood of the House of Saul, in whose stead you became king, and Yahweh has placed the kingship in the hands of Absalom, your son. Now you find yourself in troubles, because you are a man of Blood."

21. Jeremiah the prophet was born in Benjamin (Jem. 1: 1) but was more likely a Levite.

   Mordechai (Mardocheus), the hero of the Book of Esther, was a Benjaminite (Est. 2: 2) whose enemy was – pertinently enough – none other than Haman 'the Agagite', a descendant of King Agag of Amalek.

   But perhaps, in the context of this study, a far more interesting, and hitherto virtually ignored fact was that *Saul* of Tarsus (later, Paul) was proud to proclaim his own Benjaminite heritage (Rom. 11:1 / Ph. 3:5). This boast is remarkable when we consider the date in which it was made, more than a thousand years after the death of King Saul and around six-hundred years after the last historical references to extant non Judahite tribes. This would seem to indicate that Saul of Tarsus' Benjaminite identity was far more than incidental to him and his story. Indeed, those commentators who detect a virulent anti-Jewish/Judahite streak running through the words and teachings of St. Paul, might do well to investigate further his claim to Benjaminite heritage. In the light of this work, it would be tempting to see him possibly as being a proud and embittered descendent of King Saul of Israel, wreaking a brilliant revenge upon the House of Judah – in the form of a new religion whereby Zion is sidelined and the God of David is appropriated for the entire gentile world. It is an attractive construction:

· King Saul is "martyred" by David;
· King David mutates his Saulide inheritance;
· 'David' (i.e. Jesus) is "martyred" through the teachings of Saul of Tarsus;
· Saul/Paul mutates his Davidic inheritance.

22. See Appendix A, n. 5.

Appendices

Appendix A: Who Wrote Samuel?

1. 2 K.22:8-10 is cited as evidence that *Deuteronomy* and much else besides was laid down at Josiah's dictate – For perhaps the most comprehensive recent scholastic discussion on the origins of the Deutenronomistic cannon see M.A. Sweeney. 2001. *King Josiah of Judah – the Lost Messiah of Israel*, cf: ch. 1.

2. Ibid pp. 256-273 and cf: Hos. 5: 1

3. For a discussion of Ezra's alleged role in formulating biblical texts see A. Gelin. 1960. *Le Livre d'Esdras et Néhémie*, p. 24, 2nd ed. and H. Donner. 1986. *Geschichte des volkes Israel und seiner Nachbarn in Grundzügen*, II, p. 249, Göttingen.

4. A typical example is Baruch Halpern's graphic *A* and *B Source* construction – 2001. *DSD*, pp. 277-9.

5. See G.W. Wade, 1928, *OTH*, pp. 177-8 and M. Noth. 1958. *THOI*, pp. 42-50.

6. *Septuagint* (abbreviated in Latin as LXX) is named after the alleged 'seventy + Jewish translators' – the *Septuaginta* – who, according to tradition, were commissioned by Ptolemy II (285-246 BCE) to translate the Holy Scriptures into Greek. However, most modern scholars believe the story to be fictitious. For a comprehensive discussion pertaining to all the current theories with regard to the origins and the content of the Septuagint see M.K.H. Peters, 1992, in *ABD*, V, pp. 1093-1104.

7. According to the "Tiberian Tradition", the *Masoretic Text* was compiled by a group of scholars – the *Masoretes* – working in Tiberius in Palestine over a period ranging from as early as 500 CE to as late as the middle of the ninth century. For more information on all aspects of the subject see F.M. Cross and S. Talmon [eds], 1975, *Qumran and the History of the Biblical text*, Cambridge, Middle Assyrian; C.D. Ginsberg [ed], 1897, *Introduction to the Massoretico-Critical Edition of the Hebrew Bible*, London. Reprint with prolegomenon by H.M. Orlinsky, New

York, 1966 and I. Yeivin, 1980, *Introduction to the Tiberian Masorah*, Society of Biblical Literature Masoretic Studies, 5, Missoula, Masoretic Text.

8. If Baruch Halpern is correct in his highly persuasive claim that Bathsheba and Solomon were responsible for the original finished version of the Books of Samuel, then one would need to add a fifth 'mood' to the construction presented here. However, their influence is mostly reserved for 2 Samuel and has only an incidental affect on anything recorded before the Uriah episode (cf 2001, *DSD*, pp. 391-424).

Appendix B / Psalms of David?

9. For a full and comprehensive analysis of the *Book of Psalms* see J. Limburg. 1992, in *ABD*, V, pp. 522-36.

10. For example, some commentators have detected strong literary similarities between *Psalm 104* and Pharaoh Akhenaton's (Amenhotep IV) *Hymn to the Sun Disc*. See M. Auffret, 1981, *Hymnes d'Égypte et d'Israël*, Orbis biblicus et orientalis 34; K.-H. Bernhardt, 1969, *Amenophis IV and Psalm 104*. Mitteilungen des Istituts für Orientforschung, 15: pp. 193ff; M. Lichtheim, 1971-80, *Ancient Egyptian Literature*, pp. 96-107 and E. von Nordheim, 1979, 'Der grosse Hymnus des Echnaton und Psalm 104' *Studien zur Altägyptischen Kultur*, 7, pp.227ff.

11. Cf J.T. Willis. 1973. *The song of Hannah and Psalm 113*, *CBQ*, Washington D.C., 25/2: pp. 139-54.

Appendix C / Heterodoxy v. Orthodoxy & Revision v. Convention

12. Abraham Cohen's biblical commentaries are typical of the Jewish style of theological literature (cf. 1952, *Samuel I & II*, Soncino Press. London) while Joyce Baldwin employs a similar methodology from the Christian standpoint (cf. 1988. *TOTC*, 1 and 2 Samuel).

13. Fleming James probably represents the most eloquent amongst this school of commentator in the Christian world (cf. 1939, *POT*, pp. 75-165), while the writings of Hayim Tadmor present a similar – if dryer – analysis from the Jewish perspective (cf. 1976, in *AHOTJP*, pp. 91-109).

14. Ever since the late nineteenth century when the brilliant German Semitist Julius Wellhausen (1844–1918), developed his revolutionary method of biblical analysis known as "Biblical Critical Theory", there has existed an undercurrent of suspicion, especially amongst Jewish theological scholars and some historians, that modern biblical scholarship was/is bent upon undermining the veracity of the Tanakh (see J.H. Hertz [ed], 1960, *Pentateuch and Haftorahs*, pp. 397-9: C).

15. Prominent examples amongst the former group in the contemporary debate vis-à-vis Saul, David and Solomon, would be Israel Finkelstein and N.A. Silberman (cf. 2001, *TBU*, pp. 123-145) and the pre-eminent example amongst the latter is Baruch Halpern (cf. 2001, *DSD*, pp. III: pp. 107-226).

16. Originally published by Macmillan, but then dropped following the 'scandal' and taken up by Doubleday.

17. The astonishing and shocking story of *Worlds in Collision*, told with his typical eloquence and forcefulness, can be found in Velikovsky's autobiographical 1983

memoirs *Stargazers and Gravediggers*, published by William Morrow. New York.

18. Cf. J.J. Bimson, 1978, *Re-dating the Exodus and Conquest*, *JSOT*, Supplement, Series 5, P. James, 1991, *Centuries of Darkness*. D.M. Rohl, 1995, *ATOT*, Century.

Appendix D / Methodology

19. Cf. W.O.E. Oesterley, 1909, in *DOTB*, p. 427.
20. The *Qumran scrolls* constitute the earliest biblical texts found in Hebrew, and are remarkably similar to the text of the 'modern' Hebrew Tanakh. See J.M. Allegro, 1968, *Qumran Cave 4 1 (4Q158-4Q186)*, Discoveries in the Judean Desert 5.
21. E.g. the famous *House of David* reference contained in the Hazael Victory Inscription discovered at Tel Dan in northern Israel: "[I killed Jeho]ram son of [Ahab] king of Israel, and [I] killed [Ahaz]iahu son of [Jehoram kin]g of the House of David." (After I. Finkelstein and N.A. Silberman)

    While this exciting find, dating to a century or more after the death of David does prove that he was the founder of a royal dynasty, it tells us nothing whatsoever about David himself or his reign. (See I. Finkelstein and N.A. Silberman, 2001, *TBU*, pp. 128-30).
22. K.M. Kenyon, 1952, 'Excavations at Jericho, 1952', *Palestine Exploration Quarterly*, London, pp. 62-82. K.M. Kenyon, 1957, *Digging Up Jericho*, London.
23. See n. 21 above.
24. Several scholars believe Merneptah's 'Israel boast' to be false in any event, believing it to be a 'rounding off' of a list of names, or a means by which he appropriated the conquests of his forerunner, Ramesses II. For this and other theories concerning the 'stele Israelites' see G. Ahlström, 1986, *Who Were the Israelites?*; G. Ahlström and D.V. Edelman, 1985, *Merneptah's Israel, Journal of Near Eastern Studies*, 44: 59-61; H. Engel, 1979, *Die Siegesstele des Merneptah, Biblica,* 80: p. 373ff; G. Fecht. 1983. *Die Israelstele*, Gestalt und Aussage, pp. 106ff in *Fontes atque Pontes*, and E. Hornung, 1983. *Die Israelstele des Merenptah*, pp. 224ff in *Fontes atque Pontes.*

Bibliography

Ackroyd, P.R., 1993, *The Books of Samuel*, in *TOCB*, pp. 674-677

Ahlström, G., and Edelman, D.V., 1985, *Merneptah's Israel, Journal of Near Eastern Studies*, Chicago

Ahlström, G., 1986, *Who Were the Israelites?* Winona Lake

Albright, W.F., 1924, Excavations and Results at Tell el-Ful (Gibeah of Saul), *Annual of the American Schools of Oriental Research*

Albright, W.F., 1925, The Assyrian March on Jerusalem, *Annual of the American Schools of Oriental Research*, 4: p. 139)

Albright, W.F., 1933, *A New Campaign of Excavation at Gibeah of Saul*, Bulletin of the American Schools of Oriental research

Allegro, J.M., 1968, *Qumran Cave 4 1 (4Q158-4Q186)*, Discoveries in the Judean Desert 5

Allegro, J.M., 1970, *The Sacred Mushroom and the Cross*, Hodder & Stoughton, London

Amarna Letters: EA: 252

Freedman, D.N., Editor-in-Chief, *Anchor Bible Dictionary*, 1992, Doubleday, New York

Arnold, P.M., 1992, *Mizpah*, in *ABD*, II, pp. 879-881

Auffret, M., 1981, *Hymnes d'Égypte et d'Israël*, Orbis biblicus et orientalis 34, Freiburg and Göttingen

Avalos, H.I., *Goliath*, in *TOCB*, p. 258

Baldwin, J., 1988, *Tyndale Old Testament Commentaries* (Wiseman, D.J., General Editor) – *1 and 2 Samuel*, Inter-Varsity, Leicester

Ben-Sasson, H.H., Editor, *A History of the Jewish People*, 1977, Weidenfeld & Nicolson, London

Bernhardt, K.-H., 1969, Amenophis IV and Psalm 104, *Mitteilungen des Instituts für Orientforschung*, Berlin, 15, p.p. 193ff

Berginer, 2000, *Neurological aspects of the David-Goliath battle: restriction in the giant's visual field*, Israel Medical Association Journal: Imaj, 2(9): 725-7, Dept' of Neurology, Soroka University Centre, Beersheva, Israel

Bimson, J.J., 1978, *Re-dating the Exodus and Conquest*, JSOT, Supplement, Series 5, Sheffield

Birch, B.C., 1976, *The Rise of the Israelite Monarchy: The Growth and Development of 1 Samuel 7-15*, Society of Biblical Literature Dissertation Series

Boling, R.G., 1992, *The Book of Judges*, in *ABD*, III, pp.1107-17

Brookes, S., 2005, *Saul and the Monarchy: A New Look*, Ashgate, Aldershot

Brueggemann, W., 1992, *Samuel, Book of: 1-2 Narrative & Theology*, in *ABD*, V. pp. 965-73Buttrick, G.A., Editor, *Interpreters Dictionary of the Bible*

Cohen, A., 1932, *Everyman's Talmud*, Dent, London

Cohen, A., 1952, *Samuel I & II*, Soncino, London

Conder C.R., 1877, *Saul's Journey to Zuph, Palestine Exploration Society* – Quarterly Statement, pp.37-40, C3

Connolly, P., 1977, *The Greek Armies*, Macdonald, London

Coogan, M.D., 1993, *Samuel*, in *TOCB*, Oxford

Coogan. M. D. & Metzger. B. M., *Oxford Companion to the Bible*, 1993, Oxford University Press

Cross F.M., & Talmon, S., Editors, *Qumran and the History of the Biblical text*, 1975, Cambridge, Middle Assyrian

Dalman, G., 1930, *Jerusalem und sein Gelände, Schriften des Deutschen Palästina-Instituts 4, Gütersloh* C3

Day, J., *Ashtoreth*, in *ABD*, I, A. p. 492

Delcor, M., 1978, *Les Kéréthim et les Crétois, VTS*, Leiden, 28: pp. 409-22

Dempster, S.G., 1992, *Elhanan*, in *ABD*, II, pp.455-6

DeVries, L.F., 1992, *Keilah*, in *ABD*, IV, p. 14

Donner, H., 1986, *Geschichte des volkes Israel und seiner Nachbarn in Grundzügen*, II, Göttingen

Dothan, T., & Gitin, S., 1990, *Ekron of the Philistines, British Archaeological Review* 16/1: 20-25

Edelman, D.V., 1984, *Saul's Rescue of Jabesh Gilead* (1 Sam. 11: 1-11) *Sorting Story from History, ZFDAW*, Berlin, 86: 195-209

Edelman, D.V., 1992, *Ahinoam*, in *ABD*, I, pp. 117-8

Edelman, D.V., 1992, *Eshbaal*, in *ABD*, II, p. 615

Edelman, D.V., 1992, *Saul*, in *ABD*, V, pp. 980-99

Eissfeldt, O., 1943, 120-22 *Israelitisch-philistäische Grenzverschienbungen von David bis auf die Assyrerzeit, Zeitschrift des deutschen Palästina-Vereins* 66: 115-128, Reprinted. Kleine Schriften 2: 453-63

Eissfeldt, O., 1975, *The Hebrew* Kingdom, in *CAH*, II, 2B, pp. 537-605

Engel, H, 1979, *Die Siegesstele des Merneptah, Biblica* 80: p. 373ff

Eslinger, L., 1985, *Kingship of God in Crisis: A Close Reading of 1 Samuel 1-12,* Bible and Literature 10, Sheffield

Ewing, W., 1909, *Shiloh*, in *DOTB*

Feather, R., 1999, *The Copper Scroll Decoded*, Thorsons, London

Fecht, G., 1983, *Die Israelstele*, Gestalt und Aussage, pp. 106ff. In *Fontes atque Pontes*, Wiesbaden

Finkelstein, I, & Silberman, N.A., 2001, *The Bible Unearthed*, Free Press, New York

Flanagan, J.W., 1992, *Samuel, Book of: 1-2 Text Composition & Content*, in *ABD*, V, pp. 957-65

Gelin, A., 1960, *Le Livre d'Esdras et Néhémie*, 2nd ed., Paris

Gichon, M. &Herzog, C., 1997, *Battles of the Bible*, 1997 Greenhill, London

Ginsberg, C.D., Editor, *Introduction to the Massoretico-Critical Edition of the Hebrew Bible*, 1897, London, Reprint with prolegomenon by H.M. Orlinsky, New York

Grant, M., 1996, *The History of Ancient Israel*, Weidenfeld & Nicolson, London

Gunn, D.M., 1980, *The Fate of King Saul*, *JSOT*, Supplement 14, Sheffield

Gunn, D.M., 1993, *Saul*, in *TOCB*, p. 680

Halpern, B., 1981, *The Constitution of the Monarchy in Israel*, Harvard Semitic Monographs 25, pp. 125-48

Halpern, B., 2001, *David's Secret Demons: Messiah, Murderer, Traitor, King*, W.B. Erdmans, Grand Rapids, Michigan / Cambridge, UK

Hamilton, J.M., 1992, *Naioth*, in *ABD*, IV, p. 1001

Hastings, J., Editor, *Dictionary of the Bible*, 1909, T.&T. Clark, Edinburgh

Herodotus, circa 440 BCE, *The Histories*, Thuria, Italy. (Translated by de Sélincourt, A., [1954] & revised by Burn, A.R., 1974, Penguin, London

Hertz, J.H., (Editor) 1960, *Pentateuch and Haftorahs*, pp. 397-9: C. Soncino, London

Homer, *Iliad* 2: 819

Honeyman, A.R., 1948, The Evidence for Regnal Names among the Hebrews, *Journal of Biblical Literature*, 67; pp. 13-25

Hornung, E., 1983, *Die Israelstele des Merenptah*, pp. 224ff. In *Fontes atque Pontes*, Wiesbaden

Introduction to the Tiberian Masorah, 1980, Society of Biblical Literature Masoretic Studies, 5, Missoula, Masoretic Text. (I. Yeivin.)

Isserlin, B.S.J., 1998, *The Israelites*, Thames & Hudson, London

James, F., 1939, *Personalities of the Old Testament*, Scribners, New York

James, F., 1966 *The Iron Age at Beth Shan*

James, P., 1991, *Centuries of Darkness*, Jonathan Cape, London

Jobling, D., 1978, *Jonathan: A Structural Study in 1 Samuel*, pp. 4-25 in *The Sense of Biblical Narrative*, *JSOT*, Supplement 7, Sheffield

Josephus, F., circa 80-90 BCE, *Antiquities of the Jews*, Rome. (Translated by W. Whiston, Routledge, New York.)

Kent, C.F., 1910, *A History of the Hebrew People (Vol: I)*, Smith, Elder, London

Kenyon, K.M., 1952, *Excavations at Jericho, 1952, Palestine Exploration Quarterly*, London

Kenyon, K.M., 1957 *Digging Up Jericho*, London

Kittel, R., 1929, *Great Men and Movements in Israel*, Leipzig (translated by C.A. Knoch and C.D. Wright, Printed by Macmillan, New York for Williams & Norgate, London)

Kitchen, K.A., The Exodus. In *ABD*, II, pp. 700-708

Kochavi, M., & Demsky, A., 1978, *An Israelite Village from the Days of the Judges*, *Biblical Archaeologist Review*, 4/3: 19-21

Koizumi, T., 1976, *On the Battle of Gilboa*, *Annual of the Japanese Biblical Institute*, Tokyo 2: pp. 61-78

Kotter, W.R., 1992, *Gilgal*, in *ABD*, II, pp. 1022-24

Kurtz, D., and Boardman, J., 1971, *Greek Burial Customs,* Ithaca

Langenscheidt's (Old Testament) Hebrew English Dictionary (Feyerabend, K., Editor, New York

Lemche, N.P., 1992, *Hebrew* in *ABD*, III, p. 95

Levenson J., 1978, *1 Samuel as Literature and History, CBQ,* Washington DC

Lichtheim, M., 1971-80, *Ancient Egyptian Literature*, Berkeley

Limburg, J., 1992, *Psalms, Book of, in ABD,* V, pp. 522-36

Livy, T., *The History of Rome from its Foundation, Books XXI-XXX (The War with Hannibal)*, Rome. (Translated by de Sélincourt, A., & edited by Radice, B., 1965, Penguin, London.)

Macalister, R.A.S., 1965, *The Philistines, Their History and Civilization,* Chicago, Reproduced for *Philistine History*

Mafico, T.L.J., 1992, *Judge, Judging,* in *ABD* III, pp. 1104-06

Malamat, A., 1977, *The Struggle Against the Philistines,* in *AHOTJP*, p. 86

Mayes, A.D.H., 1978, *The Rise of the Israelite Monarchy, ZFDAW*, Berlin

Mazar, B., 1963, *The Military Elite of King David, VTS*, Leiden, 13: pp. 310-20

Mazar, B., 1986, *The Early Biblical Period*, Jerusalem

McCarter Jr., P.K., 1980, *1 Samuel, AB*

McGovern, P.E., 1993, Beth-Shan: Archaeological Sequence, in *ABD*, I. p. 695

Meyers, C., 1999, *Sacral-Royal Ideologies of the Monarchic State*, in *TOHBW*, pp. 261/262

Miller, J.M., 1974, *Saul's Rise to Power: Some Observations Concerning 1 Sam* 9: 1-10: 16; 10: 26-11: 15 and 13: 2-14: 46, *CBQ*, 36: 157-74

Miller, J.M., 1974. In *A History of Ancient Israel and Judah*, Philadelphia

Negev, A., & Gibson, S., Editors, *Archaeological Encyclopaedia of the Holy Land, 2001*, Continuum, New York

New English Bible (Old Testament), 1970 Edition, Oxford University Press (1970)

Noth, M., 1958, *The History of Israel*, Vandenhoeck & Ruprecht, Göttingen, (English Edition: Xpress Reprints, London)

Noth, M., 1981, *The Deutenronomistic History*, Sheffield, *Old Testament*, 1961 Edition, The British and Foreign Bible Society

Oesterley, W.O.E., 1909, *Jashar, Book of*, in *DOTB*, p. 427

Peters, M.K.H., 1992, *Pentateuch*, in *ABD*, V, pp. 1093-1104

Polzin, R., 1989, *Samuel and the Deuteronomist*, San Francisco

Press, R., 1938, *Der Prophet Samuel, ZFDAW*, Berlin

Pritchard, J.B., 1955, *Ancient Near Eastern Texts Relating to the OT*, Princeton

Pritchard, J.B., 1969, *Ancient Near Eastern Texts relating to the OT*, Princeton, 2nd edition with supplements, p. 291

Qumran Scrolls: Qumran Cave 4 I-4Q158-4Q186; QS. 9:1

Ramsey, G.W., 1992, *Samuel*, in *ABD*, V, pp. 954-7

Rehm, M.D., 1992, Levites and Priests, *ABD*, IV, pp. 297-310

Robertson, E., 1944, *Samuel and Saul*, Bulletin of the John Rylands Library

Rohl, D.M., 1995, *A Test of Time: The Bible: From Myth to History*, Century, London

Schult, H., 1965, *Ein inschriflicher Beleg für "Plethi"? Zeitschrift der deutschen Palästina-Vereins Zebahim*, 81: pp. 74-9

Schunk, K.-D., 1992, *Benjamin – Tribal History*, in *ABD*, I, B, pp. 671-2

Schiley, D.G., 1992, *Adoni-Zedek*, in *ABD* I, p. 75

Seow, C.L., 1992, Ark of the Covenant, in *ABD*, I, pp. 389ff

Singer, I., 1992, *Sea Peoples*, in *ABD* V, pp. 1059-61

Spencer, J.R., 1992, Levitical Cities, in *ABD*, IV, pp. 310-311

Stern, P., 1993, *Ephod*, in *TOCB*, p.189

Stoebe, H.J., 1956, *Die Goliathperikope 1 Sam 17 & 18; 27-28: 5 und die Textform der Septuaginta*, *VTS*, Leiden

Sweeney, M.A., 2001, *King Josiah of Judah: The Lost Messiah of Israel*, Oxford

Tadmor, H., 1976, *The United Monarchy*, in *AHOTJP*, pp. 92-109, Weidenfeld & Nicolson, London

Tanakh: The Holy Scriptures, 1985 Edition. (Orlinsky, H.M, Ginsberg, H.L., and Speiser, E.A., Editors) Jewish Publication Society, Philadelphia / Jerusalem

Taylor, J., 1909, *Ahijah*, in *DOTB*, p.18

Thiele, E., 1965, *The Mysterious Numbers of the Hebrew Kings*, Grand Rapids

Thomas, D.W., 1963, *bliyya'al in the Old Testament*, pp. 11-19 in *Biblical and Patristic Studies in Memory of R.P. Casey*, J.N. Birdsall and R.W. Thomson editors, Freiburg

The Times Atlas of the Bible, 1989. (Pritchard, J.B., General Editor.) Times Books, London

Twain, M., 1889, *A Yankee in King Arthur's Court*

van der Veen, P., 1989, The el-Amarna Habiru and the Early Monarchy in Israel, in *Journal of the Ancient Chronology* Forum 3, pp 72-78

van der Veen, P., 1993 *The Habiru as the 'Ibrim' of 1 Samuel and the* Implications of the 'New Chronology', in *Society of Interdisciplinary Studies Journal*, vol.15

van der Veen, P., 1999/2000, The Kingdom of Labayu, in *Journal of the Ancient Chronology Forum*, vol. 8

van der Veen, P.G., and Zerbst, U., 2002, *Biblische Archaologie am Scheideweg*

Velikovsky, I., 1952, *Ages in Chaos*, Macmillan, New York

Velikovsky, I., 1983, *Stargazers and Gravediggers*, William Morrow, New York

Vermes, G., 1962, *The Dead Sea Scrolls in English*, Penguin, London

von Nordheim, E., 1979, *Der grosse Hymnus des Echnaton und Psalm 104*, Studien zur Altägyptischen Kultur, Hamburg

von Pákozdy, M., 1956, *Elhanan-der frühre Name Davids, ZFDAW*, Berlin, 68: pp. 257-59

Wade, G.W., 1928, *Old Testament History*, Methuen, London

Whitelam, K.W., 1992, *Ahijah*, in *ABD*, I, 1 p. 111

Willis, J.T., 1973, *The song of Hannah and Psalm 113*, *QBC*, Washington D.C.

Yates, G.G., 1965, *A Guide to the Old Testament*, Epworth, London

Yeivin, I, 1980, Introduction to the Tiberian Masorah, *Society of Biblical Literature Masoretic Studies*, 5, Missoula,

Index

For references to 1 Samuel and 2 Samuel, see Samuel (book)

Printed in the United Kingdom
by Lightning Source UK Ltd.
120982UK00001B/244-447